SO-BYZ-007

LightWave 3D® 8 Cartoon Character Creation

Volume 2: Rigging & Animation

Jonny Gorden

Wordware Publishing, Inc.

Library of Congress Cataloging-in-Publication Data

Gorden, Jonny.
    Lightwave 3D cartoon character creation / by Jonny Gorden.
      p. cm.
    ISBN 1-55622-253-X (volume 1, pbk., companion cd-rom) -- ISBN
    1-55622-254-8 (volume 2, pbk., companion cd-rom)
    1. Computer animation. 2. Three-dimensional display systems. 3. Cartoon
    characters. 4. LightWave 3D. I. Title.
    TR897.7.G67 2004
    006.6'93--dc22   2004021079
                                  CIP

© 2005, Wordware Publishing, Inc.

All Rights Reserved

2320 Los Rios Boulevard
Plano, Texas 75074

No part of this book may be reproduced in any form or by any means
without permission in writing from Wordware Publishing, Inc.

Printed in the United States of America

ISBN 1-55622-254-8

10 9 8 7 6 5 4 3 2 1
0410

LightWave and LightWave 3D are registered trademarks in the United States and other countries.
Other brand names and product names mentioned in this book are trademarks or service marks of their respective companies. Any omission or misuse (of any kind) of service marks or trademarks should not be regarded as intent to infringe on the
property of others. The publisher recognizes and respects all marks used by companies, manufacturers, and developers as a
means to distinguish their products.
This book is sold as is, without warranty of any kind, either express or implied, respecting the contents of this book and any
disks or programs that may accompany it, including but not limited to implied warranties for the book's quality, performance,
merchantability, or fitness for any particular purpose. Neither Wordware Publishing, Inc. nor its dealers or distributors shall
be liable to the purchaser or any other person or entity with respect to any liability, loss, or damage caused or alleged to have
been caused directly or indirectly by this book.

All inquiries for volume purchases of this book should be addressed to Wordware
Publishing, Inc., at the above address. Telephone inquiries may be made by calling:

(972) 423-0090

Contents

Part II   Character Setup

Part III   Animation and Dynamics

Introduction

Creating characters is one of the most rewarding aspects of 3D animation. Seeing a character that started out as a 2D concept drawing come to life through animation is a real joy.

Ever since I can remember, I've been fascinated by animation. While other kids wanted to be firemen or astronauts, my greatest dream was to make animated movies. I was constantly getting in trouble for being late for school because I was watching the morning cartoons and for drawing in my schoolbooks. Years later when I first got the chance to play with 3D animation, I was disappointed that the software wasn't capable of doing everything I imagined. I saw the potential was there, and although movies like *Jurassic Park* and *Toy Story* were still a few years away, it was enough to make me want to persevere. I'd been creating 2D animation for a while before that, but I enjoyed the unique challenges involved with 3D animation and found that it offered so many more possibilities.

Since then, consumer 3D software has evolved to become everything I had wished for in those early days, and more. Over the last few years we've reached a point where it's possible to create convincing 3D characters with all the nuances that were previously only possible in 2D animation. With recent advancements in software and computer speed, it's easier than ever to create and animate 3D characters with the quality of performance that modern audiences demand.

But even with all that potential, the computer is just a tool, a vehicle to enable the expression of your creativity. It's only with knowledge and talent that great characters are born. I have always enjoyed sharing my knowledge and teaching people what I've learned, and this series gives you the knowledge you need to unleash your talent and create world-class 3D characters.

This Series Is for You

When I started in 3D animation there was very little in the way of training, and 3D character animation was still in its infancy. Because many of the techniques that are common today just weren't available, I had to figure a lot of it out for myself. If you're just starting out in 3D character creation I envy you, because this book and its companion, *Volume 1: Modeling & Texturing*, are the books that I wish I had so many times during my career.

If you have experience in creating 3D characters, this series teaches you how to take your characters to the next level and shows you the easy way to accomplish things that have always seemed difficult.

If you're an animator who doesn't enjoy character creation because all you want to do is animate, this series teaches you the fastest and easiest ways to create characters so you spend less time fighting with the character and more time animating, and have more fun doing it.

There are few resources available that deal with all of the aspects of 3D character creation. Many claim to but end up only scratching the surface, leaving out vital information or, even worse, teaching bad habits and inefficient techniques. This series shows you how to make a character capable of acting in every sense of the word, with the ability to express complex emotions that are essential to achieving high-quality animation, whether you're creating characters for use in your own animations or in a production environment. Many other resources use supplied content so they can skip important steps. This series guides you through every step along the way toward creating successful characters so you only need to use the supplied content if you choose to.

While short movies are often created by a single person, commercial animation productions usually involve a number of animators working with the characters. This series teaches those extra steps that are vital to ensure that an animator understands the animation controls, that the character is easy to animate, and that the character looks good when animated. Even if you're just creating characters for your own animation, those extra steps make posing and animating the character much quicker and easier.

There is rarely just one way to accomplish something in 3D creation or animation. While I have preferred methods that have evolved over a number of years of production experience, they're not necessarily the right way — just my way. Everyone has different preferred methods for creation and animation, and every character has different requirements. This series does what no other resource does; instead of just teaching my preferred methods, I provide many examples of alternate techniques and how and when to use them, and explain why I choose my preferred techniques.

Character creation is largely about problem solving, but as much as I'd like to, I can't give you a solution for every problem that you'll come across. My solution to this is to make sure that you have the knowledge and understand the techniques that you need to solve any problem that may arise. Most resources tell you *how* to accomplish a specific task, but the same technique is difficult to apply to your own work unless you know *why* it's used, and *when* it should and should not be used. My teaching philosophy is that why something is done a certain way and when it should be done are as important as how it's done. That way you have a solid understanding of the theory and practical knowledge behind the techniques so you can easily apply them to your own work.

This series gives you the knowledge to take what you've learned and build upon it, refining existing techniques and developing new techniques. Character creation and animation is a constantly evolving art form and thinking outside the box is how the evolution takes place. If you can take a technique further or find a more efficient way of accomplishing a task, then do it. Like everyone else, I'm always learning, and will continue to refine and develop the techniques that I've shared with you. It's what keeps this job fun and interesting, and makes ours the best job in the world.

Why LightWave 3D?

LightWave 3D is uniquely adapted to speed and ease of use while retaining the power and depth of features that are required for character creation and animation. It's easy to learn and doesn't require complex, advanced knowledge to do the basic tasks necessary for character creation. Using LightWave 3D you can create and rig characters for animation more quickly and easily than in any other package.

LightWave 3D has a very strong online community. Whenever you need help with any aspect of the program or any technique, there will always be someone there to help. This is especially important when you're first learning, but is invaluable even to experienced users. There are hundreds of plug-ins available to make your job even easier, and most of them are free. If you need something even more powerful, you can be sure that there's a commercial plug-in available to suit the task, at a reasonable price.

LightWave 3D 8 expands the character creation toolset even further, making the work involved in character creation faster and easier than ever before. This book and its companion volume take full advantage of the existing features as well as the features new to LightWave 3D 8 to ensure that you use the most efficient methods available for creating your characters.

Although it uses the toolset in LightWave 3D 8, this book is just as valuable if you're using an earlier version of LightWave or another package entirely. The essential principles and required tasks of character creation remain the same for all 3D characters, even though the steps to achieve a certain task may differ between packages. What I teach are theories that are program independent and character creation methods and techniques that are applicable to the creation of all 3D characters no matter what package is used.

How to Use the Books

I originally set out to write a single book on cartoon character creation. I knew it would be a fairly large book due to the number of topics relevant to the subject matter, but little did I realize just how big it would become. As I was nearing completion it became apparent that as one book it was far too big to publish, and I had a decision to make — either reduce the content to fit in a single book, or separate it into two books. It wasn't too difficult a decision to go with two books, as the last thing I wanted to do was to reduce the learning potential for you, the reader. So what was originally one book is now a two-volume set: *Volume 1: Modeling & Texturing* and *Volume 2: Rigging & Animation*.

Volume 1: Modeling & Texturing

Volume 1: Modeling & Texturing explains the process of creating 3D characters. Character design, modeling, and texturing are the fundamental building blocks of character animation. This book guides you through creating two characters, explaining the techniques for every step of the process including subpatch modeling, UV mapping, surfacing, and image mapping.

- **Part I — Preparation** explains what to do before you start the creation process. It shows you how to set up LightWave for character creation and what steps you need to take in the character concept, design, and planning stages.

- **Part II — Morfi** is an introduction to character creation, catering to the reader who has little or no prior experience in creating characters. It provides a quick entry to character creation so you can jump into the practical, creative work straight away, while at the same time giving you the opportunity to learn multiple techniques. Part II also includes a bonus chapter that provides a quick start to rigging.

- **Part III — Hamish** starts at a more advanced level, assuming the reader has a good understanding of the basic techniques described in Part II. It explains the process of modeling and texturing characters, including UV mapping, surfacing, and image map creation and application.

Volume 2: Rigging & Animation

Volume 2: Rigging & Animation follows on directly from Volume 1, explaining the process of preparing characters for animation. Proper rigging and animation preparation is vital for creating characters that can truly act and make an audience believe they are living, emotive beings. Volume 2 guides you through multiple rigging techniques, including bipeds and quadrupeds, advanced and alternate animation controls, and using dynamics for clothes and secondary motion, and includes a comprehensive explanation of facial animation.

- **Part I — Morph Creation** explains how to create and use morphs effectively. It describes the morphs that are necessary for facial expressions and lip sync, with examples from multiple characters, and explains the most efficient ways of creating those morphs.

- **Part II — Character Setup** explains the process of setting up characters for animation, including making the character deform well and making it easy to animate. It describes methods for automating motion to complement the animation controls, alternate rigging techniques for different control methods, and applying an existing rig to different characters. This section expands on the quick-start rigging chapter from Volume I, including all the theories behind the techniques.

- **Part III — Animation and Dynamics** explains the process of animating 3D characters. It explains how to use the controls for efficient animation practices, how to configure the character rig for different styles of animation, and how to animate facial expressions and lip sync, including the creation of custom morph controls. Additionally, it covers the use of dynamics for automated motion of clothing and secondary motion of the body.

The Appendix in each book contains descriptions of all the plug-ins included in the tutorials and on the CD, and provides information on other useful resources.

Both volumes contain the important theory behind the techniques and methods provided, so that when you complete the books you can continue to use them as a reference when creating your own characters. These books don't contain long-winded anecdotes or long, drawn-out explanations, but provide concise and complete explanations of every technique so you can learn quickly and effectively.

Each chapter starts with the most general theory, the techniques that apply to all characters and to all 3D packages. Following, are the theories and techniques that are more specific to LightWave 3D. Finally there are detailed steps in the tutorials, making use of the theories and techniques described earlier. The tutorials explain proper and efficient workflow practices and how to make the most of the LightWave 3D 8 toolset.

These books are companions to rather than replacements for the LightWave 3D manual. No matter what program you use, I highly recommend reading the manual every six months. It's only possible to learn and retain what you can comprehend. Many people only read the manual when they first learn a package, and even then rarely read it all. At that stage in the learning process you can only comprehend a certain amount of what is revealed. By reading the manual every six months you take advantage of your increased experience because you're able to comprehend more. Each time you read the manual you learn much more and retain that knowledge longer.

CD Content

Everything you need to follow the tutorials is included on the companion CD.

- There are sample objects, scenes, and images for every step along the way, enabling you to jump ahead to learn a specific topic.
- All the plug-ins used in the book are supplied, as well as many other plug-ins that can be helpful in character creation, including demo versions of some useful commercial plug-ins.

- All the images and illustrations from the book are supplied in full color.
- There are sample animations and images to inspire and delight you.

For a more complete list of the content, see the readme.txt file on the root of the CD.

Contacting the Author

You can contact me and see more of my work through my web site at www.zerogravity.com.au.

If you have any questions regarding this book, if you get stuck, or if you want some advice about a character you're creating or a technique you're developing, be sure to check out the support site at www.zerogravity.com.au/cartoon.

You can also find me loitering on a few popular forums under the name Kretin.

Chapter 1

Getting Started

Before starting on the tutorials, it's useful to set up a few preferences for working in LightWave. I've structured the following steps starting from the default installation. If you've been using LightWave for a while, you've probably already made some of these changes to suit your own way of working. If your own preferences differ from these, you may need to reinterpret some instructions along the way, as the tutorials in this book assume you have set the interface and options as specified here.

> **Note:** If you've followed the Getting Started chapter in *Volume 1: Modeling & Texturing* you will already have the options and settings configured. You just need to copy the files and load the plug-ins unique to this book.

1.1 Files and Folders

LightWave works with content directories. When working on a model or a scene, LightWave looks in the Content Directory for any files it needs. Using this functionality is a great way to keep your projects separate, and also allows you to store your projects separately from the main program. Figure 1.1-1 shows the folder structure that LightWave uses.

Figure 1.1-1. LightWave's content folder structure.

When you open a new scene, the Scenes folder within the specified Content Directory is where LightWave looks first. From there you can specify a different directory, but it's always good to keep within the Content Directory if you can. Working this way makes it much easier to copy a specific project to send to someone else or to back up your work.

1. Copy the **LWProjects** folder from the CD to your hard drive, preferably somewhere other than in the LightWave folder. This is a good folder to keep all your LightWave projects in. If you open the folder you'll find the working files for the tutorials in this book, as well as a Project Template folder that you can copy and rename for each new project.

Note: In Windows, after you copy the folder to the hard drive, right-click on it and select Properties at the bottom of the context menu. In the Properties window, uncheck Read-only, then click Apply. In the following dialog box, choose Apply changes to this folder, subfolders and files and click OK, then OK again to close the Properties window.

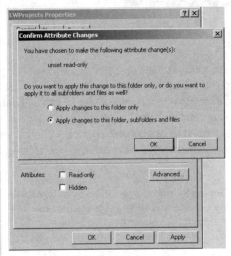

Figure 1.1-2. Changing attributes.

When copying files from a CD, they're copied to the hard drive as read only. This step changes the attributes of the copied files so you can edit or modify the files.

2.   To start a new project, make a copy of the **Project Template** folder and rename the copied folder appropriately for the project. This gives you all the folders LightWave needs, as well as some useful starting scenes.

You'll also see a folder in LWProjects called NewPlugins. This is where I've included the third-party plug-ins used during the course of this book. It's always a good idea to keep your third-party plug-ins separate from the plug-ins installed with LightWave. If you already have a third-party plug-ins folder, feel free to copy these plug-ins to your existing folder. If you do not, I recommend using this folder to store your third-party plug-ins from now on.

1.2 Modifying Shortcuts

Next we'll customize the shortcuts for Modeler and Layout. LightWave stores its settings in config (.cfg) files. If you don't specify where these are kept, they default to Documents and Settings in Windows or System:Preferences on Macintosh. It's better to have the configs stored in their own folder so they can more easily be modified and backed up. Additionally, you may want to have different configs for different projects or different installations of LightWave (if you have multiple versions of LightWave on the same machine).

1. Create a **Configs** folder in your LightWave directory.

2. Right-click on the shortcut for Modeler and change the **Target** to read: **C:\LightWave\programs\modeler.exe -cC:\LightWave\Configs**, changing **C:\LightWave** to the drive and directory where you have LightWave installed.

3. Repeat with the shortcut for LightWave, adding **-cC:\LightWave\Configs** to the Target.

Using these shortcuts, both Modeler and Layout will look in the C:\LightWave\ Configs folder for their config files.

If you have been using LightWave for a while and already have configs that you wish to continue using, make sure you copy your existing config files to the Configs folder.

If you want to use different configs, you can copy the shortcuts and point them to a different Configs folder, being sure to rename the new shortcuts appropriately.

> **Note:** You can also specify to disable the Hub in the shortcuts by adding -0, but since we're using the Hub we won't do that. This option can be useful to include in a copy of your main shortcuts so you can run a second copy of LightWave independently of the Hub if you want to quickly do something in a different content directory without interfering with other work you're doing.

1.3 Configuring Modeler

Options

There are two types of options in LightWave: General Options and Display Options. The shortcut keys for these are the same for both Modeler and Layout: **o** for General Options and **d** for Display Options.

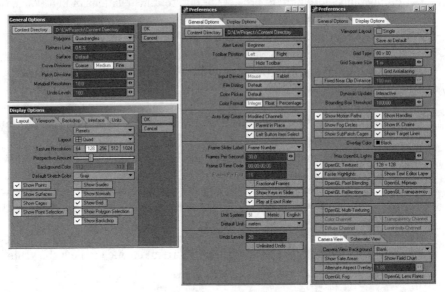

Figure 1.3-1. General Options and Display Options. Left: Modeler, right: Layout.

Launch Modeler from the shortcut so we can set up the options and window layout.

1. Press **o** to open General Options.

2. Change Patch Divisions to **3**. The reason for doing this is that Layout defaults to a subpatch level of 3. You can change this setting while working in Modeler, but if you model using a subpatch level of 3 it's easier to know if you need to adjust this setting when you import the model into Layout.

3. Change Undo Levels to a nice high number; somewhere between 50 and 100 is good.

> **Note:** General Options is also where you set the Content Directory in Modeler. Keep in mind that the Content Directory is a global setting that is the same for Modeler and Layout.

4. Click **OK** or press **Enter** to close General Options.

5. Press **d** to open Display Options. There are five tabs at the top of the window, each relating to different types of options. We'll start with the default tab, Layout.

6. The default Perspective Amount is very high, and can cause distortion in your modeling if you frequently work in Perspective view. I prefer to set it to about the middle of the 128 button (in the Texture Resolution setting). This is a more natural perspective amount to work with.

7. See Figure 1.3-2 for which Show option check boxes I have set as a default. The illustrations in the tutorials reflect my settings, but feel free to set them however you wish to best suit your preferences.

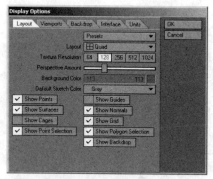

Figure 1.3-2. Display Options>Layout.

8. Click the **Viewports** tab. Here you can adjust the default settings for each view independently. The only one we'll change is the Perspective view, or TR.

9. Click on **TR** and check **Independent Zoom** and **Independent Visibility**. You can also check **Independent BG Color** and change that to a color that best shows the models. I usually like to use a desaturated dark blue, but for the purposes of clear illustrations I've left it the default gray.

10. Notice that when you check Independent Visibility the lower options become active. Now you can adjust the way models are viewed in the Perspective view. See Figure 1.3-3 for which check boxes I have set.

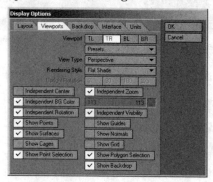

Figure 1.3-3. Display Options>Viewports, Viewport TR.

11. We'll look at Backdrop a little later, so there's just one more setting to change now. Click the **Units** tab and change Grid Snap to **None**.

12. Click **OK** or press **Enter** to close Display Options.

Interface

The next step is to open all the panels and arrange them on the right side of the display. Having these panels open all the time makes it much easier to use the advanced tool options, select points or polygons, select and modify layers, and select and modify vertex maps, all of which is done in later chapters.

1. Select the right edge of Modeler and drag it in from the side of the display.

2. Open the Numeric panel using the button at the bottom of the interface or by pressing **n**.

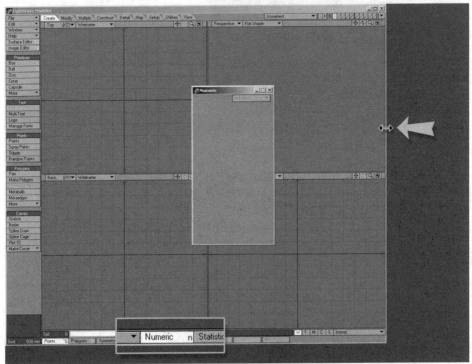

Figure 1.3-4. Drag the Modeler window to the left to make room for the panels.

3. Open the Statistics panel using the button at the bottom of the interface (or by pressing **w**).

4. Open the Vertex Maps and Layers panels from the **Window** pull-down (or press **Ctrl+F5** and **Ctrl+F6**).

5. Arrange the four windows as shown in Figure 1.3-5.

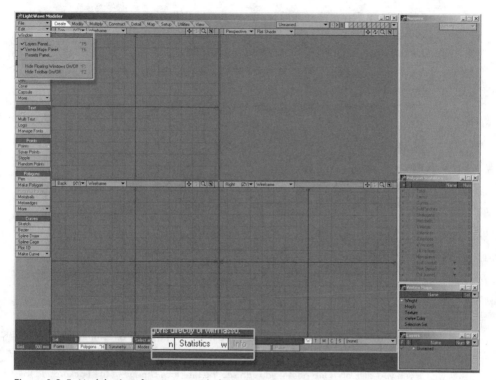

Figure 1.3-5. Modeler interface set up with the Numeric, Statistics, Vertex Maps, and Layers panels.

Now we'll install the plug-ins included on the companion CD and set up a place for them in the menu.

1. Open the Edit Plug-ins window by selecting **Utilities**≻**Plug-ins**≻**Edit Plug-ins** (or press **Alt+F11**).

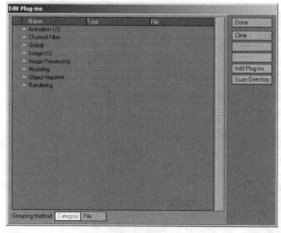

Figure 1.3-6. Edit Plug-ins window.

2. Click **Scan Directory** and browse to the **LWProjects\NewPlugins** folder on your hard drive. Select the folder and click **OK**.

3. Click **Done** to close the Edit Plug-ins window.

4. Open the Configure Menus window using **Edit**➤**Edit Menu Layout** (or press **Alt+F10**).

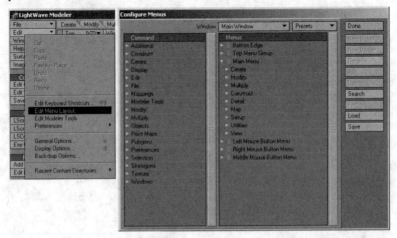

Figure 1.3-7. Configure Menus window. The left panel has a list of commands or tools, and the right panel has a list of menus. The listing under Main Menu in the Menus panel is what we are editing. This includes the tabs and tools of the main interface. When you click on a tab name, you can see the interface change in the background to display that tab, so you can see the interface update as you make changes.

5. Open the **Construct** group in the Command panel, and open **Main Menu**➤**Map**➤**General** in the Menus panel.

6. Drag **Unweld Points** from the Command panel to just below **Clear Map** in the Menus panel.

Figure 1.3-8. Adding Unweld Points to the Map tab.

7. Select **Main Menu≻View** and click **New Group**. Making a new group at this level creates a new tab.

8. Double-click on the new group and choose a name. I call it **Plugs**.

9. Expand **Main Menu≻Utilities≻Plug-ins** and drag **Additional** down to **Plugs**. If you select Plugs now, you can see all your new plug-ins under the Additional heading on the interface. Feel free to organize the plug-ins on the Plugs tab into different groups.

Figure 1.3-9. Moving Additional to the new Plugs tab.

1.4 Configuring Layout

Options

Launch Layout either from the shortcut (if it's the first time you're running it) or from Modeler via the pop-up menu button to the right of the layer buttons (see Figure 1.4-1).

Figure 1.4-1. Modeler can communicate with Layout through this menu. Once you've launched Layout from the shortcut (telling the Hub where to find it), you can also launch Layout from this menu.

First we'll set up the viewports and other options. How you configure your viewports can be a very personal preference. Almost everyone I've seen has it set differently. Because I'm doing the storytelling here, it's best to stick to my preference for now, but as always, if you're experienced enough with LightWave, feel free to use your own setup and adjust the instructions to suit. Even if you have an existing preference, I recommend trying this configuration. As we go through the tutorials I explain more about why I use this viewport layout.

1. Press **d** to open Display Options.

Figure 1.4-2. Default display options.

2. Change Viewport Layout to **2 Left, 1 Right.**
3. Change Grid Square Size to **0.25 m** (or 250 mm).
4. With Display Options still open, change the top-left viewport to **Camera View** and the right viewport to **Perspective.**
5. Change the Top (XZ) Maximum Render Level to **Front Face Wireframe.**

Figure 1.4-3. Changing Maximum Render Level.

6. Back in Display Options, check **Show Safe Areas** in the Camera View settings.
7. Click **Save as Default.**

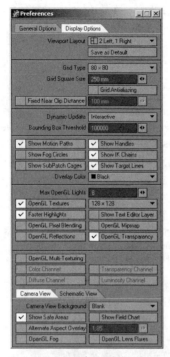

Figure 1.4-4. Adjusted display options.

We'll revisit some of these settings during the course of our work, but these are a good starting point.

Take a look at the setting for Alert Level in Modeler➤Display Options and in Layout➤General Options.

This defaults to Beginner, and controls how you're alerted to errors and warnings. Even if you're new to LightWave I'd recommend changing this to Intermediate; once you're comfortable with LightWave, change it to Expert. You

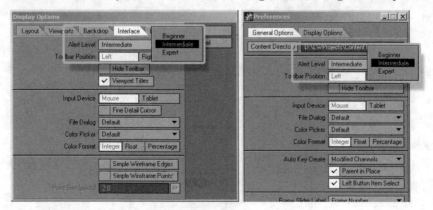

Figure 1.4-5. Alert Level. Left: Modeler, right: Layout.

still get the messages, but they appear in the Information line at the bottom of the interface instead of pop-up dialog boxes. You'll be amazed at how much quicker you can work when you're not clicking OK on dialog boxes every two minutes.

Interface

It's useful to have the Scene Editor open all the time. If you have the luxury of two displays you can place the Scene Editor in the second display, leaving the viewports clear. One of the Scene Editor's most useful functions is easy item selection, but if you only have a single display you can just open Scene Editor when you need it.

> **Note:** I have become very accustomed to having two displays. I highly rec-
> ommend a dual display system if you're serious about doing 3D graphics or
> animation. This allows you to have the main program on one display and
> pop-up windows on the other, which can be invaluable to your work flow. Some
> people like to have Modeler on one display and Layout on the other, which can
> also be useful.

1. Select **Scene Editor**➢**Classic Scene Editor**.
2. Move and scale the Scene Editor window so it covers the Perspective viewport.

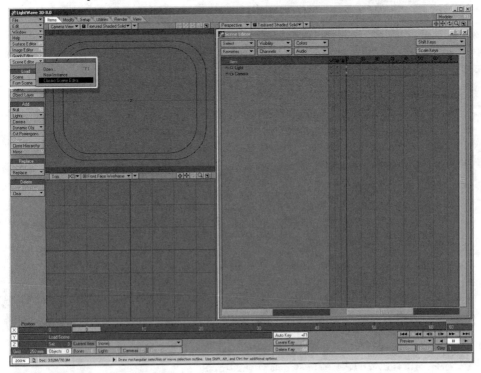

Figure 1.4-6. Classic Scene Editor.

3. If you have dual display, move the Scene Editor window to the second display; otherwise, close it.

> **Note:** There are two types of Scene Editor in LightWave 8 — the Classic Scene Editor and the new Scene Editor. The new Scene Editor is scene reliant, so there's no point in setting its position at this stage.

As we did in Modeler, we need to install the plug-ins from the CD and set up a place for them in the menu. The steps are pretty much the same for Layout as they were for Modeler.

1. Open the Edit Plug-ins window using **Utilities**≻**Plug-ins**≻**Edit Plug-ins** (or press **Alt+F11**).

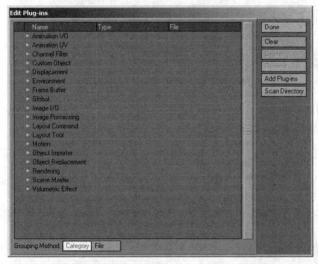

Figure 1.4-7. Edit Plug-ins window.

2. Click **Scan Directory** and browse to the **LWProjects\NewPlugins** folder on your hard drive. Select the folder and click **OK**.

3. Click **Done** to close the Edit Plug-ins window.

4. Open the Configure Menus window using **Edit**≻**Edit Menu Layout** (**Alt+F10**).

5. Open the **Preferences** group in the Command panel, and open the **Top Group** in the Menus panel.

6. Select **Scene Editor** in the Menus panel and click **New Group**. Double-click on the new group to rename it, deleting its name. This creates a small gap between buttons.

7. Drag **Parent in Place On/Off** from the Command panel to just below the new blank group in the right panel.

Figure 1.4-8. Configure Menus window.

8. Select **Main Menu▸View** and click **New Group**. Making a new group at this level creates a new tab.

9. Double-click on the new group and type in the same name as the tab we created in Modeler — **Plugs**.

10. Expand **Main Menu▸Utilities▸Plugins** and drag **Additional** down to **Plugs**. If you select Plugs now, you can see the Additional pull-down on the interface. Feel free to organize the plug-ins in the Plugs▸Additional tab into different groups.

Figure 1.4-9. Changing the Layout menu.

One last thing to do is to make sure that Auto Key, at the bottom of the Layout interface, is turned on.

Figure 1.4-10. Auto Key on.

I leave this on all the time, but I know some people like to turn it off when they're animating. Some motion modifiers require Auto Key to be on for interactive updates, and because I can't guarantee that everything will work as described with it turned off, you should keep Auto Key on while you're following the tutorials in this book.

Keyboard Shortcuts

You may have already noticed many interface changes in LightWave 8 from previous versions. Although we haven't covered keyboard shortcuts in this chapter, there are some significant changes to these as well. If you've used previous versions of LightWave 3D, then you're used to the LightWave shortcuts for undo, cut, copy, and paste:

- Undo   u
- Cut   x
- Copy   c
- Paste   v

These shortcuts have been changed in LightWave 8 to the Windows standards:

- Undo   **Ctrl+z**
- Cut   **Ctrl+x**
- Copy   **Ctrl+c**
- Paste   **Ctrl+v**

If you're used to the previous shortcuts and wish to continue using them in LightWave 8, you can easily revert to LightWave 7.5 keyboard shortcuts.

Note: Be aware that if you revert to 7.5 shortcuts you'll lose many of the updated shortcuts in the default configuration. You may find it more beneficial just to remap the old shortcuts into the new configuration.

1.   Open the Configure Keys window, **Edit▷Edit Keyboard Shortcuts** (or press **Alt+F9**).

2. Click the **Presets** pull-down and select **7.0 Style** in Modeler or **7.5 Style** in Layout.

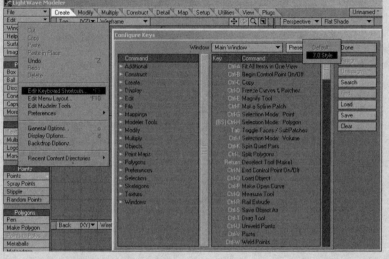

Figure 1.4-11. Edit Keyboard Shortcuts, using Presets.

Now that we've set up the basic defaults for each program, we need to save them. You can save your menu configuration separately from the Configure Menus window or, to save everything we've just done, close all three applications — Modeler, Layout, and the Hub. Closing the applications saves the settings to the config files. You can relaunch Modeler or Layout to continue working.

Part I

Morph Creation

In *Volume 1: Modeling & Texturing* we created and textured Hamish. Part I —
Morph Creation picks up from where we left off in Volume 1. If you have the
Hamish objects you created in Volume 1, you can continue to use those; otherwise, feel free to use the objects and scenes provided to jump ahead to a
specific chapter or topic.

The following chapter explains how to use morphs effectively and how to
create them efficiently. Using morphs for facial expression and lip sync animation is explained in Chapter 5, "Animation."

Chapter 2

Morphs

Morphs are the ideal way to create facial expressions for cartoon characters. While using morphs is not the only way to create facial animation, it is the easiest method for both creating and animating facial expressions. You have more flexibility using morphs than other techniques such as using bones, as you have full control over the position of every point in the model for each morph.

LightWave's implementation of morphs, called endomorphs, is unique in that it records new point positions for each point included in the morph in a vertex map. This means that all your morphs are held within the model itself instead of having a different model file for each morph. Other benefits of endomorphs are that you can adjust point positions in the base model at any time and have those changes automatically propagate through the morphs, you can add or remove geometry and the morphs update appropriately, and you can create multiple characters from a single base character without having to create new morphs for each one, as they just inherit the morphs from the base character (although they will likely need some adjustments).

The drawback to morphs is that they are linear. This means that the points move from A to B in a straight line. While it's rarely noticeable when the morphs are mixed together and moving fluidly, it can be noticed in certain situations. The eyelids are one of the most common areas you might notice this, which is why we used bones instead of morphs for Morfi's eyelids. A bit later in the book we look at some ways to overcome the linear aspect of morphs when it becomes a problem.

2.1 Planning

For every character you need to determine what morphs it needs. While the basic morph list shown later in this section is a great starting point, different characters often have different needs. Some characters may not need all the morphs in the basic list, while others may need more specialized morphs. Choosing the right morphs for your character depends on having a solid understanding of how morphs are used.

The most important resource for creating facial expressions is a mirror. Make sure you have one next to you at all times when creating the morphs. When you start to create a new morph, make the same expression while looking in the mirror to see what your face looks like and how it changes when you move back and forth from a neutral expression to the required expression. By doing this you have a much better idea of what you need to change in your model to create the same expression. Make sure you check your own face fairly regularly during the creation of the morph to make sure you haven't forgotten anything.

Modular Morphs

Morphs are most effective when they're modular. The benefit of modular morphs is that you only need a few morphs to create hundreds of different expressions by mixing them in different ways and in different amounts. The facial animation of your character will be more fluid the fewer morphs you have. By using modular morphs to their full potential you save yourself a lot of time both in creation and animation, as well as allow more flexibility and variety in your facial animation.

Often this method is described as separating each muscle of the face into its own morph, so when they're mixed they work just like our own faces do by mixing the movement of different muscles to create different expressions. While the method I use is loosely based on this idea, it's been customized for ease of use, combining the motion of some muscles into commonly used expressions such as a smile, which in reality is the combination of multiple muscles.

What is most important when creating modular morphs is to ensure that morphs can be mixed and still work properly. Morphs build on each other, so if a point moves the same amount for two different morphs, when both morphs are at full strength the point moves twice as far as each morph individually. This means you have to be careful when creating the morphs that you don't move points that may adversely affect other morphs. For example, if you include the eyelids in a frown morph, you might have to reduce the frown when the character blinks, as otherwise the eyelids will not meet properly for the blink. By excluding the edges of the eyelids from the frown morph, the character can blink while frowning, which is far more desirable.

A mistake I see often is morphs that are too specific, like emotion morphs such as a Happy morph that encompasses the entire face. Morphs like these limit your flexibility and require more work when animating. You need to think about how each morph affects the other morphs it may be mixed with. Each morph builds on the other active morphs when mixed, so if the Happy morph includes the eyelids half shut, the Blink morph would then move the eyelids far beyond closed. You could include a separate Blink morph to be used with the Happy morph, but then you'd also need a separate version of all the other morphs to be used with the Happy morph, and you'd quickly end up with hundreds of morphs, which would require significant effort to create and would be equally challenging to animate. The solution is to create the basic elements of each emotion in separate morphs so they can be mixed together to create the emotion expressions.

The modular principle applies to all the morphs, including expression morphs and phoneme morphs. If you create your phoneme morphs well, you can mix them with expression morphs to adjust the character's emotion while it is

19

talking. You can also mix phonemes to create more mouth shapes, reducing the number of specific phoneme morphs needed.

What Morphs Do You Need?

When starting a production it's a good idea to sit down with the director and animators and decide on a list of morphs common to every character. While certain characters may require unique morphs, having a common morph list helps continuity and makes the animator's job much easier.

Over time I've developed a basic morph list that I use as a starting point for all my characters. These morphs provide for all of the basic emotions and mouth shapes necessary to create convincing facial animation. Feel free to add a few more morphs to the list for your own production to add nuance or variety, but before you do, try to create the required expression using these morphs first, only adding a new morph if the expression is not possible using the basic morphs.

The basic morph list is shown here using Hamish as the example. When we look at the morphs in more detail later in this chapter, each one is shown with multiple character examples.

Eye Morphs

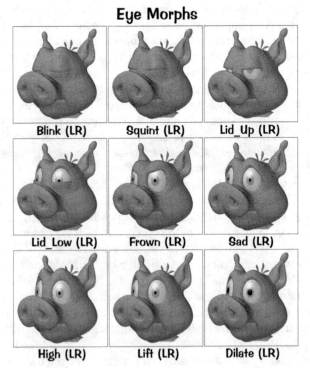

Blink (LR)	Squint (LR)	Lid_Up (LR)
Lid_Low (LR)	Frown (LR)	Sad (LR)
High (LR)	Lift (LR)	Dilate (LR)

Mouth Morphs

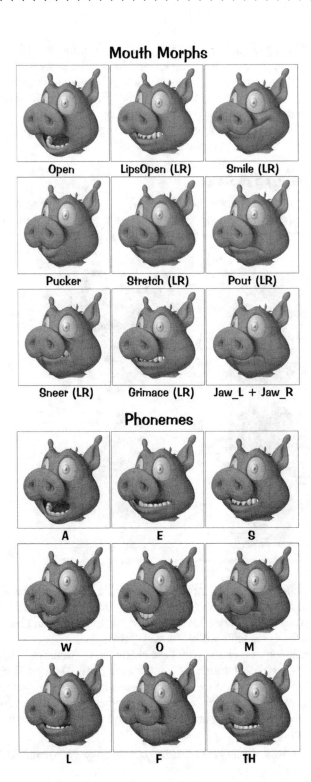

Open   LipsOpen (LR)   Smile (LR)

Pucker   Stretch (LR)   Pout (LR)

Sneer (LR)   Grimace (LR)   Jaw_L + Jaw_R

Phonemes

A   E   S

W   O   M

L   F   TH

While it's not always necessary for simple animation, the morphs listed with (LR) next to them can have the left and right sides separated into additional morphs for greater variety of expression. By including the left and right separations you can achieve asymmetrical facial animation, giving much more personality and liveliness to your characters.

So let's take a look at each of these morphs in more detail, then we'll go ahead and create the morphs for Hamish.

2.2 Eye Morphs

The eye morphs include the motion and expression of the eyelids and eyebrows.

Before we move on to the morphs, let's take a look at the base models for the characters used in the following examples.

Figure 2.2-1. Base models.

I've included a range of characters for the examples. Each character has slightly different requirements, so you can see the differences for each morph. For the eye morphs I've included Taylor* (top-right) to show examples of the eye morphs for a character without any eyebrows.

When you're creating your base character, try to make its expression as neutral as possible. Often a concept for a character shows it smiling or showing some sort of emotion. If you model emotion into the base character it makes creating and animating the facial features much more difficult, so model it in a neutral expression, allowing the morphs and animation to do the job of expressing emotion.

* Taylor appears courtesy of Live Bait Productions – www.livebaitproductions.com.

Blink

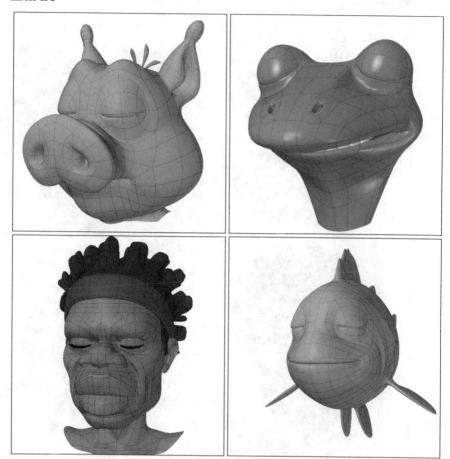

Figure 2.2-2. Eye.Blink.

When we blink, our upper lid tends to travel farther than our lower lid, creating a meeting of the eyelids about two-thirds of the way down the eye. The upper lid also tends to be slightly heavier than the lower lid, so it overlaps the lower eyelid a little bit. This also helps to define the shape of the join between lids.

Blink should only affect the eyelid geometry.

This morph is used for blinking, sleeping, feeling sleepy, or anywhere else a character closes his eyes.

Squint

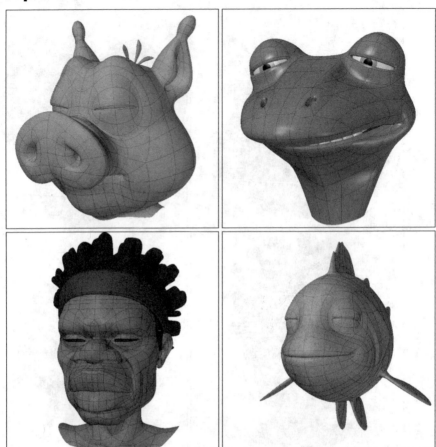

Figure 2.2-3. Eye.Squint.

The squint is very similar to the blink, except the eyelids meet in the middle of the eye.

Squint should only affect the eyelid geometry.

Squint is used to convey distrust, reacting to bright light, or trying to see something far away. It can also be used for blinking when a character's eyes are looking up.

Lid_Up

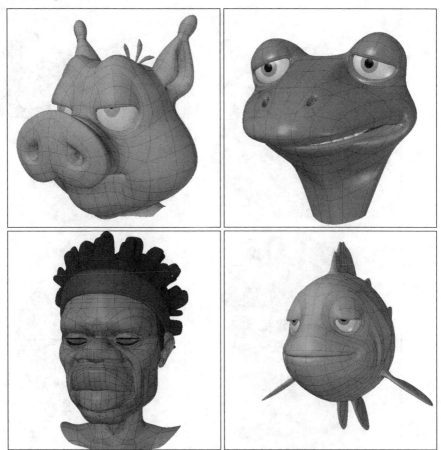

Figure 2.2-4. Eye.Lid_Up.

This is just the upper eyelid part of Squint.

Lid_Up should only affect the upper eyelid geometry.

The upper eyelid is used to convey condescension or can be used when a character is looking down. It can also enhance an angry expression when used with the Frown morph.

Lid_Low

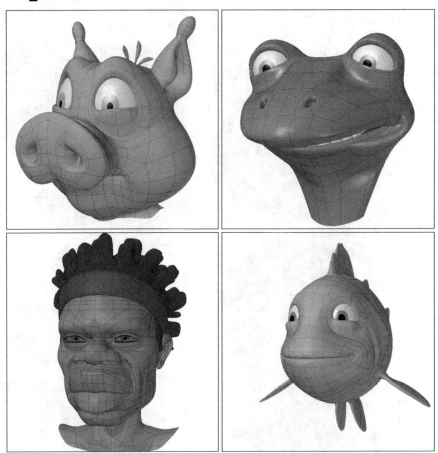

Figure 2.2-5. Eye.Lid_Low.

This is just the lower eyelid part of Squint.

Lid_Low should only affect the lower eyelid geometry.

The lower eyelid can be used to convey sadness or can be used when a character is looking up. A single lower eyelid can twitch to indicate the onset of a nervous breakdown.

Frown

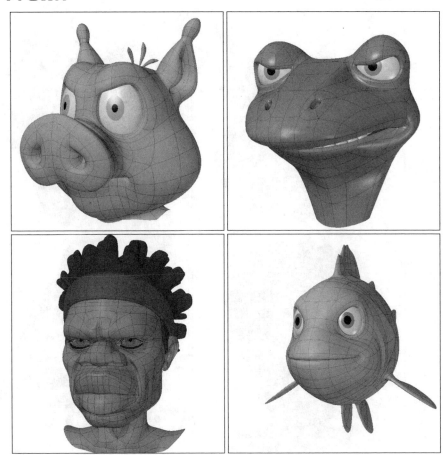

Figure 2.2-6. Eye.Frown.

The frown is the downward movement of the eyebrows. Often some of the upper eyelid geometry is employed to some degree in cartoon characters to enhance or exaggerate the expression. For most characters, take care not to move the leading edge of the eyelid or you may need an extra morph for blinking.

The exception to this is when a character doesn't have eyebrows (as in the top-right example); then it may be necessary to include the eyelids to produce the frown. In this case you need to reduce the Frown morph when blinking, but that's alright because reducing the Frown morph to blink doesn't adversely affect the expression.

Frown should mainly affect the eyebrow geometry, using the top and middle areas of the eyelid to enhance the expression if necessary.

The frown mainly conveys anger, although it can also convey confusion or surprise when used asymmetrically.

Sad

Figure 2.2-7. Eye.Sad.

The Sad morph is the upward movement of the inside of the eyebrows. To exaggerate the expression you can also move the outside of the eyebrows down a little. As with the Frown, be careful when using the eyelid geometry to enhance the expression.

Sad should mainly affect the eyebrow geometry, using the top and middle areas of the eyelid to enhance the expression if necessary.

The Sad morph can convey sadness, pleading, or fear.

High

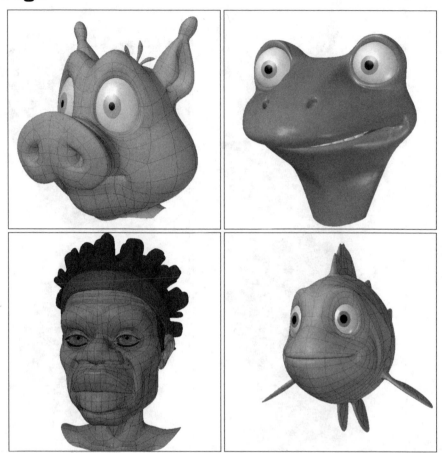

Figure 2.2-8. Eye.High.

The High morph is the upward movement of the entire eyebrow.

High should only affect the eyebrow geometry.

The High morph can convey fear or disbelief, or confusion when used asymmetrically. It can also be used to emphasize a point.

Lift

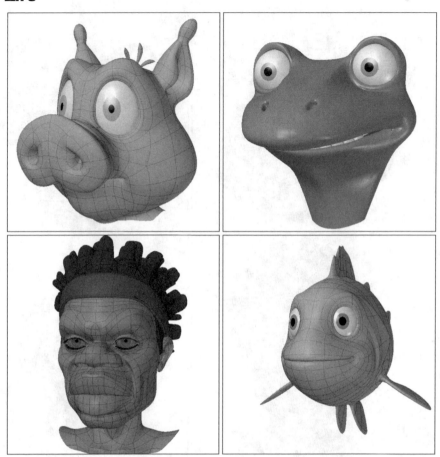

Figure 2.2-9. Eye.Lift.

The Lift morph is the upward movement of the outside of the eyebrows.

Lift should only affect the eyebrow geometry.

The Lift morph can convey frustration or disbelief, or confusion when used asymmetrically.

Dilate

Figure 2.2-10. Eye.Dilate.

Dilate is the dilating of the pupil. If you've created the pupil small, then you need to make it larger; if the pupil is large, then you should make it smaller. When the eyeball is a single sphere, as we have in Morfi (see *Volume 1: Modeling & Texturing*) and Hamish, make sure you adjust the geometry once you've scaled the pupil to retain the same curvature of the eyeball as the base. Pupil dilation is a subconscious reaction to the amount of light hitting the eyeball. The pupil becomes larger in lower light and smaller in bright light. It's usually a good idea to default to somewhere in between the two extremes.

Dilate should only affect the pupil and iris of the eyeball.

As well as indicating the level of light, offsetting the amount of dilation for each pupil can convey insanity.

2.3 Mouth Morphs

The mouth morphs include the motion and expression of the lower part of the face including the mouth, jaw, cheeks, and nose.

Don't forget about the inner mouth geometry when creating the mouth morphs. You need to adjust the inner mouth to match the movement of the lips and cheeks, even though it's not always immediately obvious.

Make sure you don't move the top teeth or roof of the mouth, unless it's for a very specific reason. The top teeth and roof of the mouth are attached to the skull and only move with the head. While many real-life rules can be broken when dealing with cartoon characters, this is rarely one of them. If the top teeth move separately from the head when a character is animated, it looks strange and detracts from the believability of the character.

Open

Open is the opening of the jaw. This motion is really quite complex when you look at it closely. The main movement is in the jaw and lower mouth, but the result includes stretching of the lips, cheeks, nostrils, neck, and in human characters, a bulge just in front of the ears at the top of the jawbone. The jaw primarily rotates, but also moves down a little. You can adjust the amount of rotation and downward movement to suit your character. Notice that the lips stretch evenly as the jaw opens, with the corners of the mouth roughly halfway between the top and bottom, but keeping the same distance from each other horizontally. You can exaggerate the squash and stretch aspect of a cartoon character by stretching the cheeks in more as the mouth opens.

Depending on the type of character, you can exaggerate the jaw opening quite a lot as we've done with Morfi (see top-right in the following figures), or keep it to more realistic proportions as with Hamish. If you don't make it too extreme in the morph, you can always give it an extra boost during animation by pushing the morph beyond 100%.

Open affects most of the geometry of the lower face, often including the neck, especially for fat characters where the open jaw creates a double chin effect.

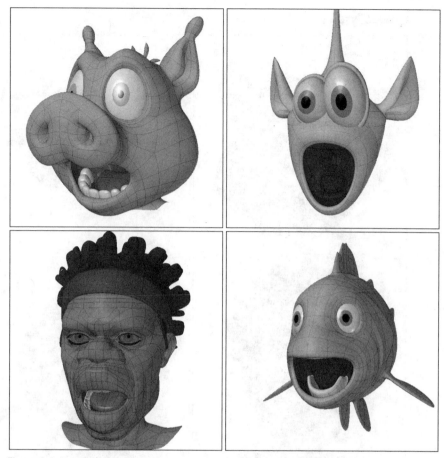

Figure 2.3-1. Mouth.Open.

Open is involved to some degree in almost every expression, and is often used in conjunction with the other mouth morphs. It's also the basis for the phoneme A.

Par

LipsOpen

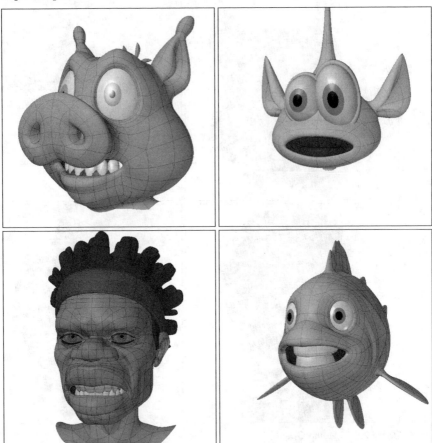

Figure 2.3-2. Mouth.LipsOpen.

The LipsOpen morph is the opening of the lips with the jaw closed, baring the teeth.

LipsOpen affects the lips and some of the area around the lips from the nose down to the chin.

LipsOpen is used for any expression where you want the teeth to show, and is most often used in conjunction with other morphs. It's also the basis for the phoneme S.

Pucker

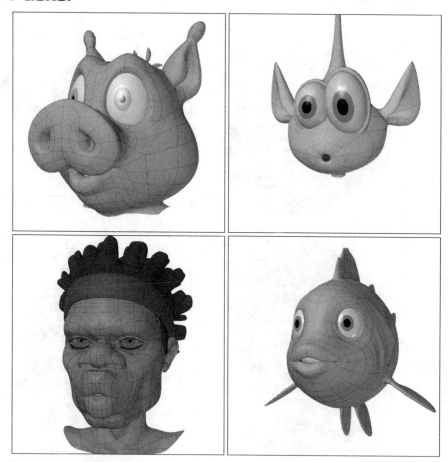

Figure 2.3-3. Mouth.Pucker.

Pucker is the pursing of the lips. Depending on the style of character and type of mouth, you can either create a perfect circle with the lips as we did with Morfi, or create a rounded opening in the middle with the lips pushed forward. The cheeks are fairly heavily involved in the pucker, both moving toward the mouth and sinking in a little, generally stretching in a fair amount for cartoon characters.

Pucker mainly affects the lips and cheeks, with some effect on the nostrils and chin.

Pucker is used for a kiss or can convey surprise. It's also the basis for the phoneme W.

Stretch

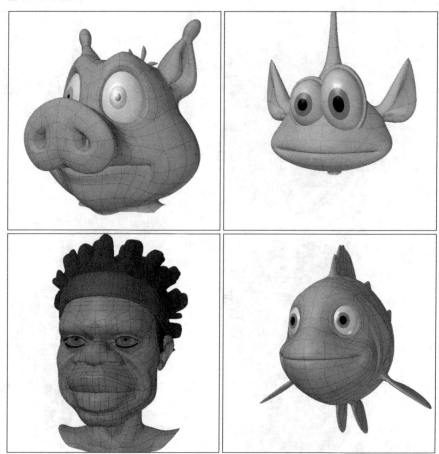

Figure 2.3-4. Mouth.Stretch.

The Stretch morph is the horizontal stretching of the lips. The stretch involves some backward motion of the corners of the mouth and bunching of the cheeks as the lips wrap around the teeth. If your character has dimples, this is one of the expressions that would accentuate them.

Stretch affects the lips and cheeks, including some of the area around the lips from the nose down to the chin.

Stretch can be used to convey frustration and is often used in conjunction with other morphs. It's also used together with Open to create the phoneme E.

Smile

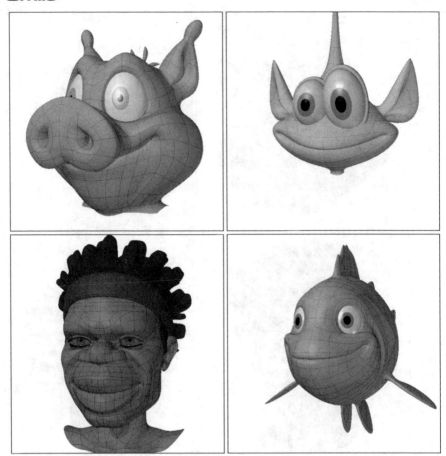

Figure 2.3-5. Mouth.Smile.

The Smile morph is the stretching of the mouth with upward motion of the corners of the mouth, cheeks, and nostrils. The cheeks play a large part in a convincing smile. Make sure you push the cheeks right up under the eyes, even employing some of the lower eyelid geometry to really sell the expression. Dimples are also accentuated with a smile. For cartoon characters, pushing the cheeks outward helps the squash and stretch.

Smile affects the lips and cheeks, with some effect on the nostrils and chin. The Smile is an emotion morph, used to convey happiness.

Pout

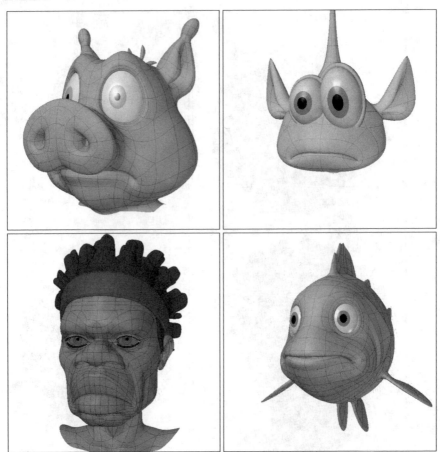

Figure 2.3-6. Mouth.Pout.

The Pout morph is a slight stretching of the mouth with downward motion of the corners of the mouth, cheeks, and nostrils; it is basically the opposite of Smile.

Pout affects the lips and cheeks, with some effect on the nostrils and chin.

The Pout is an emotion morph, used to convey sadness or anger.

Sneer

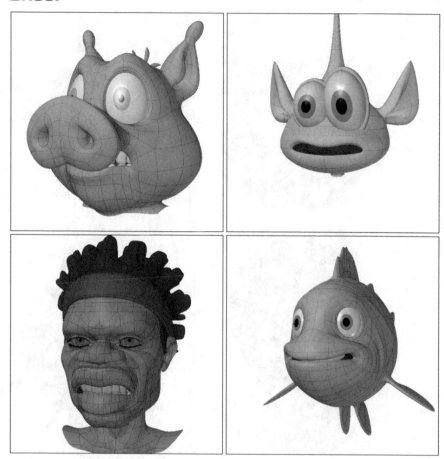

Figure 2.3-7. Mouth.Sneer.

The Sneer morph is the upward movement of the upper lip, accentuating the upward motion at the edges of the lip, baring the upper teeth. The nostrils and cheeks are pushed up toward the eyes.

Sneer affects the upper lip, nose, and cheeks.

The Sneer is an emotion morph, used to convey disgust or anger, or disbelief when used asymmetrically.

Grimace

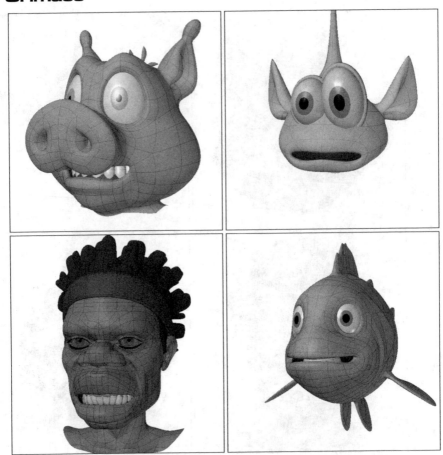

Figure 2.3-8. Mouth.Grimace.

The Grimace morph is the downward movement of the lower lip, accentuating the downward motion at the edges of the lip, baring the lower teeth. For an extreme grimace you can also tense the tendons of the neck, which are used to pull down the corners of the mouth, although this mainly applies to human characters.

Grimace affects the lower lip and chin.

The Grimace is an emotion morph, used to convey shock, anger when combined with Sneer, or apprehension when used asymmetrically.

Jaw_LT

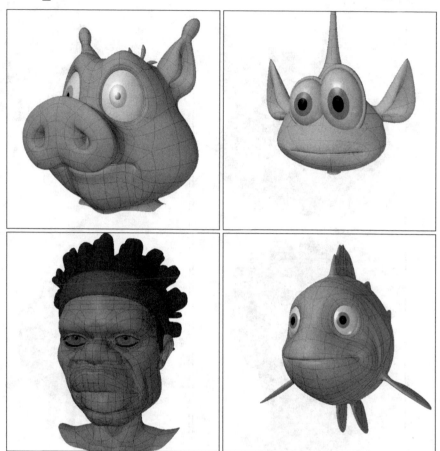

Figure 2.3-9. Mouth.Jaw_LT.

The Jaw_LT morph is the sideways movement of the jaw to the left. The lower lip moves with the jaw, while the upper lip stays in place, only compensating at the corners for the altered position of the lower lip. The jaw primarily moves to the left, but also rotates a little. You can mix the movement and rotation to suit your character. Make sure you adjust the cheeks to follow the new position of the jaw.

Jaw_LT affects the jaw, lips, and cheeks.

Jaw_LT is mainly used to enhance expressions, although it can convey heavy thought.

Jaw_RT

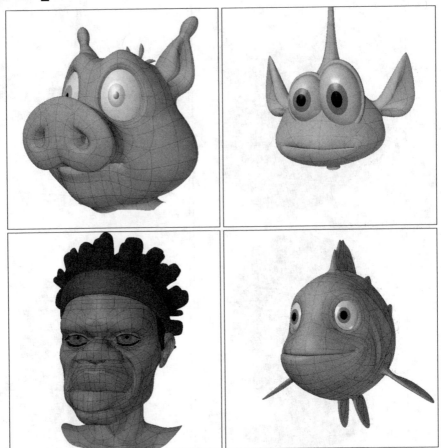

Figure 2.3-10. Mouth.Jaw_RT.

The Jaw_RT morph is the opposite motion of Jaw_LT.

2.4 Phonemes

The decision whether or not to use specific phoneme morphs in your production is an important one. The alternative to using phonemes is to use the mouth expression morphs to create your lip sync, which gives you more control and flexibility, although the benefit to using phonemes is that lip sync is a little quicker and easier to animate.

If you're fairly new to lip sync animation I recommend using phonemes, as it's a little easier to learn, but once you gain more experience, or you want to add some more zing to your animation, try using the mouth expression morphs instead.

Whichever way you choose, it's not really much extra effort to include the phonemes in your model, just in case you decide to use them. If you choose not to use phonemes for your production, you need to include some of the phoneme morphs, with slight adjustments, in the mouth shapes. I've listed those morphs with alternative names.

Many descriptions of phonemes, especially ones found on the net, were written before multiple target morphing was introduced. Many more phonemes were needed back then due to the inability to mix morphs. Now that we have the ability to mix morphs we only need a few phonemes to cover all the mouth shapes necessary for convincing speech, which also results in much more fluid lip sync animation.

Why I've chosen these morphs and how to use the phoneme morphs for lip sync is described in more detail in Chapter 5, "Animation."

A

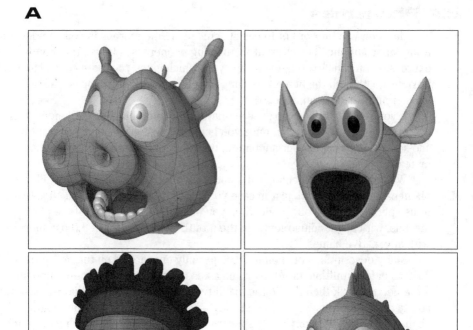

Figure 2.4-1. Phoneme.A.

The A phoneme is simply a percentage or a straight copy of the Mouth.Open morph. If your Mouth.Open morph is fairly exaggerated, then it's sometimes useful to make the A phoneme a little less extreme, especially for less experienced animators.

The A phoneme is used to pronounce a range of sounds featuring an open mouth.

E

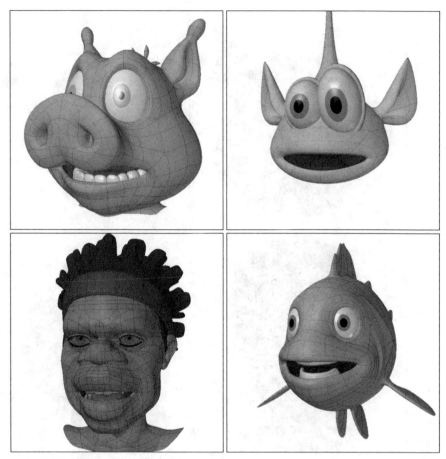

Figure 2.4-2. Phoneme.E.

The E phoneme is a mix of a little Mouth.Open, a little Mouth.LipsOpen, and a decent amount of Mouth.Stretch. If you're more experienced you might want to try just using a copy of Mouth.Stretch, which gives you more flexibility.

The E phoneme is used to pronounce a range of sounds featuring a stretched mouth.

S

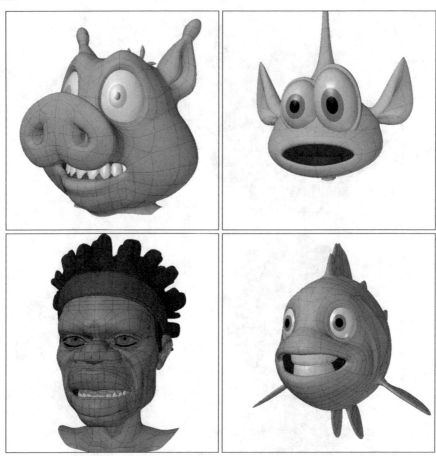

Figure 2.4-3. Phoneme.S.

The S phoneme is a copy of Mouth.LipsOpen.
  The S phoneme is used to pronounce a range of sounds featuring open lips.

W

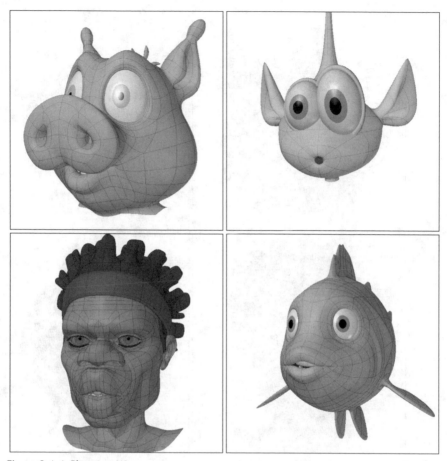

Figure 2.4-4. Phoneme.W.

The W phoneme is a copy of Mouth.Pucker.

The W phoneme is used to pronounce a range of sounds featuring puckered lips.

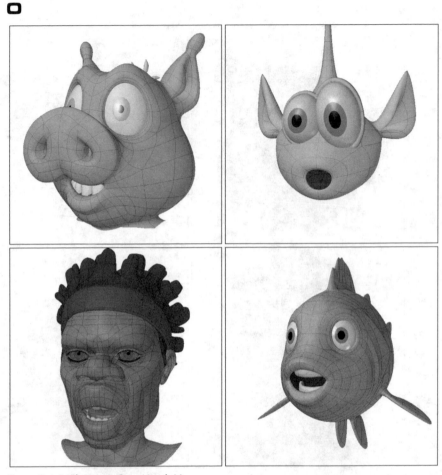

Figure 2.4-5. Phoneme.O or Mouth.Narrow.

The O phoneme is based on Mouth.Pucker with a little bit of Mouth.Open. Adjust the lips to make a nice round shape for the O. If used as a mouth morph, when you've created the shape you can apply a negative percentage of Mouth.Open to close the mouth again.

The O phoneme is used to pronounce O sounds or to bring the corners of the lips in when the mouth is open.

M

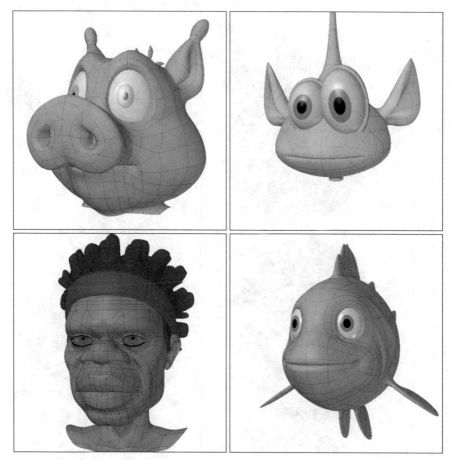

Figure 2.4-6. Phoneme.M or Mouth.LipsClosed.

The M phoneme involves the lips pressed together tightly, slightly bulging the lips where they meet.

The M phoneme mostly affects the lips.

The M phoneme is used to emphasize closed mouth consonants.

F

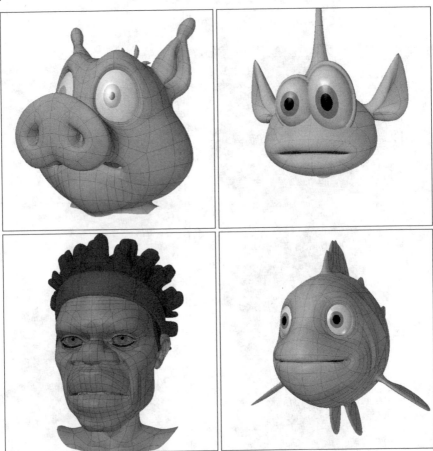

Figure 2.4-7. Phoneme.F or Mouth.F.

The F phoneme involves a little bit of Mouth.Open plus moving up and tucking in the lower lip to meet the top teeth.

The F phoneme mostly affects the lower lip and chin.

The F phoneme is used to pronounce F and V sounds.

L

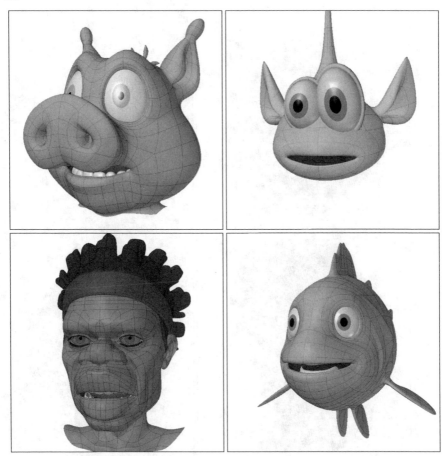

Figure 2.4-8. Phoneme.L or Mouth.TongueUp.

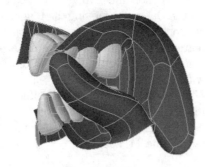

Figure 2.4-8A. Tongue position.

The L phoneme involves a little bit of Mouth.Open plus moving the tongue up so the tip is pressing behind the top teeth. If used as a mouth morph, you can just move the tongue into place without opening the mouth.

The L phoneme mostly affects the tongue.

The L phoneme is mainly used to pronounce the L sound, but can also be used as an alternative to Phoneme.S for N or D consonants.

TH

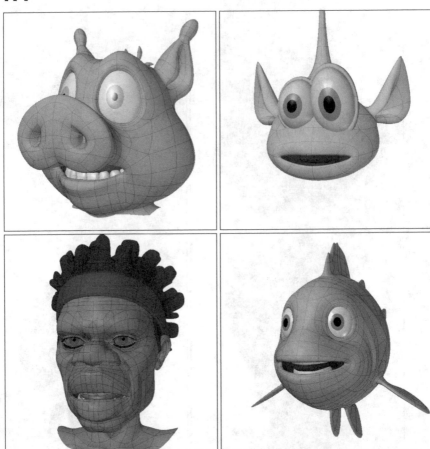

Figure 2.4-9. Phoneme.TH or Mouth.TongueOut.

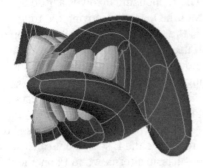

Figure 2.4-9A. Tongue position.

The TH phoneme involves a little bit of Mouth.Open plus moving the tongue up and forward to rest between the top and bottom teeth. If used as a mouth morph, you can just move the tongue into place without opening the mouth.

The TH phoneme mostly affects the tongue.

The TH phoneme is used to pronounce the TH sound.

2.5 Creating the Morphs

Now that we've had a look at the basic morph list, let's create the morphs for Hamish. First we'll create the symmetrical morphs, then use those morphs as a starting point to create the additional left- and right-sided morphs.

Sometimes when creating the morphs you'll find the geometry needs some adjusting, either refining the polygon flow or adding new geometry to better define an area. Feel free to change the geometry at this stage. Spinning quads or splitting polygons can be done at any time, but if you create new geometry, make sure you're on the (base) morph first or you'll get undesirable results.

I won't show you how to create all the morphs; instead, I show some of the techniques used to create morphs so you can continue creating the other morphs on your own.

Preparing the Object

The first step is to set up the model ready for morphing.

1. Load the Hamish model into Modeler (you can find the preprepared object in \Objects\Chapters\Hamish_Working_v003.lwo).
2. Select the eyeballs and **Cut** and **Paste** them into a new layer.
3. Select the first layer and select the polygons of the body, leaving a couple of bands under the head, and **Hide** (-) them.
4. **Fit All** and place the second layer, the template eyeballs, in the background. Make sure **Symmetry** is on and we're ready to start.

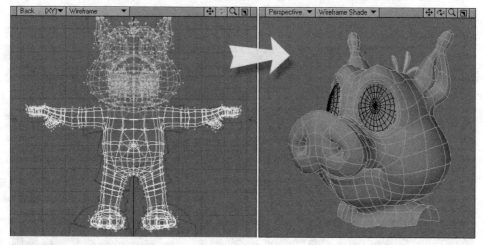

Figure 2.5-1. Prepared to morph.

Eye Morphs

The eye morphs can be quite different from character to character. In the case of Hamish, the default eyelids are wide open. This can sometimes cause problems when the eyelids are halfway closed due to their linear motion. One solution to this is making the eyelids partially closed, or relaxed, in their default position, which makes closing the eyelids easier but can require the addition of an Eye.Wide morph to open the eyelids to their full extent. Another solution is including a helper morph, which pushes the eyelids forward as they close. Using a helper morph like this is described in Chapter 4, "Advanced Rigging."

Blink

To create the Blink we just need to adjust the polygons of the eyelids.

1. Select the **Morph** (**M**) button at the bottom right of the interface. Create a new morph by clicking the pull-down menu to the right of the button and choosing (**new**). Change the name to **Eye.Blink** and click **OK**.

> **Note:** If you create a new morph, then switch to another morph or back to the base without altering any geometry, the new morph will disappear. This is a housekeeping feature of vertex maps so you don't end up with redundant maps with no information in them. If this happens to you, don't panic; you just need to recreate the new morph when you're ready to adjust the geometry.

2. Zoom up on the left eye and select the four middle polygons of the top eyelid geometry, shown in Figure 2.5-2.

3. **Rotate** the Perspective view so you're looking side on to the eye, then rotate the selected polygons about **40°** with the cursor centered on the eye.

4. Deselect the top two polygons and rotate again about **40°**.

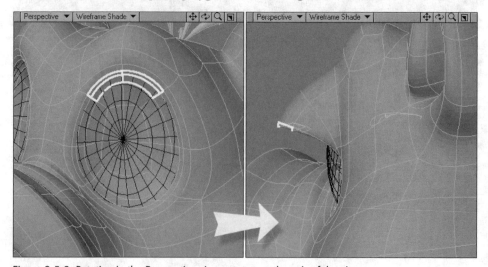

Figure 2.5-2. Rotating in the Perspective view rotates on the axis of the viewport.

5. **Shift+select** the two upper polygons again and, from the Top view, **Move** the selected polygons in toward the middle of the eyeball, then **Move** them down a little.

6. Deselect the top two polygons and, from the Top view, adjust the edge of the eyelid to match the curve of the eyeball while maintaining a small distance from the eyeball, then **Move** the polygons down a little.

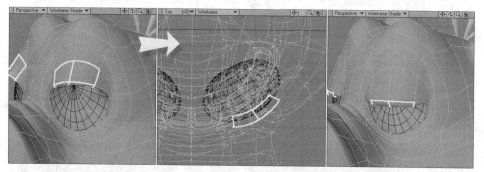

Figure 2.5-3. Try to make sure that the leading edge of the eyelid is flat.

7. Adjust the upper eyelid so it's a nice shape and maintains a roughly equal distance from the eyeball.

8. Repeat steps 2 to 7 for the lower eyelid, except only rotate by **35°** each time, and adjust the lower eyelid so it sits just under and behind the upper eyelid.

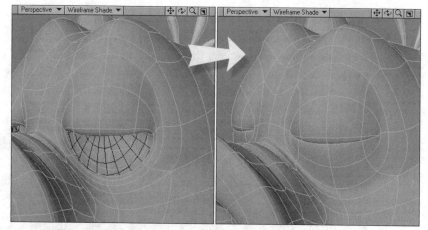

Figure 2.5-4. Create a nice rounded shape for the closed eyelids.

Well done. You've just created the blinking morph. Let's move on to a few other eye morphs.

Squint

The Squint is very similar to Blink, so we can save some effort by starting with a copy of Blink.

1. With Eye.Blink active, select **Map▷Edit Maps▷Copy Vertex Map**. Change the name to **Eye.Squint**.

2. Select the middle polygons of the leading edge of both eyelids and move them up. Adjust points if necessary to make the lids meet in a straight line in the middle of the eye.

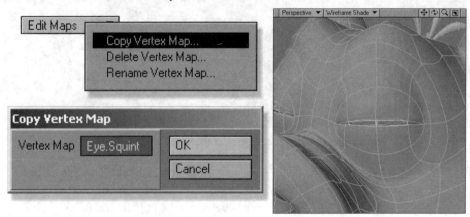

Figure 2.5-5. Squint is a modified copy of Blink.

Lid_Up and Lid_Low

The upper and lower eyelid morphs are partial copies of the Squint.

1. With Eye.Squint active, select the polygons of the upper eyelid and choose **Copy Vertex Map**. Change the name to **Eye.Lid_Up**.

2. Change back to **Eye.Squint**, select the polygons of the lower eyelid, and choose **Copy Vertex Map**. Change the name to **Eye.Lid_Low**.

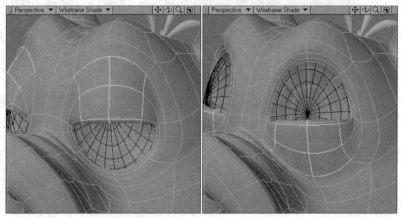

Figure 2.5-6. Check the eyelids against the eye to see if any further adjustments are needed.

Frown

The Frown is the first morph to involve the eyebrows. You can include some of the eyelid geometry in the frown, but be careful not to move the edges of the eyelids.

1. Create a new morph, calling it **Eye.Frown**. Select the polygons shown in Figure 2.5-7 and move them forward and down.

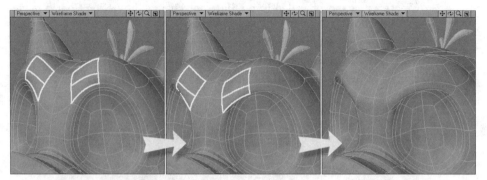

Figure 2.5-7. Create a nice furrow in the brow when creating the frown.

2. Adjust the points around the moved polygons to create a nice shape.

3. Now when we check it with the eyeballs in the background you can see there's quite a gap between the eyebrow and the eyeball. We can fix that at the same time we're enhancing the frown. Select the point at the lowest edge of the eyebrow and the point directly behind it. This second point is the middle point of the eyelid, so we can adjust it a little without adversely affecting the blink. Move the points down and forward a little.

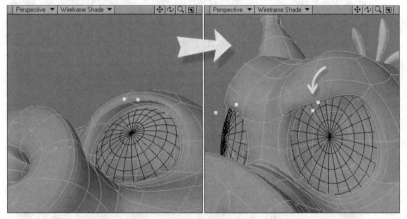

Figure 2.5-8. Adjust the middle point of the eyelid to enhance the expression.

4. Adjust any other points you think necessary to refine and shape the frown.

Dilate

The Dilate morph is a little different from the other eye morphs, affecting the eyeball itself rather than the flesh around the eyeballs.

1. Select the final eyeball layer and **Copy** and **Paste** it into a new layer. Place the original layer in the foreground and the copied geometry in the background.

2. Create a new morph called **Eye.Dilate** and change the Action Center mode to **Selection**.

3. Select the pupil and the first band of the iris around the pupil. From the Back view, **Stretch** to about **120%**.

4. **Contract Selection (Shift+[)**, then **Stretch** again, this time to about **150%**.

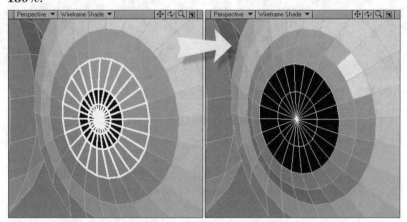

Figure 2.5-9. Action Center:Selection is useful for scaling sections like these.

5. Looking at the morphed eyeball from the side, we can see it's quite out of shape from the original. To fix that, move the polygon bands back so the curve of the morphed eyeball matches the background geometry.

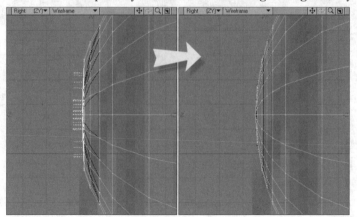

Figure 2.5-10. Adjust to retain the original curve of the eyeball.

6. Delete the copied eyeballs in the reference layer and change back to the **(base)** morph.

From here I'll let you finish creating the rest of the eye morphs: **Eye.Sad**, **Eye.High**, and **Eye.Lift**. You can use the images in the Eye Morphs section as reference, or create your own versions of the morphs.

Mouth Morphs

The mouth morphs for Hamish are unusual in that his nose or snout extends down to his top lip. It's a good example of the differences between many characters and the unique challenges involved with each character. The same rules still apply when adjusting the nose for the morphs, but some of the morphs are a little different because of the snout.

Open

Opening the jaw is one of the trickiest morphs to accomplish. It involves so much of the geometry and, because much of that geometry is hidden in the mouth, it can be quite fiddly. Luckily, once you've got the jaw open you won't have to worry about doing it again until the next character.

1. Create a new morph called **Mouth.Open.**
2. Select the polygons of the **Mouth** surface in the Polygon Statistics panel, then deselect the top half of the mouth and the back of the throat. Then, using the Right and Perspective views, select the polygons of the lower lip and chin. Finally, select the polygons of the **Teeth_Lower** surface.

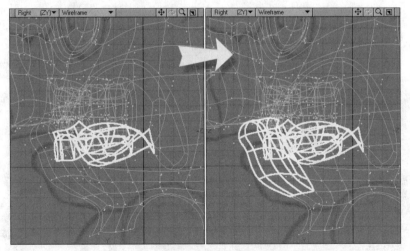

Figure 2.5-11. The most important selection is the inner mouth. The outside polygons can easily be cleared from the morph if you select and move too many.

3. Make sure the Action Center mode is set back to **Mouse** and, from the Right view, **Rotate** the selected polygons about **30%** from just behind the teeth, then move the polygons down a little.

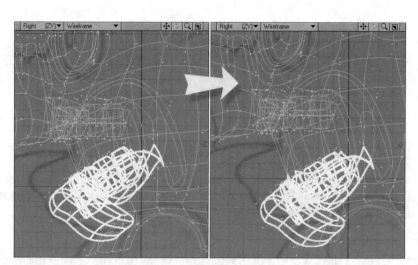

Figure 2.5-12. Rotating is the natural motion for the jaw. The movement is to enhance the expression.

4. Now we've got the basis for the open jaw, but as you can see there's quite a bit of adjusting we need to do. The first step is to adjust the lips so they're stretched nicely around the open jaw. Adjust the lips so they create a nice oval shape around the open mouth, and move the bottom lip in against the teeth.

5. Adjust the points around the mouth, including the cheeks and chin, to smooth out the shapes. You can go back to the (base) to select points and then back to the morph to adjust them if the points are hidden or difficult to select in the morph.

6. Finally, flatten the cheeks a little to promote some squash and stretch and adjust all the points to refine the shapes.

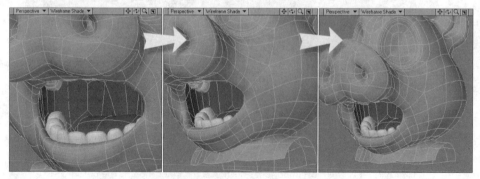

Figure 2.5-13. Adjust the points, making sure you check them from all angles.

Smile

The Smile morph can be another tricky one, involving most of the geometry of the cheeks, lips, nose, and chin.

1. Create a new morph called **Mouth.Smile**.

2. Start by moving the cheek area above the mouth up and out.

3. Change to **Mouth.Open** and select the three polygons around the corner of the mouth. Switch back to **Mouth.Smile** and move the polygons up and out, rotating them a little to match the polygon flow.

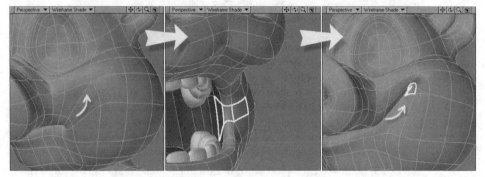

Figure 2.5-14. Move the cheeks first to give you room to move the corners of the mouth.

> **Tip:** Now that we have the open mouth morph, it's a great place to select points when editing the other mouth morphs.

4. Change to **Mouth.Open** and select the points on either side of the previously selected lip polygons. Switch back to **Mouth.Smile** and move the points up and out toward the corners of the smile.

5. Now that the smile is taking shape, adjust the cheek area below the mouth, being careful to position the mass of the cheek up and out from its original position. Feel free to tweak the points above the mouth to compensate for the new position of the lips.

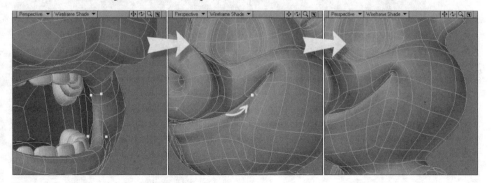

Figure 2.5-15. The cheeks make a smile.

61

6. Select the next set of lip points and move them out, then adjust the points around those to compensate.

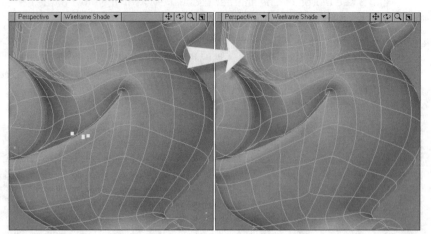

Figure 2.5-16. Adjust one row at a time.

7. Select the points of the lips on either side of the middle and move them out a little, then adjust the points of the lips and chin to indicate the stretching that's occurring.

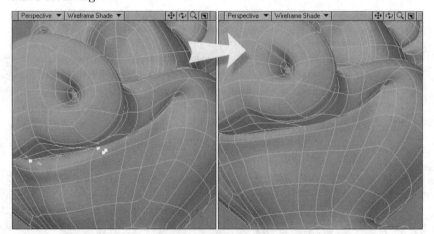

Figure 2.5-17. Push the chin in a little bit to indicate that the skin is stretching over it.

8. Move the nose and upper lip up a little, stretching the base of the nose a little smaller vertically and a little wider, then move the bottom lip up to meet the new position of the top lip.

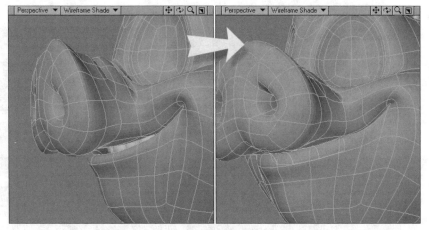

Figure 2.5-18. Moving the mouth and nose up helps sell a smile.

9. Now let's look at the eye area. I haven't adjusted any points around the eyes yet, so there's quite a dip from the cheeks to the eyes. Select the polygons at the outside of the lower eyelid and move them up. With the template eyeball in the foreground, check that the cheeks flow nicely up to the eyes. Remember to make sure not to move the leading edge of the lower eyelid.

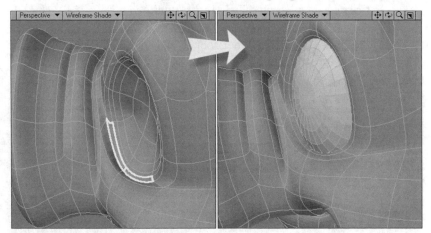

Figure 2.5-19. Including the eyes.

10. Select the polygons of the mouth, then deselect all but the inside of the cheeks. Adjust the points so the insides of the cheeks compensate for the new lip and cheek positions.

11. Finally, tweak all the points to create a nice shape for the smile.

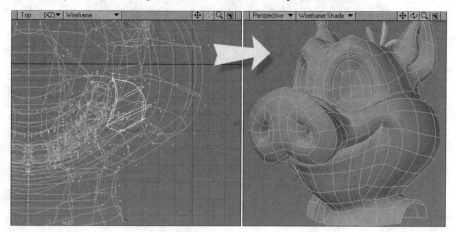

Figure 2.5-20. Inner cheeks are always important.

Pucker

Pucker is probably the morph most different from average or human characters, due to the snout. We don't want to deform the snout too much, so most of the definition of the pucker is formed by the lower lip.

1. Create a new morph called **Mouth.Pucker.**
2. Select the two front polygons of the lower lip and **Expand Selection**. From the Back view, **Stretch** horizontally to about **55%**, then from the Right view, **Rotate** about **35°** and move forward and down.

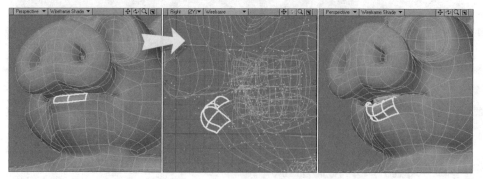

Figure 2.5-21. Creating the initial shape.

3. Select the outside polygons of the lips and move them in and forward.

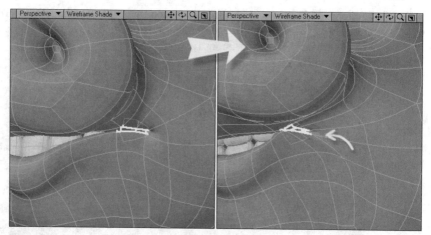

Figure 2.5-22. Stretching the corners of the mouth in.

4. This is the basis of the pucker. All that needs to be done now is to adjust the points to compensate for the new lip position. Select the polygons of the lower lip and adjust them, smoothing and evening out their shape.

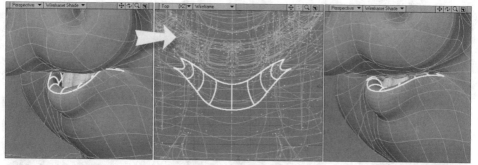

Figure 2.5-23. Make sure the polygons are evenly spaced.

5. Adjust the top lip, smoothing and evening out its shape.

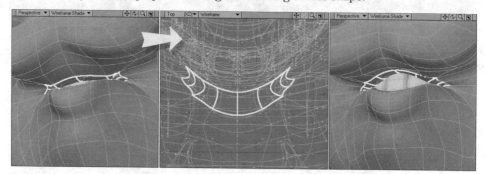

Figure 2.5-24. Move the middle of the top lip up a bit to help create an O shape.

6. Adjust the bottom of the snout to match the upper lip shape and stretch the sides in a bit, making sure to deform mostly the base of the snout so as not to affect the front of the snout too much.

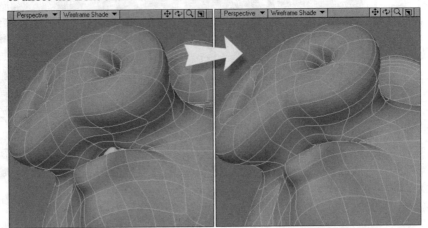

Figure 2.5-25. Don't deform the nose too much or it'll appear too rubbery.

7. Adjust the cheeks, moving points in toward the mouth and stretching the mass of the cheeks in a little.

8. Adjust the bottom lip and chin to compensate for the lip position.

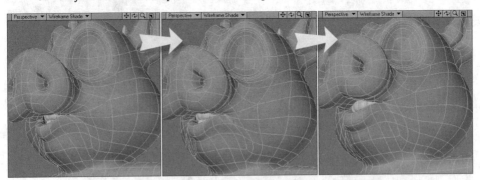

Figure 2.5-26. Adjusting the cheeks and chin. The important thing is to create nice shapes.

9. Finally, check the inside of the mouth, stretching the inner cheeks a little toward the corners of the mouth.

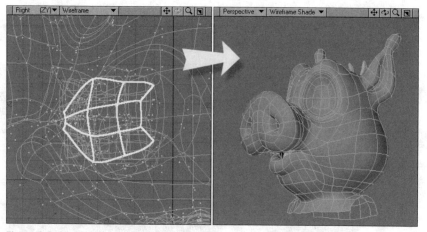

Figure 2.5-27. Remember the inner cheeks.

Jaw_LT and RT

Because Hamish has large jowls, or cheeks, the sideways movement of the jaw won't affect them too much, mostly just the lower lip and chin area.

1. Create a new morph called **Mouth.Jaw_LT**.
2. Select the same polygons we used for opening the mouth — the lower half of the inner mouth, lower lip, chin, and lower teeth.
3. Turn off Symmetry and **Center** the viewports on the selection (**Shift+a**).
4. From the Top view, **Rotate 3°**, making sure the cursor is centered on the X axis, just behind the selected area.
5. **Move** the selected polygons about **10.5 mm** to the left.
6. Before we adjust the points, let's use the reverse values to create the jaw's right movement. Create a new morph called **Mouth.Jaw_RT**.
7. Choose **Rotate**, and click the **Apply** button in the Numeric panel. The jaw should rotate toward the right using the same values as the rotation for Jaw_LT. If it rotates to the left, undo and change the Angle in the Numeric panel to **–3°** and try again.

8. Choose **Move**, and place a minus sign (–) before the X value in the Numeric panel, then click **Apply**. The jaw should move to the right the same amount as Jaw_LT moved to the left.

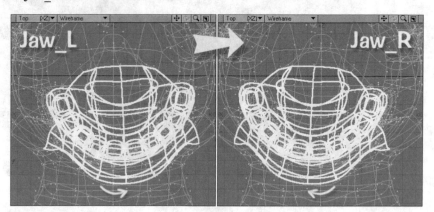

Figure 2.5-28. Major jaw movement.

9. Now with the basic movement done for each morph, adjust the points for each to compensate for the new positions.

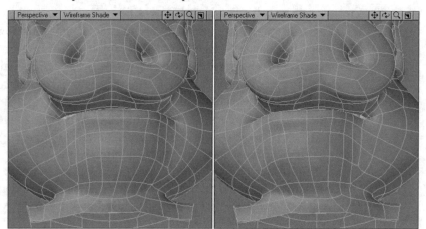

Figure 2.5-29. Resulting morphs after adjusting the points around the mouth.

When you're finished creating the jaw morphs remember to turn Symmetry back on to create the remaining mouth morphs. The mouth morphs still to create are **Mouth.LipsOpen, Mouth.Stretch, Mouth.Pout, Mouth.Sneer,** and **Mouth.Grimace.** You can use the images in the Mouth Morphs section as reference, or you can create your own versions of the morphs.

Phoneme Morphs

The first few phoneme morphs are really easy to create, as they're just copies of existing mouth morphs. To help us do this we'll use a plug-in called MorphMap Mixer, by DStorm.

1. Create a new morph called **Phoneme.A**, and select **Plugs➤Additional➤ MorphMap Mixer**. Check the Numeric panel and if necessary make it a bit longer so you can see all the morphs.

> **Note:** If you don't find the button, make sure you have followed the instructions on installing the plug-ins in Chapter 1.

2. Because our open mouth isn't too extreme in this case, move the Mouth.Open slider in the Numeric panel all the way to the right. If your character has an exaggerated open mouth, it may be better to use just a percentage of the Mouth.Open morph. Click the **MorphMap Mixer** button again when you're done to close it.

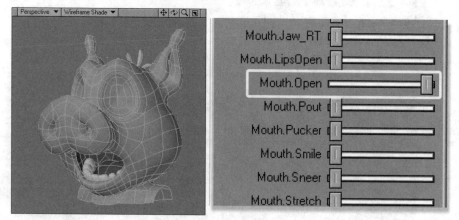

Figure 2.5-30. A is just a copy of Mouth.Open.

3. Create a new morph called **Phoneme.E**.

4. Select **MorphMap Mixer** and, in the Numeric panel, move the Mouth.Open slider to about **25%**, Mouth.Stretch to about **75%**, and Mouth.LipsOpen just a little bit, about **10** to **15%**.

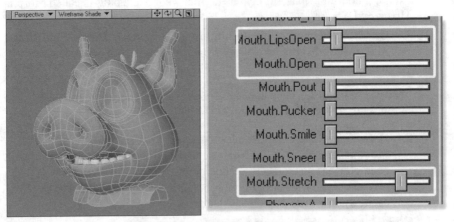

Figure 2.5-31. E is a mix of morphs.

5. Create a new morph called **Phoneme.S**, select **MorphMap Mixer**, and move the Mouth.LipsOpen slider all the way to the right.

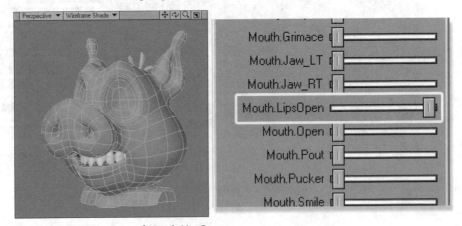

Figure 2.5-32. S is a copy of Mouth.LipsOpen.

6. Create a new morph called **Phoneme.W**, select **MorphMap Mixer**, and move the Mouth.Pucker slider all the way to the right.

Note: In this case, where Phoneme.A, Phoneme.S, and Phoneme.W are exact copies of the mouth morphs, you could also copy those morphs to create the phonemes.

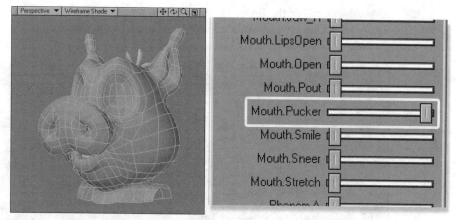

Figure 2.5-33. W is a copy of Mouth.Pucker.

7. That's the easy phonemes done; now we need to do some more work for the others. Create a new morph called **Phoneme.O**, select **MorphMap Mixer,** and move the Mouth.Open slider to about **25%** and Mouth.Pucker to **100%.**

8. Move the corners of the lips in and adjust the lips to make a nice round shape.

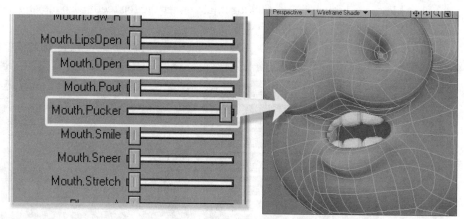

Figure 2.5-34. Make sure you get a nice round shape for the lips.

9. Create a new morph called **Phoneme.M.**

10. Move the points of the lower lip up and forward a little and move the points just outside the corners of the mouth forward a little to show the lips pressed against each other.

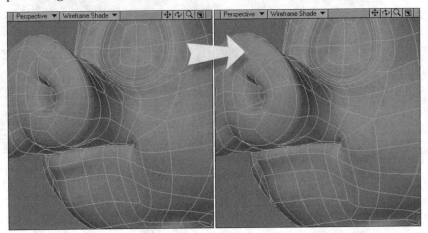

Figure 2.5-35. Pressing the lips together.

11. Create a new morph called **Phoneme.F**, select **MorphMap Mixer**, and move the Mouth.Open and Mouth.Sneer sliders to about **20%**.

12. Move the bottom lip up, tucking it just under the top teeth, also moving the chin up and back a little to compensate.

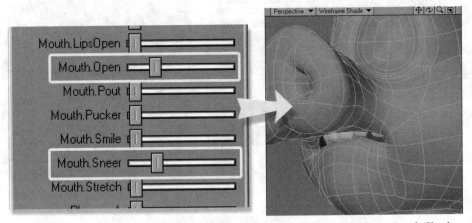

Figure 2.5-36. Don't tuck the bottom lip in too far behind the teeth or it'll look unnatural. Check your face in the mirror to see how far your bottom lip goes when pronouncing F's.

13. Create a new morph called **Phoneme.L**, select **MorphMap Mixer**, and move the Mouth.Open slider to about **25%**.

14. Move the tongue up, pressing the tip against the top teeth.

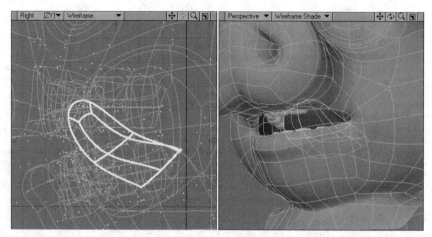

Figure 2.5-37. The important aspect of L is the tongue.

15. Create a new morph called **Phoneme.TH**, select **MorphMap Mixer**, and move the Mouth.Open and Mouth.LipsOpen sliders to about **20%**.

16. Move the tongue forward so the tip is sitting between the top and bottom teeth and stretch the tip of the tongue to make it a bit wider.

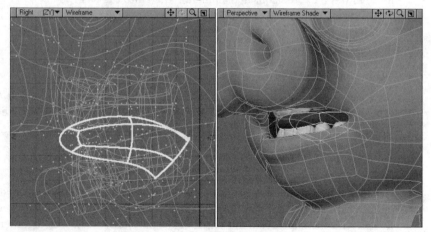

Figure 2.5-38. Notice the shape of your tongue when you pronounce different things. It changes shape quite a lot for different phonemes.

That's all the phonemes done. It was pretty easy using MorphMap Mixer, wasn't it?

Now that all the symmetrical morphs are created, MorphMap Mixer is also useful for testing that your morphs mix well. Create a new morph called UV.Test and mix various morphs to see how they behave together.

> **Note:** I call the test morph UV.Test because the morphs created for UV mapping are in the UV morph group. This ensures that all the morphs are grouped and makes it easier when finalizing the model to delete all the unnecessary morphs.

Adjust the morphs if necessary to ensure they mix together nicely.

Asymmetry

Now that our morphs are complete it's a good time to talk about asymmetry. Most people's faces are asymmetrical to some degree. Some faces are quite noticeably asymmetrical at rest, but most people's faces become more asymmetrical in their expressions or when they talk. For example, a smile may have one side higher than the other or one side of the lips may open more when a person is talking. This type of asymmetry is a great way to inject personality and individuality into your character.

Quite often we subconsciously distinguish attractive people from ugly people by the amount of symmetry in their faces. We can use this stereotype to our advantage with our characters, keeping faces of attractive or appealing characters symmetrical, and making faces of bad or mean characters more asymmetrical, although for most cartoon characters asymmetry is introduced more into the expressions and animation than into the base pose.

You can use the left- and right-sided morphs to enhance asymmetry in the animation, but for common asymmetrical expressions it's easier to add them into the morphs themselves. Let's look at the two types of asymmetry.

Base Asymmetry

Base asymmetry is the asymmetrical nature of the face when it's at rest. This type of asymmetry is usually modeled into the base pose for the character. The trouble with doing this is that you lose the ability to edit the model using Symmetry mode.

The best way to make your character's base pose asymmetrical is to model the asymmetry within a morph. You can then apply the morph at full strength at all times during animation, but you still retain the ability to edit your model using Symmetry mode. You can use MorphMap Mixer to test the asymmetrical morph with the expression morphs to make sure they work well together.

Expressive Asymmetry

Expressive asymmetry is the introduction of asymmetry when the face moves with expression or speech. There is a difference between making an expression asymmetrical on purpose and the subconscious asymmetrical nature of an expression. For example, if your character is angry, you might just make him sneer using one side of the face to add more interest to the animation — this is forced asymmetry. When one side of a person's lips subconsciously open wider than the other side when he is talking, it's quite different — let's call it subconscious asymmetry. It's the subconscious asymmetry that you want to model into the morphs, leaving the forced asymmetry for the animators to put in themselves.

Once you've finished the symmetrical versions of the morphs, if you want to introduce some asymmetry into the expressions or phonemes, turn off Symmetry and have a ball. It's a good idea to copy the symmetrical morph to a test morph and then model your asymmetry in the test morph until you're happy with it, just in case you mess up and want to start again. Once you're happy with the asymmetrical version you can just copy it to the original morph.

Left and Right Morphs

Now that we've created the base morphs it's time to separate the left and right sides into their own morphs. There are a few ways to accomplish this, but the technique shown here is the quickest and most efficient I've found to date. It involves creating a weight map for the left and right sides of the face, then using those weight maps to apply the morphs. This ensures a smooth transition from the deformed side to the non-deformed side of the face, as well as making sure that the deformation, when the left and right morphs are combined, is the same as the original symmetrical morph.

1. Change the Perspective view to **Weight Shade** and select the points along the middle of the model at X=0. Don't worry if you select a few points just either side of the middle; they're okay to include. Create a new weight map called **Morph_LR**, with an initial value of **50%**.

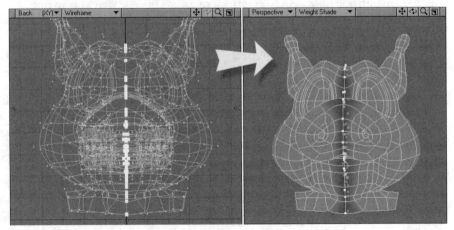

Figure 2.5-39. The start of the gradient weight.

2. Expand Selection (**Shift+]**) and select **View➤Selection➤Maps➤ Select by Map**. Select the **Morph_LR** vertex map in the pull-down and change Action to **Deselect**. This deselects the points down the center.
3. **Map➤General➤Set Map Value** to **75%**, then turn off **Symmetry**, deselect the left points, and **Set Map Value** to **25%**.

4. **Select by Map**, this time selecting all the points belonging to Morph_LR. Invert the selection (**Shift+'**) and **Set Map Value** to **100%**. Deselect the left points and **Set Map Value** to **0%** for the remaining selected points.

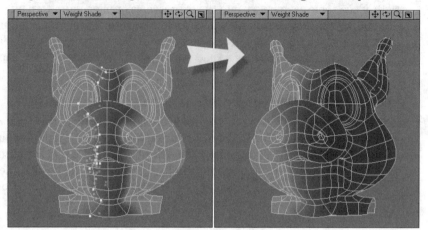

Figure 2.5-40. It's important that the weight values are opposite values on either side of X=0.

Now we have a nice gradient weight map with the gradient between 0% and 100% occurring across the middle of the mouth. If you have a more detailed mouth you may wish to create more values in your weight map (e.g., 0-16-33-50-67-84-100), whereas a less detailed mouth like Morfi's might have fewer values (e.g., 0-50-100). Just be sure the end points of the gradient (0% and 100%) fall at roughly the one-quarter and three-quarter points along the mouth.

Before we move on we need to adjust the weight values around the eye area. We want the gradient to cover a smaller area between the eyes than at the mouth; otherwise we might find that when we create the left blink morph, the left eyelid doesn't quite close properly and also affects the right eyelid a little, which we definitely don't want.

5. Turn on **Symmetry** and select the four polygons at the center of the eye. Expand the selection four times to select all the polygons of the eye, then select the two bands of polygons above the eye to the ear.

6. **Set Map Value** to **100%**, then turn off **Symmetry** and deselect the polygons on the left side. **Set Map Value** to **0%** for the remaining selected points.

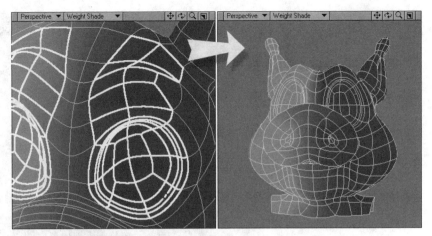

Figure 2.5-41. Adjusting the weights for the eye area.

Now we have the same 0 to 100% gradient between the eyes, but it covers a smaller area than at the mouth.

Before creating the morphs for the left and right sides, check through all the morphs again to make sure none of them need more tweaking. If you decide after this step that you want to adjust a morph it's a lot more work because then you have to adjust or recreate the left and right sides as well.

Layout

Okay, you've checked that your morphs are fine, so let's continue. The next part is done in Layout, so let's send the object over.

> **Note:** Since writing this section, the Masked Morph Copy plug-in was released by Kevin Phillips, making the following steps possible in Modeler. Instead of incorporating the plug-in into the steps, I've left this section as is because editing morphs in Layout has many other uses in addition to separating left and right morphs. See the Appendix for a description of Masked Morph Copy.

1. If you already have Layout open, clear the scene to make sure there are no objects loaded. In Modeler, select the Layout pull-down at the top-right corner of the interface and choose **Send Object to Layout.**

> **Note:** If you're not running the Hub, you need to save the object and then load it from within Layout instead of sending it over from Modeler.

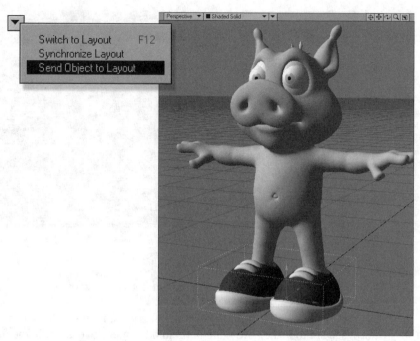

Figure 2.5-42. Send Object to Layout opens Layout if it isn't already open.

2. We're only working with Layer 1, so hide or clear Layers 2, 3, and 4 from Layout.

3. Open the properties for Layer 1 and set SubDivision Order to **Last**.

4. Select the **Deform** tab and **Add Displacement**➤**Normal Displacement**. Double-click the **Normal Displacement** instance to open its properties window.

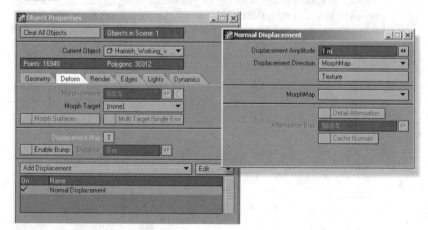

Figure 2.5-43. Normal displacement works on point normals or morph maps.

5. Change Displacement Direction to **MorphMap** and click the **Texture** button.

6. In the Texture Editor change Layer Type to **Gradient**. Change Input Parameter to **Weight Map**, and set Weight Map to **Morph_LR**.

7. Now we need to create keys in the gradient to tell it what values to use. We want the gradient to follow the weight map values so click in the middle of the gradient bar and click again at the bottom, creating two new keys. With the bottom key still selected, set its values to Value **100%**, Alpha **100%**, and Parameter **100%**. Select the middle key and set its values to Value **0%**, Alpha **100%**, and Parameter **0%**. Select the top key and set its values to Value **0%**, Alpha **100%**, and Parameter **–100%**. This gradient allows deformation of the left side of the face.

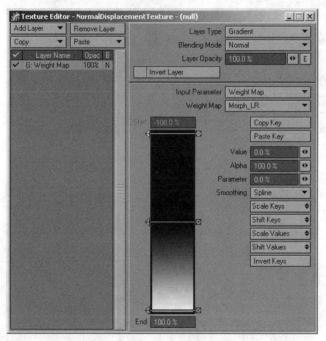

Figure 2.5-44. The gradient for the left side.

8. We need to create a second gradient to deform the right side of the face, so select **Copy**➤ **Selected Layer(s)** and **Paste**➤**Add to Layers**. In the new gradient, change the Value entries for each key from top to bottom to **100%**, **100%**, and **0%**. Click the check mark next to the second gradient Layer Name, turning it off, and click **Use Texture** to close the Texture Editor.

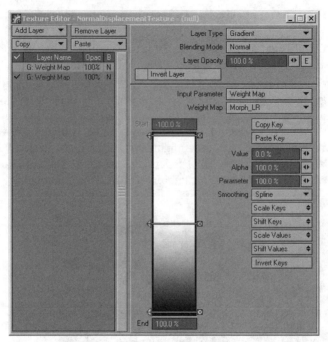

Figure 2.5-45. The gradient for the right side.

9. Now we're ready to start morphing. Back in the Normal Displacement prop-
    erties, select **Eye.Blink** in the MorphMap pull-down. You should see the
    left eye close on the model.

10. Select **File⯈Save⯈Save Endomorph** and call it **Eye.Blink_LT.**

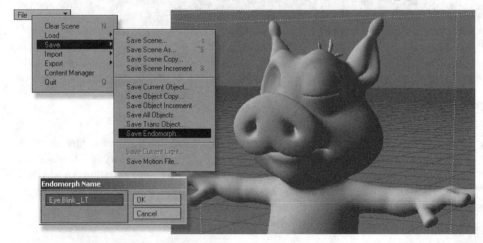

Figure 2.5-46. Saving the left blink.

11. Select the MorphMap pull-down and you can see Eye.Blink_LT has been added to the list of morphs. Choose **Eye.Frown** and **Save Endomorph**, calling it **Eye.Frown_LT**.

12. Continue down the list, saving a left-sided copy of all the eye morphs except **Dilate**, then save a left-sided copy of all the mouth morphs except **Open, Pucker, Jaw_LT**, and **Jaw_RT**.

13. Before we move to the right side **File➤Save➤Save Current Object**, saving the object with its new morphs.

Now we need to save the right-sided copies.

1. Click the **Texture** button in the Normal Displacement properties. Check the top gradient and close the Texture Editor. You should see the selected morph switch to the other side of the face.

2. Select **Eye.Blink** in the MorphMap pull-down and **Save Endomorph**, calling it **Eye.Blink_RT**.

3. Continue down the list of morphs, saving a right-sided copy of all the morphs that have accompanying left-sided copies. When you're done, **Save Current Object** and return to Modeler.

The last step is to create separate left- and right-sided versions of the Dilate morph, if you choose to create them.

1. Select the eyeball layer and, with Symmetry off, select the left eyeball (the right eye when looking at the Back view). Then select the **Eye.Dilate** morph.

2. **Copy Vertex Map**, changing the name to **Eye.Dilate_LT**.

3. Select the right eyeball and reselect the **Eye.Dilate** morph. **Copy Vertex Map** to **Eye.Dilate_RT**.

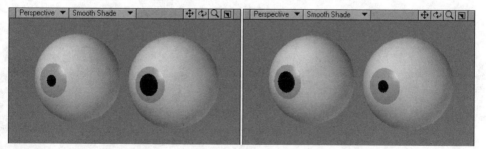

Figure 2.5-47. Left and right dilated pupils.

4. Save the object.

That completes the facial morphs for Hamish. I always enjoy morph creation, as you start to see the personality of the character emerge, but it can be a fiddly and tedious process at times. The real reward for your effort is when you start to animate the facial expressions and lip sync to really bring the character to life.

Part II

Character Setup

The following chapters explain the process of setting up characters for animation, including making the character deform well and making it easy to animate. Chapter 4, "Advanced Rigging," describes methods for automating motion to complement the animation controls, alternate rigging techniques for different control methods, and applying an existing rig to different characters.

Chapter 3

Rigging

Rigging is the process of setting up a character for animation. This includes creating a skeleton to deform the character and creating animation controls to enable easy posing of the character.

3.1 Planning

What Makes a Good Rig?

There are two major components to rigging: making the character deform nicely and making the character easy to animate. These components are vital, and only when you've accomplished both do you have a good character rig. A rig with good deformations that's difficult to animate causes wasted time during the animation process, not to mention frustrating the animators beyond all reasonable limits. A rig that's easy to animate but doesn't deform the character nicely results in substandard quality, and more frustration from the animators when they can't make the character look good in certain poses.

Character Deformation

Good character deformation means that the character looks good in any pose and that all the joints deform nicely in any position possible within the skeletal constraints. This is accomplished through the bones and how the character is attached to those bones, and is heavily influenced by your knowledge of anatomy.

The first step is making sure the bone joints are in the correct positions. If your bones aren't in the right places, it's impossible to achieve good joint deformation. Whether you're rigging human or animal characters, it's important to research the anatomy of the real-life equivalent of that character to get a solid understanding of where to place the bones. To achieve the best deformation, the bones of your character should mimic the bones of the real-life equivalent of that character, both in what bones are used and where they're positioned.

The next step is to understand the mechanics of how each joint works. This is what I meant when I said "any position possible within the skeletal constraints." Too often I see people complain that they can't achieve nice deformation of a joint, when they've manipulated the joint into a position it was never meant to reach. Before you can make joints deform well, you need to understand what positions each joint is capable of reaching and how it should move to reach that position. Only once you've done this can you pose the character properly to test the deformations.

A solid understanding of how bones affect the muscles and how the muscles in turn affect the skin is important to defining your deformations. Knowing what parts of a real body each bone affects and how it affects it means you can more easily determine what areas of your character are affected by each bone. You can learn a lot just by standing in front of a mirror and moving each joint around, seeing how the movement of your bones affects the muscle and flesh around the joints.

The last step is deciding how the character model is affected by the bones and what parts of the geometry are manipulated by each bone. This can often be the most time-consuming step, but once the bones are in the right positions it's much easier to get right.

It's also important to know when to give yourself control of the deformation of a joint and when to let the software have control. You have the ability to take complete control of every joint in the character, but in many cases the software does a good job all by itself. You should only give yourself extra control of the joints that the software doesn't handle well on its own. The trick to this is to keep it simple. The more complex your bone structure and weight maps are, the more difficult it is to create nice deformation.

Animation Controls

There are certain things that an animator should take for granted in a rig — the ability to manipulate every joint, the ability to fix the feet and hands in place while other parts of the character move, and the ability to control facial expression. Beyond those basic requirements it's up to you to make the job of posing and animating the character an easy and enjoyable experience.

The best rigs give an animator complete control of the character with the least amount of work. This means an animator has to move the fewest number of animation controls to manipulate the character into any pose possible. Fewer controls mean faster animation production, and it's up to you as a character rigger to work out the most efficient uses for each animation control.

85

Complete control might sound like an obvious requirement, but it's an important one. Beyond the basic joints, including spine, arms, legs, feet, and hands, there are usually many other poseable areas of a character. Fingers are rarely forgotten, but what about toes? If your character has toes, it's more than likely that an animator will want to manipulate them at some point. Even areas of the model that may use automated animation techniques such as expressions or dynamics often need to be posed by an animator — things like long ears, tails, hair, and clothes. By excluding any potentially poseable area of the character from the animator's control you will restrict the quality of animation possible with the character.

Having fewer controls is important for a number of reasons. It means that the character can be posed more quickly, as modifying one item is much faster than modifying multiple items. It also means less clutter on the screen and easier selection both in the viewports and in item lists, all of which results in faster animation production. It also means there are fewer items for the software to keep track of. Every extra item in a scene slows down the response rate. You may not notice any speed decrease when you're animating a single character, but once you have 10 or 20 characters in a scene you quickly realize that every item counts.

It's important to stress here that you should never sacrifice control for ease of use. Where you can, use one instead of multiple items to increase the efficiency of the rig, but only if it doesn't detract from the ability to fully and easily pose the character.

Consistency

Consistency is very important for character animation. Every character in a production should have the same control methods where possible, with the same name and selection order for all of the morphs, bones, and controls. This way an animator can seamlessly switch from character to character, knowing the name of every control and where to find every control for the character. If you press the down arrow twice to switch from the left foot control to the right foot control, an animator should be confident that this will work no matter which character he is animating.

It's important to decide right at the beginning what controls to include. If you can, sit down with the animators before you start and work with them to decide on a single control method that keeps the majority happy (you'll rarely keep everyone happy). While you may have some animators wanting unique control methods, this often results in more time spent during setup than is saved during animation. If all the characters in a production have the same basic controls, animation will be a fast and smooth process, and any animator can work on any scene, knowing exactly what he is doing.

Naming Conventions

A consistent naming convention is important. It allows the animator to quickly and easily distinguish items, and is necessary for efficient character creation.

A consistent naming convention makes it easier to perform editing, especially if you come back to the character after a period of not using it. If the name of each morph, bone, and control is the same for every character in a production, at least items common to all the characters, you know immediately what's what. It also makes it easier for others in the chain of production to make adjustments.

Make sure all the references to left and right sides are the same for every aspect of the character. _LT and _RT are good to use as they are short and easily recognizable. _L and _R are easier but not so good because when the _L string is replaced with _R, mirroring an item named Arm_Lower_L is changed to Arm_Rower_R. _Left and _Right can be more difficult to distinguish because the words blend in with the item name, whereas _LT is obvious at a glance.

Making the left and right references the same for every aspect of the character is necessary to take full advantage of time-saving features such as Mirror Hierarchy. When you mirror the rig, the weight maps associated with the bones are determined by the same replace string used to rename the bones. If the left and right references for the weight maps are different from the bones, then you need to manually apply the alternate weight maps.

Anatomy and How It Relates to Rigging

Studying the anatomy of the creature that your character is based on is very important to creating a good rig for that character. Whether your character is human, anthropomorphic animal, or caricatured animal, a good understanding of the anatomy of the corresponding real-life equivalent is essential.

Human and Anthropomorphic Characters

The human anatomy is the reference from which the rigs of every human or anthropomorphic character should be created. Most cartoon characters have the same skeletal mechanics as real humans, so having a good knowledge of the human skeleton is very important. Knowing how the movement of the bones affects the muscles and skin in real humans is also important so you can allow for it in the rig and have a good basis for knowing how to attach the character to the bones.

You don't need every bone in the human skeleton in your character rig, but you do need to make sure you can simulate the motion of every bone. The spine is a good example of this: The human skeleton has 24 separate bones, or vertebrae, but you certainly don't need 24 bones in your character's skeleton to simulate the motion of the spine. Four or five bones are usually plenty to enable the posing of a character's spine. It's also useful to just use a single bone for the metacarpus (hand) and metatarsus (foot) bones, as these bones don't have much independent movement.

Skeleton

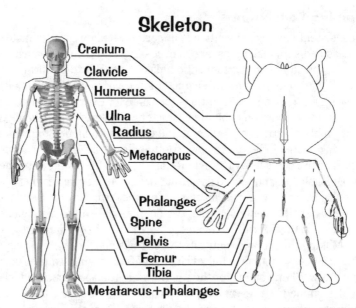

Figure 3.1-1. All the major bones of the human skeleton should be represented in your rig.

The pivot points of the bones for your character should be in the same places as the pivot points of a real skeleton. Most cartoon characters have quite different proportions than a human, so you need to adjust the joints to suit the character, but as long as the joints are in the same positions relative to the proportions of your character, then your deformations will be accurate.

Bone Joints

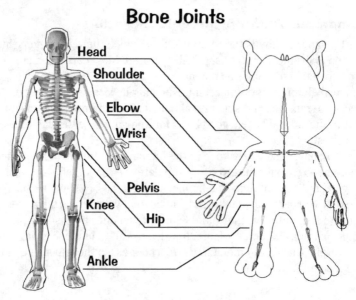

Figure 3.1-2. Although Hamish's body has very different proportions, the bone pivot points are in the same places relative to a human skeleton.

The difference between a real skeleton and a 3D character's skeleton is that it's not just the bone movement that you need to emulate but the effect of the combined bone and muscle movement on the skin. So while you need bones in the same places as a real skeleton, you also need additional bones to simulate the effect that muscles have on the skin.

Muscle Helpers

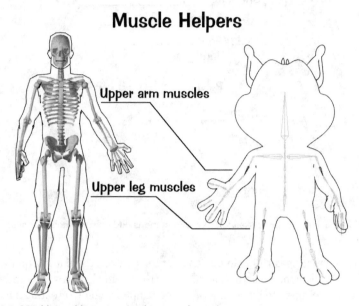

Upper arm muscles

Upper leg muscles

Figure 3.1-3. Additional bones to simulate muscle motion.

So you can see there's really not much difference between a character rig and the human skeleton, but as with most things, you need to understand the rules before you can break them, and the same thing applies with rigging. Only when you have a solid understanding of the rules of human anatomy can you know when and how you can break the rules to allow for exaggeration in cartoon character rigs.

Anthropomorphic animals sometimes need a little extra work. Often they have both human and animal characteristics. You need to apply human physiology to the human features, and study and apply animal physiology to the animal features.

Caricatured Animals

Humans and animals have the same basic bone structure, although each animal has bones in different places and sometimes there are slight mechanical differences. So we can often use the same bones and similar rigging methods as humans, with the main difference being in the initial position of the bones. It's important to study the anatomy of an animal before creating the character to gain a solid understanding of where the bones should be positioned, how they move, and what differences there are between the human and animal skeleton.

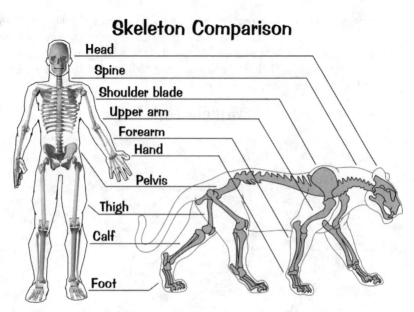

Skeleton Comparison

Head

Spine

Shoulder blade

Upper arm

Forearm

Hand

Pelvis

Thigh

Calf

Foot

Figure 3.1-4. The basic skeleton between humans and most animals is similar.

When creating cartoon animal characters it's even more important to create the same basic bone structure, as many cartoon animals have the ability to switch from quadruped to biped motion. For example, if you're creating a more realistic animal you might only need rudimentary controls for the front feet, but cartoon animals who sometimes use their front feet like human hands and fingers need the ability to pose the fingers in a more human manner.

It's up to you whether you create the default character and rig in an upright position or on all fours, but generally you should create the default pose in the form the character spends the most time in. An anthropomorphic character that sometimes moves like an animal is usually best created upright, but a caricatured animal that sometimes moves or expresses in a more human way would probably be best created on all fours. When creating such a character, you need to do a little more work to make sure that your bone placement and deformations work for both forms of movement, but if you've studied the anatomy of the animal the work is made much easier.

Joint Mechanics

There are only a few types of joints in a skeleton. The type of joint between each bone determines what axes of rotation to allow for each of the bones in a character rig. If you move a bone outside the limitations of its joint type, your character's movement might be noticeably strange. The audience may not know exactly what is wrong but will notice that something is not quite right. Besides the visual aspect, restricting joint rotations makes the job of rigging and posing a character much easier.

In reality there is a larger range of joint types than described here, but these are enough for our rigging needs.

Hinge Joint

A hinge joint is the most simple of joints, only able to rotate on a single axis.

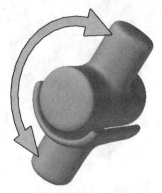

Figure 3.1-5. A hinge joint can only rotate on one axis.

The elbow, knee, and fingers are hinge joints. The bone of a hinge joint should only rotate on its pitch.

Saddle Joint

A saddle joint allows one major and one minor axis of rotation. It has less restriction, or can rotate farther, on its major axis, but has very limited rotation on its minor axis.

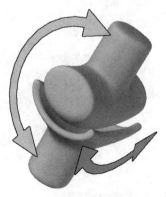

Figure 3.1-6. A saddle joint can rotate on two axes.

The wrist, ankle, and knuckles are saddle joints. The bone of a hinge joint should only rotate on its pitch (major) and heading (minor), although there are special considerations for the wrist and ankle joints, as they're most often controlled with IK.

Ball Joint

A ball joint is able to rotate on all axes.

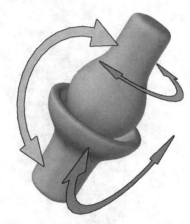

Figure 3.1-7. A ball joint can rotate on all axes.

The shoulder and hip are ball joints. The bone of a ball joint can rotate on all axes, but it's often best to limit the rotation to two axes and use another bone for rotating the third axis.

Pin Joint

A pin joint allows one major and two minor axes of rotation. It has less restriction on its major axis, but has limited rotation on its minor axes.

Figure 3.1-8. A pin joint can rotate on all axes.

The vertebrae of the spine and the pelvis are pin joints. The bone of a pin joint can rotate on all axes, and there isn't as much restriction as in the real spine because we use fewer bones than occur in a human skeleton.

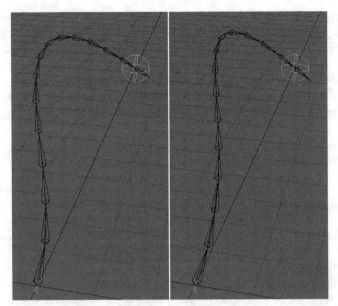

Figure 3.2-10. Left: No stiffness. Right: Gradual increase of stiffness toward the base of the chain.

When to Use IK

The choice to use FK, IK, or even motion modifiers to control the hierarchies in a character can come down to personal preference, but there are established requirements for a character rig that will affect your decision for some hierarchies. As a rule, I like to use IK for the legs and arms of a character and FK for the spine as I find this gives me the best combination of control and ease of use.

It's usually taken for granted that the legs will be controlled using IK. This is because the feet, more than any other part of a character, need to stay in position while the rest of the character moves.

For the arms, some people prefer FK and others prefer IK. I find that sometimes people who prefer FK for the arms make the decision based on the method of animation they first learned or a lack of awareness of the best methods for posing or animating using IK, but in the end it's about using the method you (or your animation team) feel most comfortable with. Keep in mind that if you choose FK for the arms you will need to apply or use IK at times when the character's hands need to interact with the environment.

Some people like to use IK for the spine so they can position the upper torso and/or the head using an animation control item. Because the spine is a complex chain of bones with many subtleties in its poses and motion, I find using IK can limit the flexibility or ability to pose the spine so I prefer to use FK unless there's a specific movement the character needs to do that is made easier by using IK.

IK is often useful for tails, tentacles, and other more freely moving append-
ages, but is not always the best solution. IK allows for easy and precise posing,
but for long chains other animation methods, such as using motion modifiers,
can create more effective motion.

It's best to use just one method of control for each hierarchy in a scene or
shot, but there are times when you want to control a hierarchy using different
methods at different times within the same scene. It's possible to interactively
switch control methods during a scene, or even allow a combination of control
methods for the one hierarchy. These techniques and some alternate control
methods for different hierarchies are explained in Chapter 4, "Advanced
Rigging."

3.3 Weight Mapping

Weight maps are very versatile and have many useful functions in character creation. The function described here is their ability to control which areas of a
model are affected by each bone.

You can use bones to deform a model with or without weight maps. It's
quite possible to rig a character without using any weight maps at all. If you
don't use weight maps, the bone falloff setting largely determines how the bones
affect the geometry. This may seem like an easy way out of doing extra work,
but it takes control away from you and gives control to the software, which is
never an ideal solution and often results in needing even more work to achieve
good joint deformation. To achieve some level of control when not using weight
maps you need *hold bones*, bones that exist just to hold an area of the mesh in
place so surrounding bones don't adversely affect it. Hold bones can sometimes
do the job, but you don't have nearly the level of control as you do when using
weight maps unless you include a large number of hold bones, which tends to
defeat the purpose. Using too many hold bones reduces the efficiency of a rig,
which can increase calculation times and reduce the update speed of a scene,
especially a scene featuring multiple characters.

Efficient Weight Mapping

The golden rule for weight mapping is to only use as many weight maps as you
absolutely have to. Fewer weight maps are faster and easier to create. You're
also more likely to achieve nice joint deformation when using fewer weight
maps, which sounds a bit silly, but it's true.

The benefit to bones not needing weight maps to work is that bones can
also share weight maps. When bones share weight maps, they use the falloff setting to determine how to share control over the area. This means that you don't
need a separate weight map for every single bone, just the areas where you
want or need extra control. You can use this to your advantage by letting the
software control the joints that it deforms well and using weight maps for the
other joints, minimizing the workload.

> **Note:** I strongly recommend *against* using the automatic weight generation tool Bone Weights. This tool creates a weight map for every bone, which makes it much more difficult to create nice joint deformations, increases your workload immensely, and is far less efficient. Creating a weight map for every bone also creates additional deformation problems that don't exist otherwise.
>
> The only time you should use the Bone Weights tool is if you're creating a character for a computer game, and its game engine requires every bone to have a weight map.

There are two reasons to give an area of a model a separate weight map: to keep the surrounding bones from influencing an area and to control joint deformation.

Bone Influence

A weight map ensures that an area is only deformed by the bones that you choose. This prevents parts of the model that are close to each other from being affected or deformed by the other's bones. It also makes sure those areas of a model that shouldn't deform, like the head, remain solid.

Areas of a model with a weight value of 100% follow the exact motion of a bone with that weight map assigned. The same bone has no influence on areas with a weight value of 0%.

> **Note:** A point that is not assigned to a weight map is not the same as a point with a weight value of 0%, although in the Weight Shade view mode they are often indistinguishable. Depending on how it's used, the behavior of a weight map can be quite different between unassigned points and points with a value of 0%, although when weight maps are used for bone deformation control, the behavior of the two points is the same.

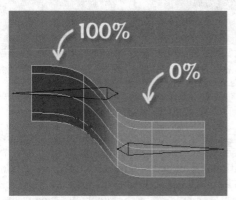

Figure 3.3-1. The points with 100% weight follow the exact motion of the bone, leaving the area with 0% unaffected.

Keep in mind that when you use weight maps, every point in your object should have at least one weight map applied at a value higher than 0%. Ideally every point should have a combined total value of 100% for all its weight maps. In most cases every bone should have an assigned weight map. If that is the case, any points that don't have a weight map applied or only have 0% weight value, are not affected by any bones. The points appear to be left behind as the character is moved.

Deformation Control

A weight map gives you control over the deformation of joints that the software may have trouble with. By adjusting the weight values, you can give each competing bone more or less influence over each point in the weight map, giving you precise control of how a joint is affected by the surrounding bones.

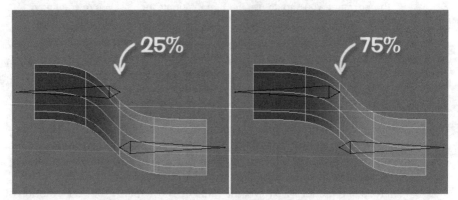

Figure 3.3-2. The bones affect the points to different degrees depending on their weight values.

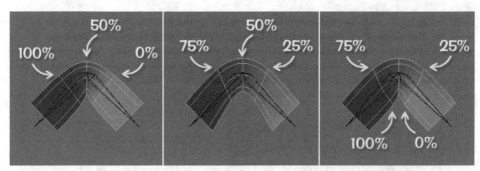

Figure 3.3-3. You can control how sharp or smooth the deformation is by adjusting the size of the blended area between adjoining weight maps.

Hard Bodies

You can use bones and weight maps to rig *hard bodies*, or areas of a model that need to move independently. By assigning each unattached piece of geometry its own full-strength weight map (with no influence on any other areas), the bone or bones for that weight map only affect that piece. This is useful when rigging props, such as objects that a character is holding or the mechanical joints for a robotic character.

It's possible to rig hard bodies as separate objects so you don't need bones or weight maps. The trouble with this is that you can end up with a lot of unnecessary items in your object list, making animation much more difficult. Using bones and weight maps not only keeps your scene file much more manageable, but it also gives you more flexibility, allowing you to choose whether or not a hard body can deform.

In cartoon animation you often need a hard body to bend or become longer or shorter to exaggerate the pose or motion. By using bones and weight maps, you can separate the motion of the joint between hard bodies while still allowing them to deform by including multiple bones for each hard body.

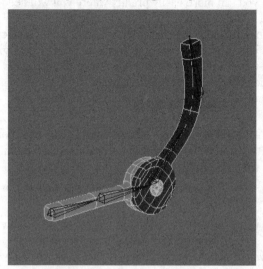

You will also come across situations where a hard body is attached to a soft body, or deformable area. Consider a robot arm, made up of two solid pieces — the upper arm and lower arm — with cable attached to either side of the elbow joint. There are a number of ways you could rig this using separate objects, but it's far easier to use a single object with weight maps. You can assign each solid piece its own full-strength weight map, then blend the two weight maps on the cable.

Figure 3.3-4. Multiple bones using a single weight map allow deformation while keeping the joint solid.

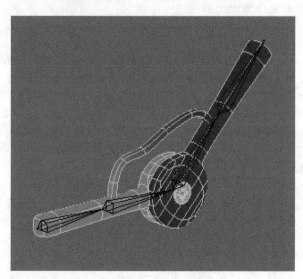

Figure 3.3-5. The solid area is at full strength, and the deformable area has blended weight values.

What Weight Maps Do You Need?

There are problem areas that are common to most characters. You can address these early on by starting with a basic set of weight maps. Once the character is rigged, you can test the deformations and adjust weight values or create more weight maps where they're needed.

As you gain experience you can more easily predict where you will need more weight maps and what values to apply, reducing the amount of work in the adjustment stage. Even then, if in doubt it's best to err on the side of simplicity. If you're unsure about what initial values to apply to adjacent weight maps, give the points between bones a value of 50% for each weight map. You can see where you need to tweak the values when the joint is posed.

Let's look at a basic set of weight maps and why they're good starting points.

- The head should be solid in most cases, deformed only by the head bone and morphs. Giving the head its own weight map ensures that only the head bone affects it, keeping it solid.

- The neck is separated so the shoulder and head bones don't affect the neck area.

- The shoulders are a joint the software often has trouble with, partially because a character's skeleton lacks a rib cage. The arm weight map creates a separate weight map on either side of the shoulder so you have control over how the joint is deformed.

- The wrists can also be a difficult area. The weight for the hands gives you control of the wrist deformation.

- The weight maps on the legs give control of the deformation at the hips, but having a separate weight map for each leg also makes sure that the bones of one side don't affect the other. The arms don't have that problem as they're far enough away from each other that their bone influences don't intersect, but the legs are often close enough to each other that this can be a problem.

- The foot and toe weights give control of the ankle and foot deformation while also separating the left and right sides, even more important when your character has big feet like Hamish.

Other initial weight maps to consider are for fingers if they're fat or close together, toes if they need independent control, and any deformable or movable geometry attached to the head such as long ears, hair, or a hat.

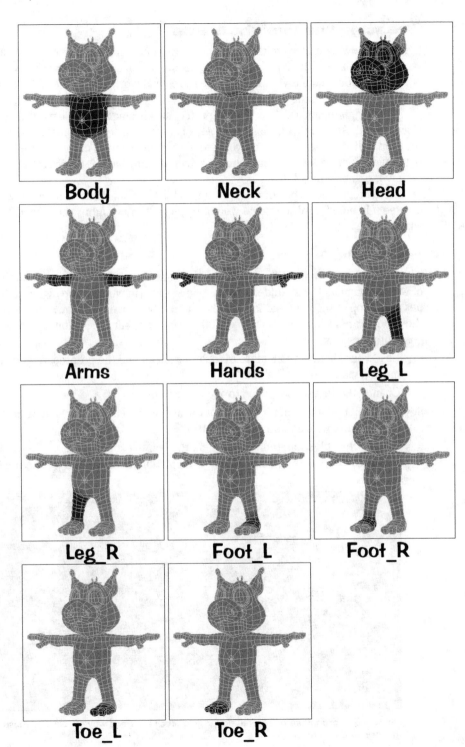

Creating the Weight Maps

Creating the weight maps without skelegons or bones as reference means that you need to plan for the position of the bone joints. You should have a pretty good idea if you've done your anatomy research and worked out where the comparative joints are in the character.

The weight maps don't have to be perfect at this stage as you have the chance to adjust them with more accuracy once you can see the bone's effect on the model. If you're uncertain of what weight values to apply, make the median of the weight maps — the point where each competing weight map is 50% — at the pivot point of the joint.

We'll create the basic set of weight maps for Hamish. Once he's rigged we can see if he needs any additional weight maps or if any weight values need adjusting.

Mapping the Arms and Hands

The arm weight map includes the often tricky shoulder region. The best method of weight mapping the shoulder joint is to give the arm weight map higher values at the top of the joint and lower values at the bottom of the joint. That way the shoulder muscle moves nicely with the arm bone, but the armpit doesn't push into the body.

1. Load your Hamish model into Modeler (you can find the preprepared object in \Objects\Chapters\Hamish_Working_v004.lwo).

2. Change the Perspective view to **Weight Shade**.

3. Select all the points in the middle of the arm and create a new weight map called **Arms** with an initial value of **100%**.

4. Expand the selection, then deselect all the points except those at the wrist and **Set Map Value** to **75%**. Deselect all points in preparation for the next step.

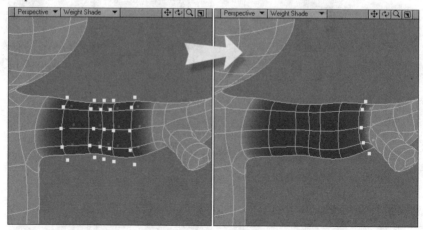

Figure 3.3-6. Expanding points that are easy to reach is a good way of selecting those that are harder to reach.

5. Select the top point at the peak of the shoulder and **Set Map Value** to **80%**. Following the row of points down from the Back view, select the two lower points and **Set Map Value** to **60%**. Give the middle points a value of **40%** and the next two points a value of **20%**.

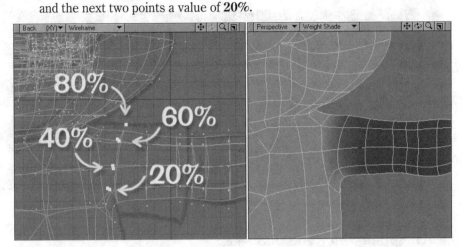

Figure 3.3-7. Adjusting weight values at the shoulder.

6. Now the shoulder weight is looking pretty good, but the higher values need a little more blending. Select the top point of the row on the inside of the shoulder and **Set Map Value** to **30%**. Give the points under that a value of **20%** and the next two points a value of **10%**.

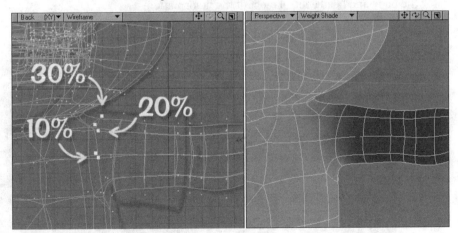

Figure 3.3-8. Smoothing the blended area.

> **Note:** Notice the area is smoothly blended by decreasing the values by equal amounts. When the blending is smooth like this the weight values are much easier to adjust later on.

7. Select the points of the hand including the wrist and create a new weight map called **Hands** with an initial value of **25%**.

8. **Contract** the selection and **Set Map Value** to **100%**.

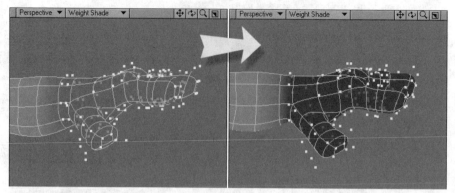

Figure 3.3-9. Weight map for the wrist and hand.

Mapping the Head and Neck

Mapping the head and neck of chubby characters is a bit different than with thin characters. Because the neck isn't as defined in chubby characters, it's more difficult to differentiate between the solid mass of the head and jaw and the more flexible areas of the neck.

What we'll do for Hamish is to give partial control to the neck, while letting the body and head control most of the deformation.

1. Select the polygons of the head, as shown in Figure 3.3-10, and create a new weight map called **Head** with an initial value of **100%**.

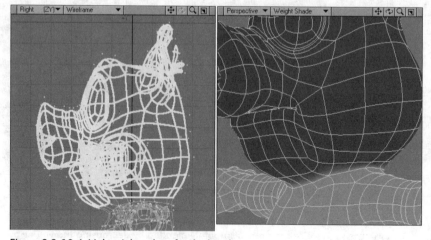

Figure 3.3-10. Initial weight values for the head.

2. With the polygon flow adjusted, we can continue with the weight mapping. Select the line of points at the neck and **Set Map Value** to **25%**.

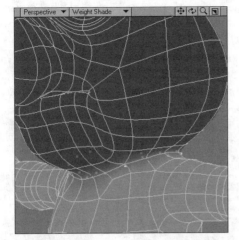

Figure 3.3-11. Weight values for the neck area.

3. With the points still selected, create a new weight map called **Neck** with an initial value of **50%**.

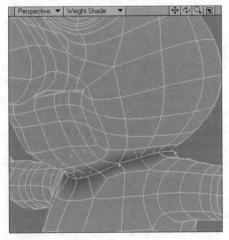

Figure 3.3-12. Neck weight map.

4. Now we need to create maps for the ears. Select the polygons of the bulb at the top of the ear, making sure you have the complete bands of polygons in the selection. **Expand** the selection until you have all the polygons of the ear selected. Create a new weight map called **Ears** with an initial value of **50%**. **Contract** the selection and **Set Map Value** to **100%**.

5. Expand the selection, select the **Head** weight map, and **Set Map Value** to **50%**. **Contract** the selection once and **Clear Map**, giving the weight map for the head the opposite values of the ears.

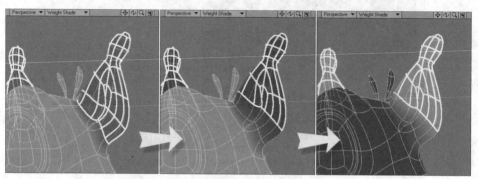

Figure 3.3-13. This weight map allows the ears to be posed.

Mapping the Legs and Feet

The leg weight map is a little more complex because of the groin area and the need for separate left and right weight maps. The groin can be a tricky area to weight map because the front and back deform quite differently. The easiest method of weight mapping the groin area is to test it and see, adjusting the values after rigging.

To create the separate left and right weight maps, it's easiest to create symmetrical weights first and separate them into left and right weight maps afterward. This is much quicker and ensures the same values on both sides.

1. Select the band of polygons above the knee and **Expand** the selection three times to select all the polygons of the leg as shown in Figure 3.3-14. Create a new weight map called **Leg_LT** with an initial value of **50%**. **Contract** the selection and **Set Map Value** to **100%**.

2. Select the four points at the base of the groin, as shown in Figure 3.3-15, and **Set Map Value** to **25%**.

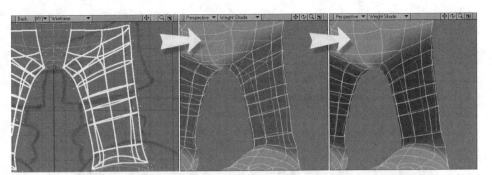

Figure 3.3-14. Initial weight values for the legs.

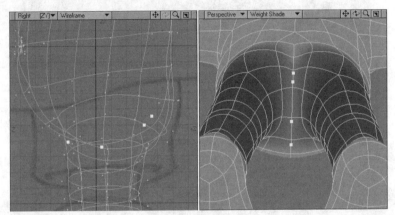

Figure 3.3-15. This allows the groin area to deform a little with the position of the legs.

3. Now we need to smooth the weight map at the edges as we did for the shoulder. Select the inner point of the triangles at the front of each leg and the points of the bum cheeks as shown in Figure 3.3-16, and set the value to 25%.

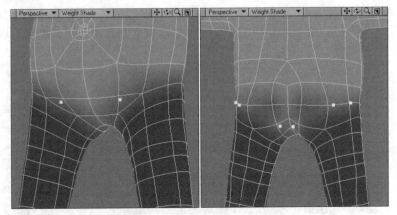

Figure 3.3-16. Smoothing the blended areas.

4. Select the three points at the bottom of the bum cheek and set the value to **50%**. Select the point at the inside top corner of the bum cheek and set the value to **10%**.

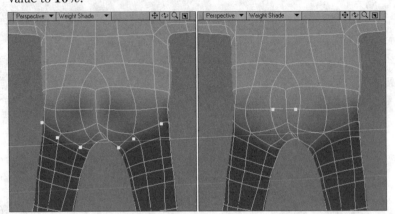

Figure 3.3-17. Adjusting the bum cheeks.

5. Select the points from the ball of the foot to the ankle and create a new weight map called **Foot_LT** with an initial value of **50%**. **Contract** the selection and **Set Map Value** to **100%**.

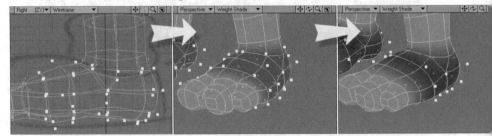

Figure 3.3-18. Weight values for the foot. Create the joint between foot and toes at the ball of the foot.

6. Select the points from the ball of the foot to the toes and create a new weight map called **Toe_LT** with an initial value of **50%**. **Contract** the selection and **Set Map Value** to **100%**.

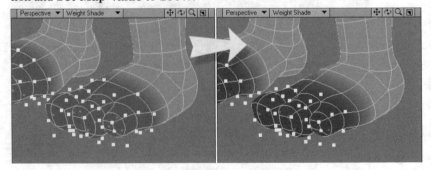

Figure 3.3-19. Weight values for the toes.

Mapping the Shoes

We'll leave weight mapping the clothes until after we've rigged the body, but we can weight map the shoes now, as they don't rely on the body as much as the other clothes do.

1. Change to the clothes layer, select the polygons of the shirt, pants, and socks, and **Hide Selected** (-).

2. From the Right view, select the points shown in Figure 3.3-20. Select the **Foot_LT** weight map and **Set Map Value** to **100%**.

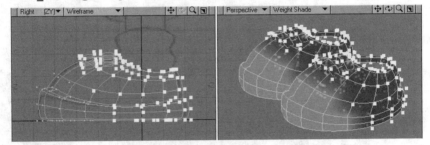

Figure 3.3-20. Initial weight values for the shoes.

3. Select the points shown in Figure 3.3-21 and **Set Map Value** to **50%**, giving us a nice straight line at the edge of the weight map.

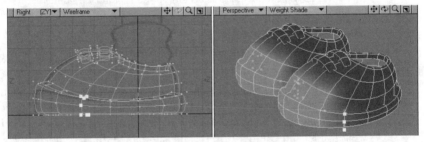

Figure 3.3-21. You can create a smooth line between weight maps even if the polygon flow doesn't support it.

4. With those points still selected, select the **Toe_LT** weight map and **Set Map Value** to **50%**. Select the remaining points at the toes and **Set Map Value** to **100%**.

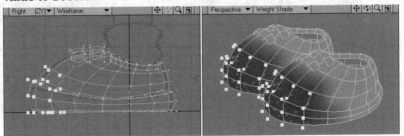

Figure 3.3-22. Weight values for the toes of the shoes.

115

Separating Left and Right Sides

Now that the legs and feet are mapped we can separate the left and right sides.

1. Still in the clothes layer, turn off **Symmetry** and select some of the polygons of the right shoe, making sure to select at least one polygon for each part — the sole, the shoe, and the laces. **Select Connected** (]) to select all the polygons of the right shoe.

2. Add the body layer to the foreground (**Shift+select**) and **Shift+select** the polygons of the right foot and leg and the right side of the groin to add them to the selection, being careful not to select any polygons of the left shoe.

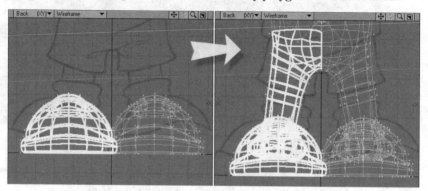

Figure 3.3-23. Be careful not to select any polygons of the left side.

3. Select the **Leg_LT** weight map and **Copy Vertex Map** to **Leg_RT**.

4. Copy the **Foot_LT** weight map to **Foot_RT**, and copy the **Toe_LT** weight map to **Toe_RT**.

5. We want the values along the center line to be the same for each side, so before clearing the right side from the original weight maps, deselect the polygons along the center line (X=0) of the model. Now select the **Leg_LT** weight map and **Clear Map**. Do the same for **Foot_LT** and **Toe_LT**.

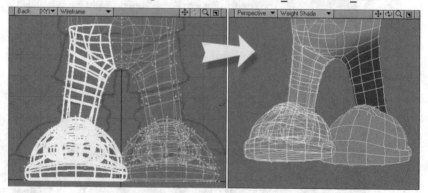

Figure 3.3-24. Deselect the middle polygons before clearing so the center values remain.

Mapping the Body

Often the blended areas of adjoining weight maps are easy to create, as there are nice even values around the rows of points. The weight map for the body at the shoulder and groin areas isn't that easy as there are lots of different weight values, making the creation of the body weight map quite fiddly and time consuming. Instead of creating the weight map manually we'll use a plug-in called Combine Weightmaps, written by Kevin Phillips, to subtract the arm and leg weight maps from the body. That way, since we created the weight maps for the arms and legs first, the weight map for the body is the easiest of the lot.

1. Select the polygons of the body including a few extra segments of the arms, legs, and head. Create a new weight map called **Body**.

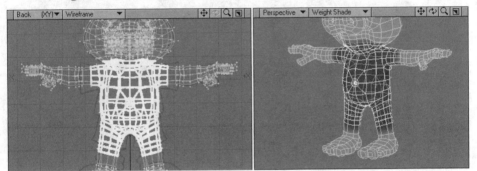

Figure 3.3-25. Make sure you overlap the selection into the previously mapped areas.

2. Making sure the polygons are still selected, select **Plugs➤Additional➤ Combine Weights**. Set "to create" to **Body**. Change "Take" to **Body**, "and" to **Subtract**, and "this" to **Arms**. Turn off **Make non-mapped points equal 0%** and press **OK**.

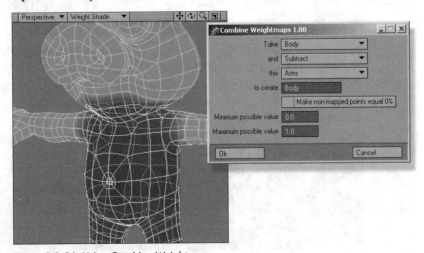

Figure 3.3-26. Using Combine Weightmaps.

117

> **Note:** If you can't find the plug-in, make sure you have followed the instructions on installing the plug-ins in Chapter 1.

3. Select **Combine Weights** again. Enter the same values as in step 2, except change "This" to **Head**.
4. Continue applying **Combine Weightmaps** until you've subtracted the **Neck**, **Leg_LT**, and **Leg_RT** weight maps from the Body weight map.

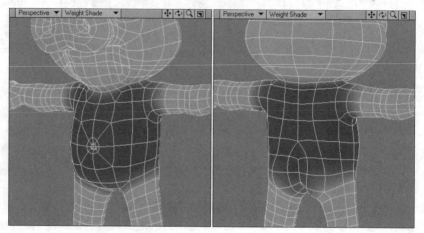

Figure 3.3-27. Final Body weight map.

Mapping the Eyes and Eyebrows

The eyebrow weight map is one that is especially important for cartoon characters. The stretch control for the eyes allows you to adjust their scale so you can give them some squash and stretch or cartoony exaggeration. This weight map isn't included in the basic list, as not all characters require stretchy eyes, but we'll deviate from the basic list and include them for Hamish.

First we'll map the eyeballs, then create the eyebrow weight map.

1. Place the eyeball layer in the foreground and turn off **Symmetry**.
2. Select the polygons of just the left eyeball (the right eye when looking at the Back view) and create a new weight map called **Eye_LT** with an initial value of **100%**.

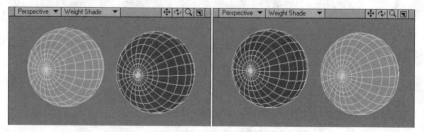

Figure 3.3-28. Left and right eye maps.

3. Select the polygons of just the right eyeball and create a new weight map called **Eye_RT** with an initial value of **100%**.

4. Place the body layer in the foreground and turn **Symmetry** back on.

5. Select the four polygons in the center of the eye socket and **Expand** the selection four times. Create a new weight map called **Eyebrows** with an initial value of **50%**.

6. Contract the selection and **Set Map Value** to **100%**.

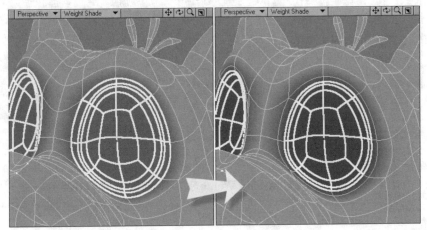

Figure 3.3-29. To ensure the eye morphs work with the stretching of the eye, we need to include the entire eye area.

7. Select the top four polygons of the eyebrow and **Set Map Value** to **50%**. Deselect all but the top one and **Set Map Value** to **100%**.

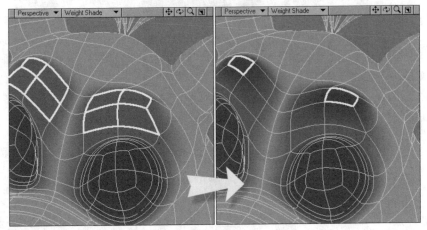

Figure 3.3-30. Initial weight values for the eyebrows.

8. Select the four points shown in Figure 3.3-31A and **Set Map Value** to **100%**.

9. Select the points shown in Figure 3.3-31B and **Set Map Value** to 25%, smoothing out the edges of the weight map.

10. Select the two points shown in Figure 3.3-31C and **Set Map Value** to 75%.

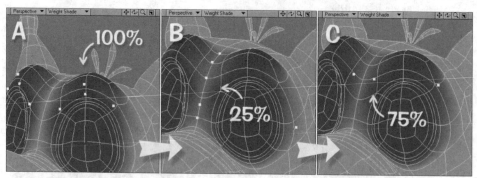

Figure 3.3-31. Adjusting the weight map.

11. Finally, select **Combine Weights**. Set "to create" to **Head**. Change "Take" to **Head**, "and" to **Subtract**, and "this" to **Eyebrows**. Turn off **Make non-mapped points equal 0%** and press **OK**.

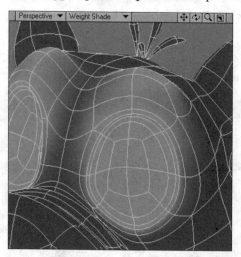

Figure 3.3-32. Weight map for the head after subtracting the eyebrows.

That completes this stage of the weight mapping. We'll revisit the weight maps to adjust the deformations after rigging and again when rigging the clothes.

3.4 Preparing for Layout

Now that we have the initial weight maps completed, we need to prepare the model for rigging in Layout. It's important to keep the final character object to as few layers as possible. A single layer is ideal and is sufficient for most cartoon characters. This keeps the scene less cluttered and makes it much easier to select objects and apply expressions.

Leave the clothes and template eyes in their own layers for now, so they're easier to work with. We'll copy the clothes into the first layer and delete the template eyes after rigging, making Hamish a single-layered object.

1. Save the model under its working title.

2. **Cut** and **Paste** the eyeballs into the first layer.

3. Select the clothes layer. Select the polygons of just the shoes and **Cut** and **Paste** them into the first layer, leaving the template eyeballs and clothes in their own layers.

4. **Save Incremental (Shift+s).**

Figure 3.4-1. Hamish object ready for rigging.

5. Select the **Layout** pull-down and choose **Switch to Layout**.

6. In Layout, load the scene **Hamish_Setup.lws**. This scene has some lights and items set up ready for Hamish.

7. Press the **Modeler** button (**F12**) to switch back to Modeler.

8. In Modeler, with the Hamish model active (you can find a preprepared object in \Objects\Chapters\Hamish_Working_v005.lwo), choose **Send Object to Layout**.

If you're not running the Hub, you need to load the object from within Layout instead of sending it over from Modeler.

1. Launch Layout and check that the Content Directory is set to **\LWProjects\LW8_CartoonCreation**.
2. Load the scene **Hamish_Setup.lws**.
3. Load your Hamish object (you can find a preprepared object in \Objects\Chapters\Hamish_Working_v005.lwo).

9. In Layout select **File**➤**Save**➤**Save Scene As** (**Ctrl+s**), calling the new scene **Hamish_Rig01_v001.lws**.

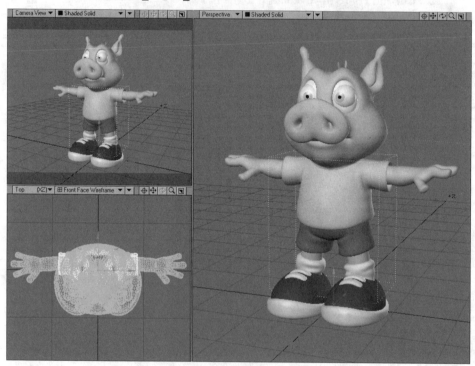

Figure 3.4-2. Hamish in Layout.

Object Properties

With the scene set up, the next thing to do is to adjust some of the properties for the objects.

1. Select **Scene Editor**➤**Open** (**Ctrl+F1**) to open the Scene Editor.
2. Select all the Hamish layers and open the Object Properties panel.
3. In the Geometry tab, change Subdivision Order to **Last**.
4. Change Display SubPatch Level to **1** so the wireframes are nice and light, making them easier to work with.

> **Note:** To make the following steps easier to follow I'll reference the layers of the Hamish object by layer name from here on, so Layer1 means Hamish_Working_v005:Layer1.

5. Select just **Layer1** and, in the Deform tab, select **Add Displacement** and choose **Morph Mixer** from the pull-down menu, activating the morphs in the object.

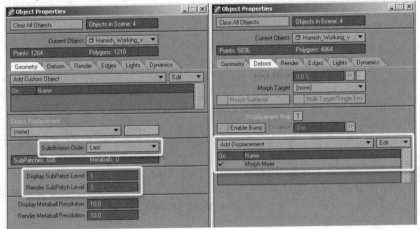

Figure 3.4-3. Object Properties panel.

6. Close the Object Properties panel.

Visibility Options

We'll adjust the visibility options for the clothing and template eye layers.

1. In the Scene Editor, select **Layer2**, the template eyes. Select the visibility icon and set to **Wireframe**. Click the active icon to uncheck it, deactivating the layer. Select the color cube next to the name and set the color to **Gray**.

2. Select **Layer3**, the clothes. Select the visibility icon and set to **Hidden**. Click the active icon to uncheck it, deactivating the layer.

3. Select **Layer2** and **Layer3** and parent them to **Layer1**.

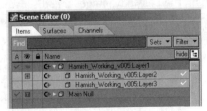

Figure 3.4-4. Visibility options.

4. Save the scene.

3.5 Bone Creation

Bones are used to deform a character so it appears to move in a realistic manner. Section 3.1 addressed the issues involved with bone deformation as it applies to rigging. This section looks at some of those issues in more detail as well as issues specific to creating the bone structure for your character.

Character skeletons are often created with every bone physically connected, or touching another bone. In most cases this results in many more bones than are necessary, and can also cause rotation problems due to a bone's parent being at an odd angle. A child bone can exist anywhere within a rig; it doesn't have to be touching its parent. Use this ability to your advantage to achieve efficiency and stability with your character's skeleton.

A character skeleton doesn't have to be a single hierarchy. Since bones can be parented to other bones or the object they're connected to, you can have multiple, separate hierarchies within an object.

Bones are very powerful and offer control and flexibility in a rig. You can use them to do all sorts of things you may never have imagined. If you have trouble with the deformation of a joint, the first thing to investigate is the possibility of solving the problem using bones. Only look at alternative solutions if adjusting the bone settings can't solve the problem. The trick is to analyze how you want an area to deform, and then figure out what combination of bones you need to accomplish the deformation.

Skelegons or Bones?

You can create the bones for a character directly in Layout or by creating skelegons in Modeler. Skelegons are temporary or fake bones. A skelegon is a special type of polygon that represents a bone in Modeler. The skelegon polygons can then be converted to bones in Layout.

When skelegons were introduced it opened up a range of possibilities for rigging that weren't available before when only bones existed in Layout. Now LightWave 8 has included many of the benefits of skelegons in Layout's Setup tools, making creating and editing bones in Layout much easier.

The choice to use skelegons to create your initial bone structure or create the bones directly in Layout really comes down to personal preference. There isn't a right or wrong way, as each method has advantages and disadvantages, so you can decide for yourself which you feel most comfortable with. It's often useful to use both methods for a single rig, utilizing the advantages of each for different sections.

The "Rigging Morfi" chapter in *Volume 1: Modeling & Texturing* describes the proper way of using skelegons to create and position the bones. For Hamish we'll create the bones directly in Layout using LightWave 8's Setup tools.

Bone Rotation

A bone has three axes of rotation: heading, pitch, and bank, or H, P, and B. To create a good bone structure for a character it's very important to understand these rotation axes and how they work. Think of the rotation axes as being a hierarchy, where bank is the child of pitch, which is in turn the child of heading. This means that rotating the heading affects the direction of the pitch and bank axes, rotating the pitch affects the direction of the bank axis but not the heading, and rotating the bank has no effect on the direction of the pitch or heading axes.

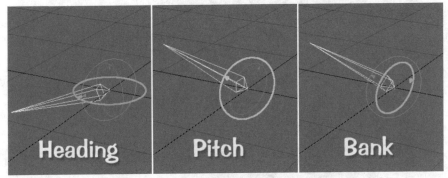

Figure 3.5-1. Heading affects pitch and bank, pitch affects bank, and bank has no effect on the other axes.

Even though heading is at the top of the axis hierarchy, it's important to make pitch the primary axis of rotation for a joint so we can make use of LightWave's internal joint deformation functions. When rotating a bone (or any item) on all axes you should rotate each axis in order. Rotate the heading until the pitch axis is correctly aligned. Then rotate the pitch as much as required, and lastly rotate the bank. You should perform rotations in this order when creating the initial position of the bones as well as when posing or animating.

The alignment of the rotation axes of a child bone are determined by the orientation of its parent. This means you can offset the rotation direction of a bone from its parent rotation direction to suit the joint it's deforming. It also means if the parent isn't oriented correctly the rotation direction of the child bone will not be correct. Where possible you should orient the parent of each bone to match the intended rotation direction of its child, ensuring a stable rig and predictable behavior of the bones.

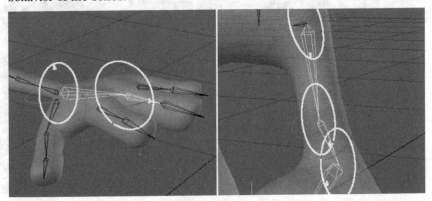

Figure 3.5-2. Left: The bank of the hand bone offsets the pitch of the finger bones. Right: Parent rotations align the rotation of the children.

125

Gimbal Lock

Gimbal lock occurs when the pitch nears 90° or 270°, causing the bank and heading to lie along the same plane. This limits the item to only two rotation axes, as the bank and heading effectively do the same thing.

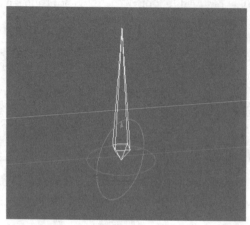

Figure 3.5-3. A bone suffering gimbal lock. Notice it can't rotate on its local heading axis.

By understanding the relationship between the rotation axes and the relationship between parent and child, you can often completely avoid gimbal lock.

If you do run into gimbal lock, you can adjust the rotation of the axes so the item is oriented correctly. You can position the item by readjusting the heading, pitch, and bank, achieving the correct orientation in a different way. This is an ideal solution for animation controls because you still have full control over the rotation and you retain the efficiency of a single control.

> **Note:** This is exactly what using local or world coordinates does, except by doing it manually you retain full control, avoiding the problems associated with changing coordinates.

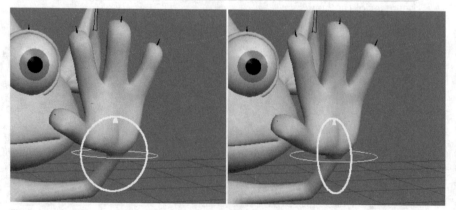

Figure 3.5-4. The orientation of the hand control can be adjusted even though it's suffering from gimbal lock.

Another solution is to create a nested control for the item. A nested control is one where there are two items — a parent and a child — performing the rotation instead of just one. Each item has different rotation axes available, so if the child reaches gimbal lock, you can use the parent to rotate on the disabled axis. This solution is most useful within the bone structure.

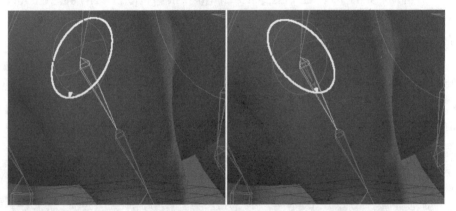

Figure 3.5-5. Left: The bone is suffering from gimbal lock and can't rotate on its local heading axis. Right: Adding a control bone aligns the rotation so its parent axes are the same as its local axes.

Gimbal Lock Solutions to Avoid

There are two solutions that LightWave provides for gimbal lock: changing the coordinate system and using Record Pivot Rotation (RPR). These can be useful in certain situations, but should never be used for character rigs.

LightWave includes the ability to rotate an item using local or world coordinates instead of the default parent coordinates. While this appears to work just fine when posing, its major flaw becomes apparent during animation when the item spins 360° between poses. Although you're adjusting the rotation using local or world coordinates, the rotation is still calculated using parent coordinates. The item will find the closest parent coordinate rotation to achieve the desired position. This is often 360° from the correct rotation, which appears correct in the current pose but causes the item to spin between keyframes.

You can use Record Pivot Rotation for an item, which adjusts the pivot rotation to match the current rotation of the item. This zeros out the initial rotation, which seems like a good idea and is often recommended for use on the bones of a character. The major flaw to RPR is that you lose control of the rotation of the item. An important feature of a good character rig is the ability to adjust it or add to it if the need arises. If you use RPR, adjusting the item becomes much more difficult, the behavior of added child items is unpredictable, and IK becomes less predictable, especially targeting. Although both solutions can work in some circumstances, it's best to avoid them since we have better solutions that provide stable and predictable results every time.

Control Bones

Control bones are used to assist the bones directly related to the skeleton, which for descriptive purposes we'll call working bones. As the name suggests, a control bone gives you more control over the character, both in the way it moves and how it deforms. Since control bones perform many different functions within a character rig, it's important to know when to use them.

Rotation Control

Rotation control bones usually have no effect on the geometry, existing merely to assist the rotation of the working bone.

A rotation control bone can align the rotation of a working bone so that it rotates in the correct direction. If the parent of a bone can't be oriented to provide the correct alignment of its child, then you can add a control bone between them to properly align the child bone.

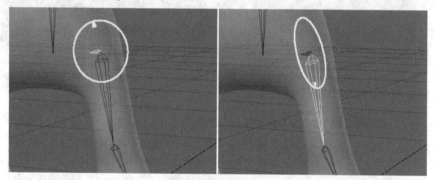

Figure 3.5-6. The bank of the hip control bone aligns the rotation of the leg bones.

A rotation control bone can be used to avoid gimbal lock on ball joints by taking the place of one of the rotation axes. If a bone suffers from gimbal lock, whether in its rest rotation or in a possible posed rotation, a control bone can be used as a parent to create a nested control for that joint. This can give you more control over the joint as well as make the rig more stable.

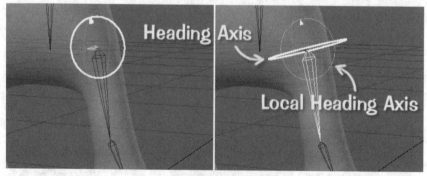

Figure 3.5-7. The upper leg bone can't rotate on its local heading axis. The bank of the hip bone rotates the upper leg bone on its local heading axis, overcoming the gimbal lock.

Muscle Control

Muscle control bones do have an effect on the geometry, and often have the benefit of providing rotation control at the same time as muscle control.

A control bone can simulate the muscle structure, providing more control over joint deformation. The muscles often move quite differently than the bones, especially on ball joints. Instead of allowing a bone to rotate on all axes, which can cause the geometry at the joint to twist undesirably, you can limit the bone to two rotation axes and use a control bone under the joint to simulate the third axis of rotation. This minimizes twisting at the joint while still providing the functionality of a ball joint.

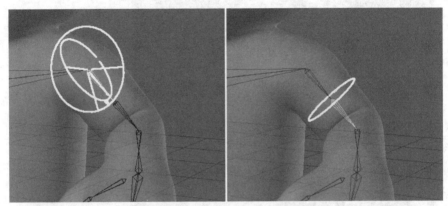

Figure 3.5-8. The first bone rotates on heading and pitch. The second bone rotates on bank, so the twisting occurs over the length of the upper arm instead of at the shoulder joint.

A control bone can also simulate muscle structure by having its position or scale linked to the rotation of a joint. This is useful for joints where the muscle stretches or slides across bones. By including a bone to control the muscle you can simulate the correct motion of the surface when the joint bends.

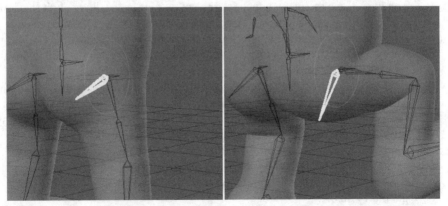

Figure 3.5-9. The bum bone simulates the motion of the muscle sliding over the pelvic bone.

What Bones Do You Need?

Every character has unique requirements, but most characters need the same basic skeletal structure. Before creating the bones for Hamish we'll take a brief look at each major hierarchy and what its bone requirements are.

Spine

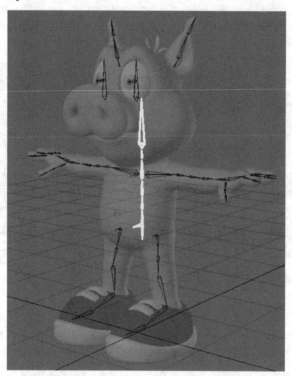

You don't need too many bones for the spine; four is usually enough to allow for the necessary poses. Position the spine toward the back of the character, especially for more realistic human characters, to follow the position of a real spine. For most characters it should be fairly straight, although you can allow for the natural curvature of the spine in more realistic characters.

The neck can be made up of one or two bones, depending on its flexibility. Make sure the joint of the head bone is at the pivot point of a real skull, just behind and below the ears in human characters. The head bone should always be vertical, as this makes parenting the eye bones much easier, as well as making its initial orientation the same as the character's head.

The pelvis consists of a control bone and a working bone. The control bone is used to rotate the pelvis and hips, and the working bone keeps the groin geometry stable.

Leg Bones

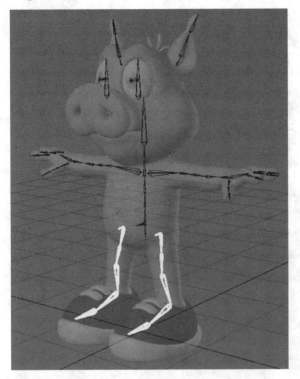

The hip bone is at the root of the leg hierarchy. The hip is a control bone that aligns and assists the rotation of the upper leg bone, as well as allowing some manual control for positioning the knee.

For simple characters a single upper leg bone is often sufficient. For more complex characters it's useful to have two upper leg bones. The first bone is used for IK calculation and the second is used to assist the positioning of the knee. Because the hip joint is quite complex, it's handy to have two options for directing the knee — each deforming the geometry differently — so you can use the one that works best or combine their use to fine-tune a pose.

Position the knee joint toward the front of the geometry rather than in the middle, as this creates nicer and more realistic deformation and gives you a slight bend in the joint to help the IK solution. Make sure the ankle joint is in the right place; if it's too high or too low the foot rotation will look odd. The toe joint can be a tricky one, especially for characters with chunky feet. To start with, position the toe joint at the ball of the foot, roughly halfway between the top and bottom of the foot. Sometimes you need to test and adjust the position of the toe joint to make sure the foot doesn't fold in on itself when the toes bend.

Arm Bones

The shoulder often seems to suffer from joint deformation problems, but many of these problems occur when the shoulder is poorly posed. The reason for this is that the upper arm bone needs to allow for the motion of the arm bones below them, the position of the elbow, and the mass of the shoulder muscle. We use two bones for the upper arm to alleviate some of these problems, but it's important to understand how these two bones relate to one another as well as the surrounding bones to be able to pose the shoulder correctly. The first upper arm bone is used to position the shoulder joint. The second upper arm bone is rotated to position the elbow, so the twisting that happens when the elbow changes position occurs in the middle of the arm instead of at the shoulder.

The forearm and wrist is another common problem area. When using IK it's easiest to have a wrist bone parented to the hand bone. This rotates the bank of the wrist with the bank rotation of the hand. Using a single wrist bone is sufficient for most cartoon characters, although it can cause twisting problems if the hand is rotated too far. If the forearm starts to collapse then you know you've rotated the hand too much. For more complex or realistic characters it can be beneficial to have multiple wrist bones, which are described in Chapter 4, "Advanced Rigging."

Position the shoulder joint in line with the peak of the shoulder muscle, just outside the armpit. Position the elbow joint slightly toward the back of the arm to give nicer deformation and to give the joint a slight bend to help the IK solution. Position the wrist joint in the center of the geometry.

Finger Bones

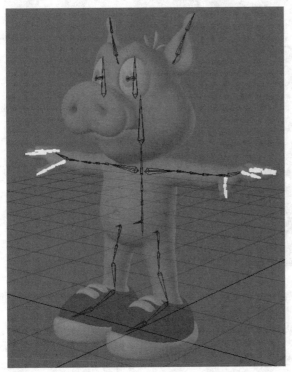

It's important to position the finger bones carefully. The positions of the joints determine the shape of the fist when the fingers close, and if the joints aren't positioned correctly, making a fist can collapse the hand.

Hamish has short stubby fingers that only require two joints, although many characters require three-jointed fingers. The principles are the same for both; you just need an extra bone for each finger.

Eye Bones

Each eye is controlled by two or three bones. The main eye bone rotates the eyeball. The base bone is used to align the rotation of the eye bone and provide the initial scale of the eyeball. The stretch bone can be included to dynamically adjust the scale of the eye for cartoon exaggeration.

Position the base and eye bones exactly in the center of the eyeball, and position the base of the stretch bone where you want the center of the stretching to occur, usually at the bottom of the eye socket so the eye only stretches upward.

Creating the Bones

Creating the bones in Layout is different from creating skelegons in Modeler. You need to create skelegons from the viewport perpendicular to the pitch of the bone. In Layout the viewport doesn't determine the orientation of the bones, but it does play a part. To create a chain of bones aligned on one axis you should create them from the viewport perpendicular to the aligned axis. The other important aspect of bone creation in Layout is that all bone editing must be done on frame 0, so it's a good idea to keep the rig in its default position on frame 0.

Creating the Spine

The pitch of the spine should be aligned along the front center line of the character. Create the spine from the Right view to keep the spine centered on the X axis.

1. Load **Hamish_Rig01.lws** into Layout (you can find a preprepared scene in \Scenes\Chapters\Hamish_Rig01_v001.lws).
2. Change the Perspective viewport to **Right (ZY)** and change its mode to **Front Face Wireframe**.

3. Select **Layer1** and change to **Bone** mode (**Shift+b**).

4. Select **Setup➤Add➤Draw Bones** and, in the Right view, click and drag to create the first bone of the spine, from the top of the pelvis to the belly button. Position the bone so it's under the center of the arms from the Right view.

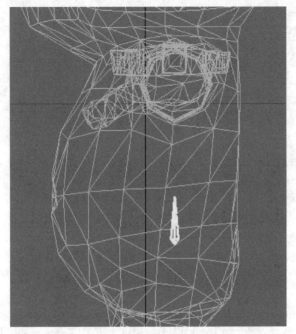

Figure 3.5-10. Draw the first bone for the spine.

5. Select the bone, press **y** to enter Rotation mode, and change the Heading (**H**) value to **180** (if it isn't already) using the numeric controls. This adjusts the rotation direction of the bone so the spine is more intuitive to control.

> **Note:** When drawing bones, Heading will always point in the direction of the bone. In most cases this is what you want. In this case, if you created the first spine bone exactly vertical, its heading would be unaltered so it would need some help to know in what direction it should rotate.

6. Select **Setup➤Add➤Draw Child Bones** and create three more bones for the spine, finishing at the top of the arm, then create a smaller bone for the neck and a long bone for the head.

7. It can be tricky to get the joints in the right position when creating bones this way. If you need to adjust the joints, change to **Object** mode (**Shift+o**) and select **Setup➤Modify➤Joint Move**. Click the right mouse button (**RMB**) on each joint to move it along the axis of the bones. Press **Spacebar** to confirm the changes.

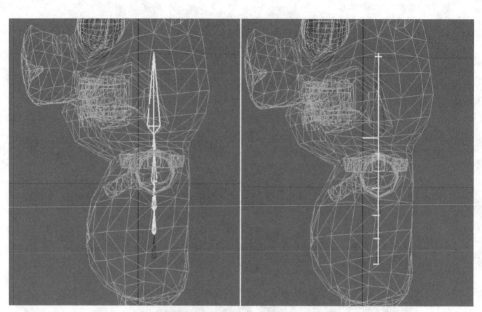

Figure 3.5-11. Draw the rest of the spine, adjusting joints if necessary.

> **Note:** Selecting the object before Joint Move lets you adjust any joint in the skeleton. Moving a joint with the left mouse button (LMB) lets you move it anywhere. Moving a joint with RMB limits the move to the Z axis of the bone.

8. Select the first bone and **Items➢Replace➢Rename** to **Back01**. Rename the other bones in order to **Back02**, **Back03**, **Back04**, **Neck**, and **Head**.

9. Select **Back01** and **Items➢Add➢Clone** (**Ctrl+c**) and create two clones.

10. In the Current Item list, select **Back01 (2)** and rename it to **Pelvis_ Base**. Change its rotation to **180, 0, 0**. Select **Back01 (2)**, rename it to **Pelvis**, and change its rotation to **180, 90, 0**.

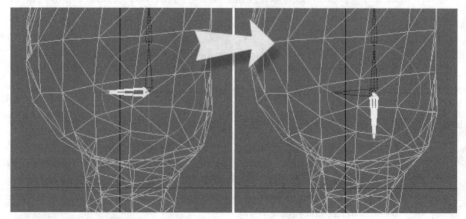

Figure 3.5-12. Pelvis bones.

Creating the Leg Bones

The pitch of all the leg bones should be aligned along the front center line of the leg.

1. Select **Draw Bones** and, in the Right view, create a bone from just below the pelvis in the middle of the leg to the knee, making its tip a little closer toward the front of the leg.

2. Select **Draw Child Bones** and create three more bones for the shin, foot, and toe. Notice the positions of the bones in Figure 3.5-13. The tip of the shin bone should be in the middle of the leg at the ankle, and the toe joint should be at the ball of the foot, about halfway between the bottom and top of the foot.

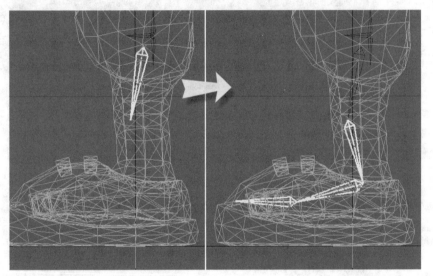

Figure 3.5-13. Draw the leg bones.

3. Rename the bones you just created to **Leg_Upper_LT**, **Leg_Lower_LT**, **Foot_LT**, and **Toe_LT**.

4. Select **Leg_Upper_LT** and clone it once. Rename the clone to **Hip_LT**.

5. Set the rotation of Hip_LT to **180, 0, 0**.

6. Select **Setup➢Modify➢Tip Move** and adjust using RMB to bring its tip to the same position as Pelvis_Base.

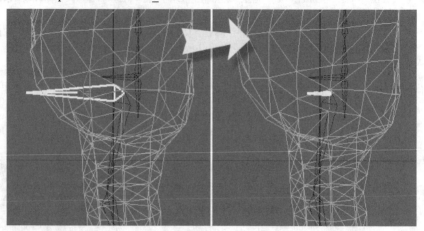

Figure 3.5-14. Creating the hip bone.

7. Select **Leg_Upper_LT** and **Setup➢Detail➢Bone Split** to create two collinear bones.

8. Rename the two upper leg bones **Leg_Upper01_LT** and **Leg_Upper02_LT.**

> **Note:**   You don't always have to change the name of split bones, as Bone Split adds a number to the end of the original name. It is good to rename them though, to keep the naming convention consistent.

9. Select **Leg_Upper01_LT** and open Motion Options (**m**). Change its Parent Item to **Hip_LT.**

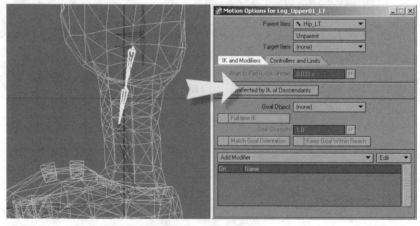

Figure 3.5-15. Split the upper leg bones and reparent.

10. Select **Hip_LT** and change the Top view to **Back (XY)**. Move (**t**) the hip bone in X to the center of the leg. Rotate (**y**) the bank so the leg bones lie along the center of the leg.

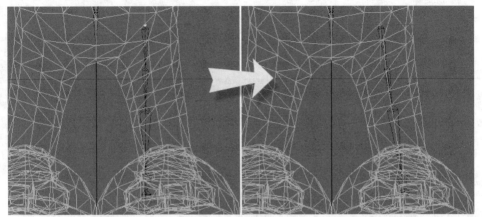

Figure 3.5-16. Adjusting the leg bone position.

11. Because of the rotation of the leg bones, the foot bones are out of alignment. We want the pitch of the foot bone to be vertical. Zoom up on the foot and adjust the bank of Leg_Lower_LT until the foot bone is vertical or the tip is in the same X position as the base.

12. Adjust the heading of Foot_LT until the pitch is aligned, then adjust the pitch until Toe_LT is pointing straight at the viewport.

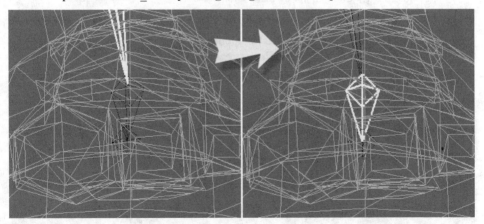

Figure 3.5-17. Adjusting the foot bones.

Creating the Arm Bones

The pitch of the arm bones should be aligned along the front center line of the arms, and the pitch of the hand bone should be aligned along the top of the hand.

1. In the Back view, select **Back04** and **Draw Child Bones**. Create a bone to the peak of the shoulder, but at a slight upward angle.
2. Move the bone down to near the base of Back04, then **Tip Move**, moving the top to the shoulder joint just above the middle of the arm.

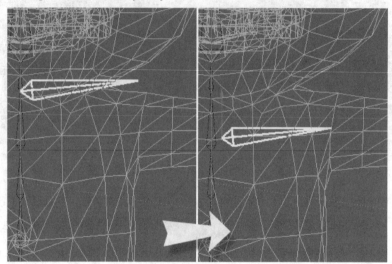

Figure 3.5-18. Creating the shoulder bone.

3. Draw two child bones, one to the elbow and one to the wrist, keeping the tips of the bones in the middle of the arm.
4. Rotate the bank of the lower arm bone to **–90°**, setting up the orientation of the hand bone.

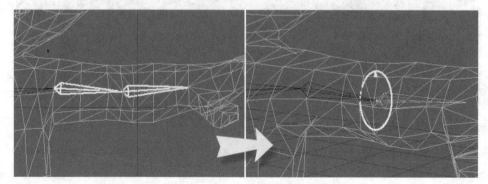

Figure 3.5-19. Adjust the bank of the parent to point in the direction you want for the pitch of the child.

5. Draw a child bone for the hand following the upward angle of the hand. Notice the pitch of the hand is vertical because we adjusted the rotation of the lower arm bone.

6. Change to Top view and change to **Object** mode. Select **Joint Move** and move the elbow joint back a little to create a slight bend in the joint.

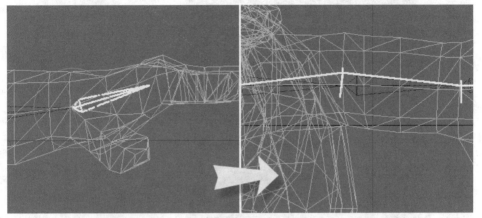

Figure 3.5-20. Create the hand and adjust the elbow.

7. Rename the bones in order: **Shoulder_LT, Arm_Upper_LT, Arm_ Lower_LT**, and **Hand_LT**.

8. Select **Arm_Upper_LT** and **Split Bone**, creating two collinear bones. Do the same for **Arm_Lower_LT**.

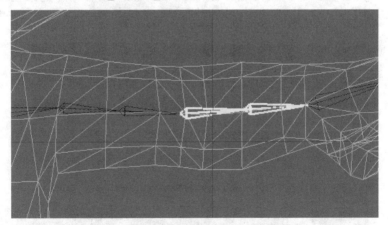

Figure 3.5-21. Split the upper and lower arm bones.

9. Open the Scene Editor (**Ctrl+F1**), right-click on **Hamish01:Layer**, and select **Expand child items (recursive)**.

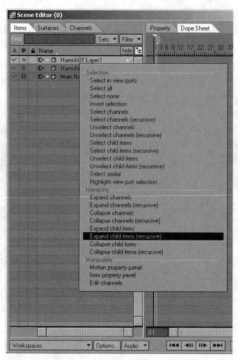

Figure 3.5-22. Scene Editor.

10. Click once to select **Hand_LT**, then click and drag it up to **Arm_Lower_ LT_1**, parenting it to that bone. Parent **Arm_Lower_LT_2** to **Hand_LT** the same way.

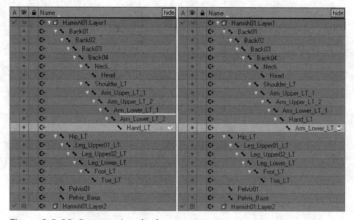

Figure 3.5-23. Reparenting the bones.

11. With Arm_Lower_LT_2 selected, switch to **Move** (**t**) mode and in the numeric panel change the X, Y, and Z values to **0**.

12. Change to **Rotate** (**y**) mode and click in the **H** setting to the right of the existing value. Type **–180** and press **Enter**.

> **Note:** In the numeric controls, the numeric keypad Enter key confirms the current setting and moves to the next. The Enter key in the main keyboard confirms the current setting and exits. Use both keys to take full advantage of this functionality. If you want to adjust a single setting, use the keyboard Enter key; if you want to adjust multiple settings, use the numeric keypad Enter key.

13. Change to Back view and rotate the pitch so the tip of Arm_Lower_LT_2 is touching the tip of **Arm_Upper_LT_1**.

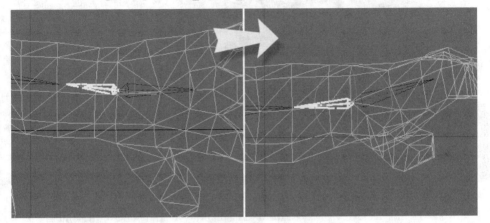

Figure 3.5-24. Adjusting the rotation of the wrist bone.

14. Open the Scene Editor, change to the **Property** tab, and change the Property view to **Motion≻General**.

15. Select the **Target** setting for Arm_Lower_LT_2 and, in the properties panel, set the target to **Arm_Lower_LT_1**.

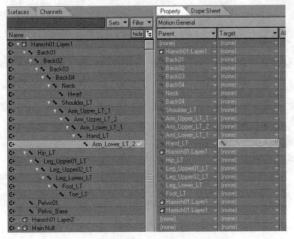

Figure 3.5-25. Setting a target for the wrist bone.

16. Rename the upper arm bones **Arm_Upper01_LT** and **Arm_Upper02_ LT**. Rename the lower arm bones **Arm_Lower_LT** and **Wrist_LT**.

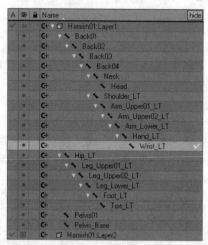

Figure 3.5-26. Bone hierarchy.

Creating the Finger Bones

The pitch of the finger bones should be aligned along the top of the fingers and thumb.

1.   In the Back view, select **Hand_LT** and draw a child bone to the end of the middle finger.

2.   Move the bone to the point of the knuckle from the Top view, and just above the middle of the finger from the Back view. Rotate the pitch so the tip of the bone comes out at the middle of the finger.

3.   Select **Bone Split**, creating two collinear bones.

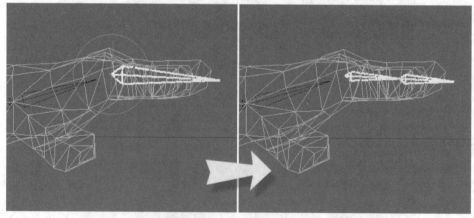

Figure 3.5-27. Creating the finger bones.

4. Select the first finger bone and move it so its base is at the point of the knuckle of the first (index) finger. In the Back view, move it down a little. Rotate the heading to align the bones with the angle of the finger.

5. Select **Setup≻Modify≻Scale Hierarchy**. Choose **No** in the requester and scale the finger bones so the tip of the second bone is just past the tip of the first finger.

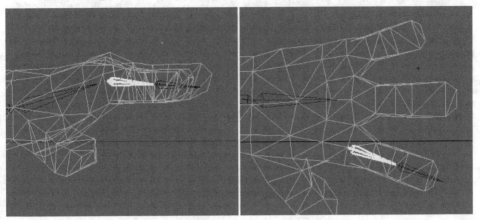

Figure 3.5-28. Position the bones in the first finger.

6. Rename the two bones **Finger101_LT** and **Finger102_LT**.

7. Select **Finger101_LT** and select **Setup≻Edit≻Copy Hierarchy**. Choose **Replace String** and replace **101** with **201**.

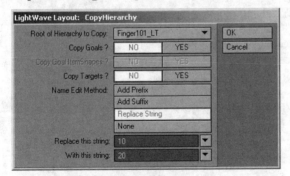

Figure 3.5-29. CopyHierarchy panel.

8. Move **Finger201_LT**, the first bone of the copied hierarchy, to the point of the knuckle of the second finger and move it up until the tip of the second bone is in the middle of the finger. Set its heading to **0**.

9. **Scale Hierarchy** until the tip of the second bone is just past the tip of the finger.

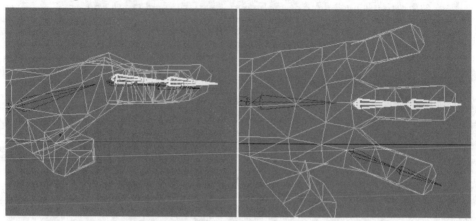

Figure 3.5-30. Middle finger bones.

10. Select **Finger101_LT** and **Copy Hierarchy**, replacing the string **101** with **301.**

11. Move **Finger301_LT** to the point of the knuckle of the third finger and adjust the heading to align the bones with the third finger. **Scale Hierarchy** until the tip of the second bone is just past the tip of the finger.

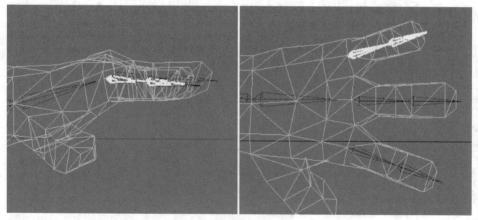

Figure 3.5-31. Little finger bones.

12. Select **Finger101_LT** and **Copy Hierarchy**, replacing the string **Finger101** with **Thumb01.**

13. Move **Thumb01_LT** so the base of the bone is a little way from the base of the hand bone, and just a little lower. Rotate the heading until it points to the middle of the thumb.

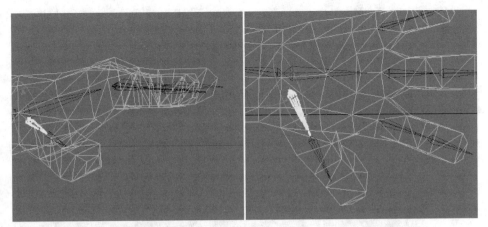

Figure 3.5-32. First two thumb bones.

14. Select **Thumb02_LT** and **Setup≻Add≻Child Bone** (=), calling the new bone **Thumb03_LT.**
15. Change to **Object** mode and select **Joint Move**. Move the joints of the thumb bones until they're aligned along the middle of the thumb. Check in the Perspective view to make sure they're in the right place from all angles. Notice the pitch of the thumb bones is correctly aligned with the angle of the thumb.

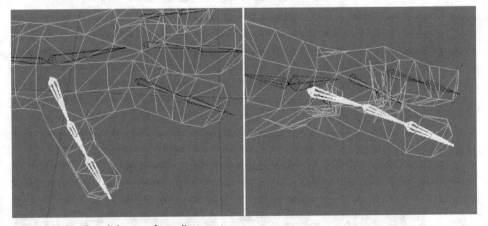

Figure 3.5-33. Thumb bones after adjustment.

Creating the Eye Bones

The pitch of all the eye bones should be aligned on the ZY plane.

1. Select **Setup≻Add≻Bone**, calling it **Eye_Base_LT.** Change the heading to **180** and, from the Right view, move it so the base of the bone is at the center of the eyeball.

2. Select **Tip Move** and move the tip using RMB until the tip is about halfway between the middle and outside edge of the eyeball.

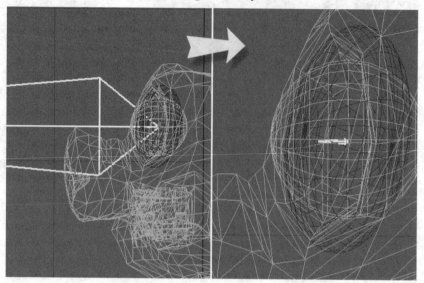

Figure 3.5-34. Base eye bone.

3. Zoom in and adjust the position of the bone so its base is exactly in the center of the left eyeball. Check from the Back and Right views.

4. Add a child bone (=), calling it **Eye_LT**. Change the Z position to **0**, then **Tip Move**, using RMB to move the tip to just outside the eyeball.

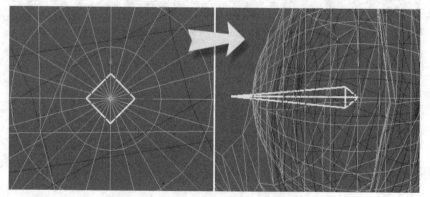

Figure 3.5-35. Position the base, then create the main eye bone.

5. Select **Eye_Base_LT** and **Items>Add>Clone (Ctrl+c)**. Rename the new bone **Eye_Stretch_LT**.

6. Move **Eye_Stretch_LT** in Y only to the base of the eye socket and change the pitch to **–90°**. Select **Tip Move** and, using RMB, move the tip to the top of the eye socket.

Figure 3.5-36. Stretch bone.

Creating the Ear Bones

We need to include bones for Hamish's ears so they can be posed. For long ears like these, the ear has a base that aligns the rotation of the main ear bones so they rotate in a different direction from the head, keeping the pitch as the major rotation axis. Make sure the pitch of the ear bones is aligned to the direction you want them to bend or rotate.

1. Select the **Head** bone, and from the Back view draw a small child bone at the same angle as the direction of the ear.

2. Move the bone to the base of the ear, making sure that it's in the center of the ear from all angles. Rotate the heading and pitch to point the bone at the tip of the ear, and rotate the bank about **–30**, or until the back is pointing at the back of the ear.

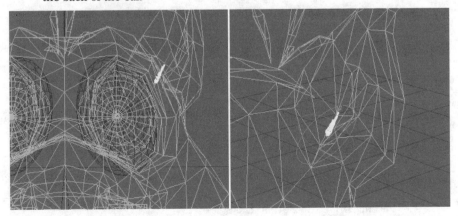

Figure 3.5-37. Base ear bone.

3. From the Back view, draw two child bones — one to the base of the bulb and the other to the tip of the ear.

4. Adjust the rotation of both bones so the joints are centered in the geometry. Check from all angles when adjusting.

5. Rename the ear bones **EarBase_LT**, **Ear01_LT**, and **Ear02_LT**.

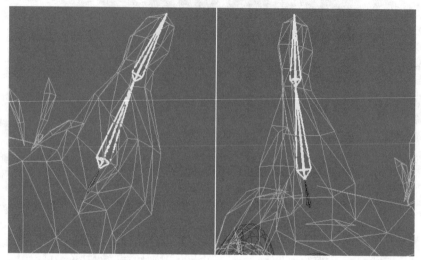

Figure 3.5-38. Ear bones.

Activating the Bones

Once the bones are created they need to be activated, or turned on, before they'll work. Activating the bones also sets their rest position and rotation. This is useful if you accidentally move or rotate a bone on frame 0, because you can easily reset the position or rotation back to the rest values.

1. Select a bone or the **Layer1** object and **View▶Select▶All▶Select All Bones of Current Object**.

2. Press **r** to activate and set the rest position and rotation of the bones.

> **Note:** Notice the bones change from dotted lines to solid lines. Inactive bones are displayed as dotted lines so you can see in the viewport whether a bone is active or not.

Organizing Hierarchies

Most of the bones are parented correctly but there are some that need adjusting.

1. Open the Scene Editor, right-click on **Layer1**, and select **Expand child items (recursive)** to make sure all the bones are visible.

2. Make sure **Parent in Place** is turned on.

3. Parent **Pelvis** to **Pelvis_Base**.

4. Parent **Hip_LT** to **Pelvis_Base**.

5. Parent **Eye_Base_LT** to **Eye_Stretch_LT**.
6. Parent **Eye_Stretch_LT** to **Head**.

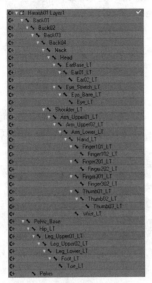

Figure 3.5-39. Bone hierarchy.

Checking the Rotations

It's a good idea once the bones are correctly parented to double-check that the pitch of the bones in each hierarchy are correctly aligned, and that all the bones in each hierarchy rotate in the correct direction. Even though the bones are rested, it's best to get into the habit of keeping frame 0 in the default pose, so make sure you check the rotations on a frame other than frame 0. Frame 10 is a good test frame to use, as it's far enough away from frame 0 that it's easy to see at a glance which frame you're on, and by scrubbing the timeline you can see the transition from the default rotation to the posed rotation.

If there are any bones that require adjusting, you can use Setup➤Modify➤ Bone Twist (Ctrl+k) to modify the alignment of a bone using a handle similar to the bank handle for skelegons. You can also use Setup➤Modify➤Orientation➤ Align Pitch to align the pitch of a bone to its parent.

If you want numeric or more exact control, you can adjust a bone within a hierarchy without altering the bones lower in the hierarchy by following these steps:

1. Make sure **Parent in Place** is on.
2. Parent the immediate child of the bone to the object.
3. Adjust the rotation of the bone.
4. Parent the child back to the adjusted bone.

Initial Bone Settings

There are some settings we can give the bones at this early stage. The rotation control bones should have no effect on the geometry, so we can set their strength to 0.

1. Open the Scene Editor, right-click on **Layer1**, and select **Expand child items (recursive)** to make sure all the bones are visible.
2. In the Property tab, change the Property view to **Bone➤Influence**.
3. Select the Bone Strength values for **Eye_Base_LT**, **Pelvis_Base**, and **Hip_LT**.
4. In the Adjust Properties panel, change the value to **0** and press **Apply**.

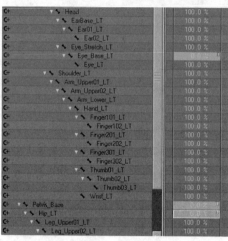

Figure 3.5-40. Adjusting bone strength.

Assigning Weight Maps

The weight maps can be assigned now, and we only have to assign weights to half the bones. When the rig is mirrored, the weight assignments will be mirrored along with it.

1. Select the Bone Weight Map values for the four back bones.
2. In the Adjust Properties panel, change the vertex map to **Body (weight map)** and press **Apply**.

Figure 3.5-41. Assigning weight maps.

Creating the Controls

We only need to create the main controls and controls for the left side of the body. When the rig is mirrored, most of the controls for the right side will be created automatically.

Adding the Controls

We'll start by adding nulls for the animation controls, then add some control bones to align the animation controls attached to the skeleton.

1. Load **Hamish_Rig01.lws** into Layout (you can find a preprepared scene in \Scenes\Chapters\Hamish_Rig01_v002.lws).

2. Select **Items≻Add≻Null** to add a null object to the scene, naming the null **Hamish_Master**.

3. Add eight more nulls, naming them: **Hamish_Mover, Hamish_Foot_LT, Hamish_Toe_LT, Hamish_Ankle_LT, Hamish_Hand_LT, Hamish_Shoulder_LT, Hamish_EyeTarget**, and **Hamish_EyeStretch**.

4. Select the **Back04** bone and **Create Child Bone** (=), calling it **Shoulder_Base**. Move the new bone in **Z** to the same level as the base of the shoulder bone and rotate the pitch **90°**.

5. Press **r** to rest the bone. Open the Bone properties and set Bone Weight Map to **Body** and change the Strength to **0%**.

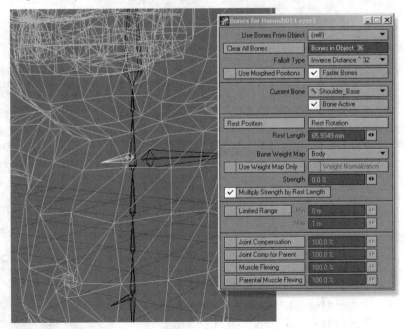

Figure 3.6-1. Shoulder_Base properties.

6. Select the **Head** bone and create a child bone, calling it **EyeStretch_ Base**. Rotate the new bone's pitch **90°**.

7. Press **r** to rest the bone. In Bone properties, adjust the Rest Length to around **30 mm**, set Bone Weight Map to **Head**, and change the Strength to 0%.

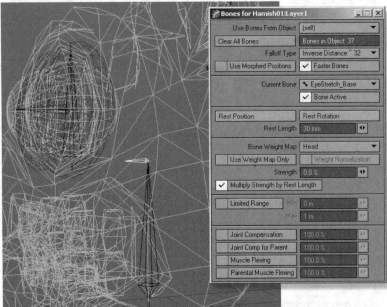

Figure 3.6-2. EyeStretch_Base properties.

Positioning the Controls

Now we need to position the controls. We can do this quickly by parenting the null objects to the bones before setting up the final hierarchy.

1. Turn off **Parent in Place** and open the Scene Editor.

2. In the Scene Editor, right-click on **Layer1** and select **Expand child items (recursive)** to make sure all the bones are visible.

3. Parent **Hamish_Mover** to the **Pelvis_Base** bone.

4. Parent **Hamish_Foot_LT** and **Hamish_Toe_LT** to the **Toe_LT** bone.

5. Parent **Hamish_Ankle_LT** to the **Foot_LT** bone.

6. Parent **Hamish_Hand_LT** to the **Hand_LT** bone.

7. Parent **Hamish_Shoulder_LT** to the **Arm_Upper01_LT** bone.

Figure 3.6-3. Hierarchy after positioning.

8. Parent **Hamish_EyeTarget** to the **Eye_LT** bone.
9. Parent **Hamish_EyeStretch** to the **Eye_Stretch_LT** bone.

Setting the Control Hierarchy

With the controls in their initial positions we can create the final hierarchies and adjust the positions of the controls where necessary.

1. Turn on **Parent in Place.**
2. Select **Hamish_Mover, Hamish_Foot_LT,** and **Hamish_EyeTarget** and parent them to **Hamish_Master.**
3. Select **Hamish_Mover** by itself. Notice that after reparenting, the heading is rotated 180°. This will reverse the transformations for its child items, which we don't want, so set the heading rotation back to **0.**
4. Select **Hamish_Foot_LT** by itself and set the Y position to **0.**

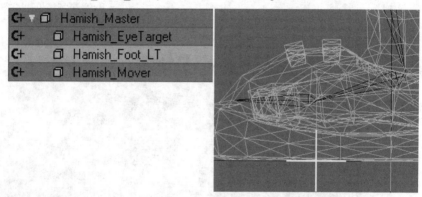

Figure 3.6-4. Adjusting the foot control.

5. Select **Hamish_Toe_LT** and **Hamish_Ankle_LT** and parent them to **Hamish_Foot_LT.** Move **Hamish_Toe_LT** to about halfway along the toe bone.

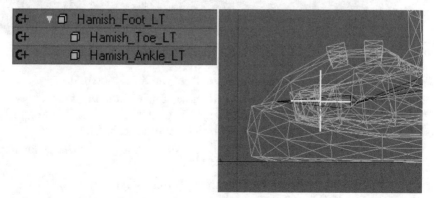

Figure 3.6-5. Adjusting the toe control.

161

6. Parent **Hamish_Hand_LT** to **Hamish_Mover.**

7. Parent **Layer1** to **Hamish_Mover.**

8. Parent **Hamish_Shoulder_LT** to the **Shoulder_Base** bone.

9. Parent **Hamish_EyeStretch** to the **EyeStretch_Base** bone.

The final hierarchy is shown in Figure 3.6-6.

10. Select **Hamish_EyeTarget** and move it in **Z** to just in front of Hamish's snout. Clone (**Ctrl+c**), making one clone. Rename the clone **Hamish_ EyeTarget_LT.**

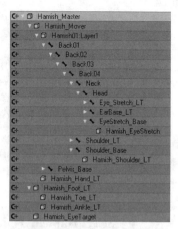

Figure 3.6-6. Final hierarchy of ItemID. To change the display order to ItemID, click in the Name bar above the item display.

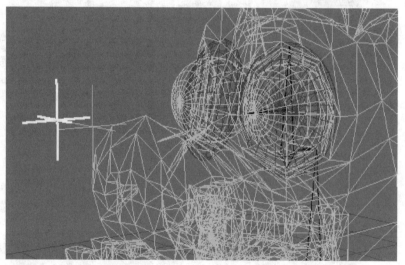

Figure 3.6-7. Eye target controls.

11. Select **Hamish_EyeTarget** and set the X position to **0**.

12. Select **Hamish_EyeStretch**, move it in **Y** to the tip of the **Eye_Stretch_LT** bone, and set the pitch to **0**. Clone (**Ctrl+c**), making one clone. Rename the clone **Hamish_EyeStretch_LT.**

13. Select **Hamish_EyeStretch** and set the X position to **0** as shown in Figure 3.6-8.

14. Back in the Scene Editor, parent **Hamish_EyeTarget_LT** to **Hamish_EyeTarget.**

15. Parent **Hamish_EyeStretch_LT** to **Hamish_EyeStretch.**

Figure 3.6-8. Eye stretch controls.

Setting the Control Appearance

Now that all the controls are in place we need to adjust their appearance so they're easily distinguishable and easy to select.

1. In the Scene Editor, change the Property view to **Item:Flags** and select the Item Color values for **Hamish_Mover, Hamish_Hand_LT, Hamish_Foot_LT,** and **Hamish_EyeTarget**. In the Adjust Properties panel, change their Item Color to **Orange** and press **Apply**.

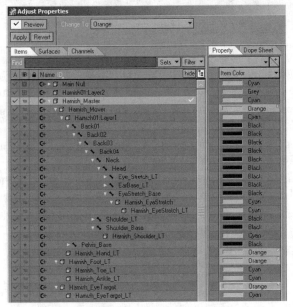

Figure 3.6-9. Changing the item color to orange.

2. Select the Item Color values for **Hamish_Master**, **Hamish_EyeStretch**, **Hamish_Shoulder_LT**, and **Hamish_Toe_LT**, change their color to **Red**, and press **Apply**.

3. Select **Morfi_Mover** and open the Object Properties panel. **Geometry➢ Add Custom Object➢Item Shape**. Double-click on the Item Shape entry to open its properties.

4. Change Shape to **Ring** and change Scale to **200 mm**. Close the properties and copy the Item Shape entry.

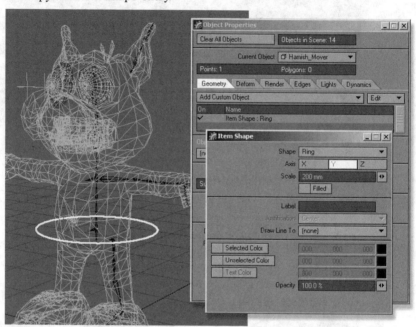

Figure 3.6-10. Item Shape settings for Hamish_Mover.

5. Select **Hamish_Foot_LT** and **Paste** the Item Shape into the Custom Object list. Open the properties for Item Shape and change Scale to **175 mm**.

6. **Paste** the Item Shape Custom Object into **Morfi_Toe_LT** and change Axis to **X** and Scale to **100 mm**.

7. **Paste** the Item Shape Custom Object into **Morfi_Hand_LT** and change Axis to **Z** and Scale to **75 mm**.

8. **Paste** the Item Shape Custom Object into **Morfi_Shoulder_LT** and change Axis to **X** and Scale to **75 mm**.

9. **Paste** the Item Shape Custom Object into **Morfi_EyeStretch** and change Shape to **Ball** and Scale to **100 mm**. **Copy** the Item Shape entry.

10. **Paste** the Item Shape Custom Object into **Morfi_EyeTarget**.

Figure 3.6-11. Final item shapes.

Adding IK

With the controls in place we can add IK to the bone hierarchies. We'll add IK to the leg and arm, adjusting the rotation channels for the bones so the animator knows which channels are available for manual control.

Adding IK to the Leg

The leg and foot position is controlled mostly by IK, with manual or FK control to position the knee.

1. Press **m** to open the **Motion Options** and select the **Controllers and Limits** tab.
2. Select the **Hip_LT** bone and change Bank Controller to **Inverse Kinematics**.

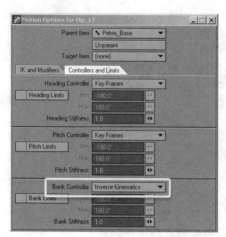

Figure 3.6-12. IK settings for the hip bone.

3. Turn off the Pitch and Bank Rotation Channel controls at the lower-left corner of the interface.

4. Select **Leg_Upper01_LT**, change Pitch Controller to **IK**, and turn off all the Rotation Channel controls.

5. Select **Leg_Upper02_LT** and turn off the Heading and Pitch Rotation Channel controls.

6. Select **Leg_Lower_LT**, change Pitch Controller to **IK**, and turn off all the Rotation Channel controls.

7. Select **Foot_LT** and switch to the **IK and Modifiers** tab.

8. Set Goal Object to **Hamish_Ankle_LT**. Turn on **Full-time IK** and **Match Goal Orientation** and set Goal Strength to **100**. Turn off all the Rotation Channel controls.

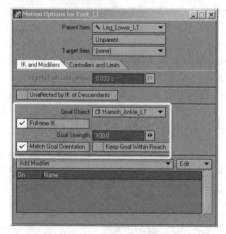

Figure 3.6-13. IK settings for the foot bone.

9. Select **Toe_LT** and set Goal Object to **Hamish_Toe_LT**. Turn on **Match Goal Orientation**, and turn off all the Rotation Channel controls.

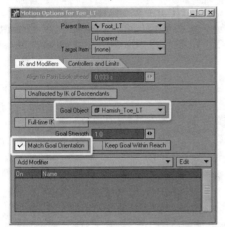

Figure 3.6-14. IK settings for the toe bone.

Adding IK to the Arm

The arm and hand position is controlled by IK with manual control to position the elbow.

1. Select the **Shoulder_LT** bone and switch back to the **Controllers and Limits** tab. Change the Heading and Pitch controllers to **IK** and turn off all the Rotation Channel controls.

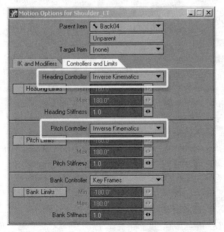

Figure 3.6-15. IK settings for the shoulder bone.

2. Select **Arm_Upper01_LT**, change the Heading and Pitch controllers to **IK**, and turn off the **H** and **P** Rotation Channel controls, leaving only **B**.
3. Select **Arm_Upper02_LT** and turn off the Heading and Pitch Rotation Channel controls.

4. Select **Arm_Lower_LT**, change the Pitch Controller to **IK** and turn off all the Rotation Channel controls.

5. Select **Hand_LT**, then select the **IK and Modifiers** tab. Set Goal Object to **Hamish_Hand_LT**, turn on **Full-time IK** and **Match Goal Orientation**, and set Goal Strength to **100**. Then turn off all the Rotation Channel controls.

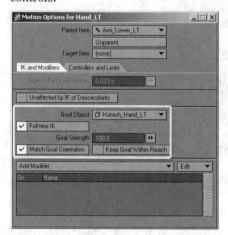

Figure 3.6-16. IK goal settings for the hand bone.

6. Select **Arm_Upper01_LT**, set Goal Object to **Hamish_Shoulder_LT**, turn on **Full-time IK**, and set Goal Strength to **100**.

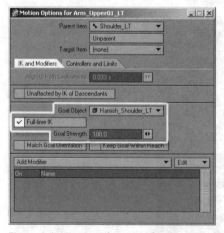

Figure 3.6-17. IK goal settings for the shoulder bone.

7. Zoom out and change the Perspective viewport to **Shaded Solid** so you can see if the eye is targeting correctly in the next step.

8. Select **Eye_LT** and, in the Motion Options, set the Target Item to **Hamish_EyeTarget_LT**.

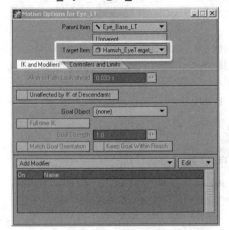

Figure 3.6-21. Target setting for the eye bone.

9. Select **Eye_Stretch_LT** and set the Target Item to **Hamish_EyeStretch_ LT**.

10. Select **Layer2**, the template eyeballs, and **Clear** (–) it from the scene.

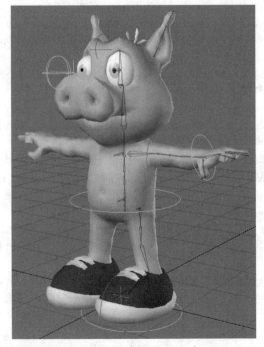

Figure 3.6-22. Left side of the rig complete.

171

Exporting the Rig File

The Rig format saves the rig and all its settings. You can save the entire rig by selecting the object before exporting or save individual hierarchies by selecting the bone at the root of the hierarchy.

Saving the rig before mirroring can make it easier to apply the rig to another character.

1. Select the Hamish object and select **Setup**➤**Edit**➤**Export RIG (Shift+j)**.
2. Select **Browse Export File** and choose a location and file name for the rig. I've chosen **\Scenes\Hamish_RIG**.
3. Enter **Hamish Rig** as the description, and choose **YES** to all the options.

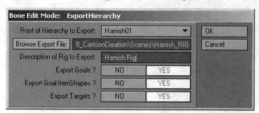

Figure 3.6-23. Export Rig options.

3.7 Finishing the Basic Rig

With the left side of the rig created we need to mirror the left-side hierarchies and organize the item order before testing the deformations. You can test the deformations before mirroring if you're unsure about your bone positions, but in most cases it's best to test after mirroring so you can see the proper effect of all the bones on the object.

Mirroring the Rig

Mirroring bone hierarchies mirrors bones, strengths, and IK settings and gives you the choice to also mirror goals and targets, so the IK goals and most animation controls are mirrored across also.

1. Select the **Hip_LT** bone and select **Setup**➤**Edit**➤**Mirror Hierarchy**.
2. In the Bone Setup: MirrorHierarchy panel, change Mirror Goals to **YES** and Name Edit Method to **Replace String**, replacing _LT with **_RT**. (See Figure 3.7-1.)
3. Select the **Shoulder_LT** bone and **Mirror Hierarchy**. Change Mirror Goals to **YES** and Mirror Targets to **YES**, and replace _LT with **_RT**. (See Figure 3.7-2.)
4. Select **Eye_Stretch_LT** and **Mirror Hierarchy**. Change Mirror Goals to **NO** and Mirror Targets to **YES**, and replace _LT with **_RT**. (See Figure 3.7-3.)

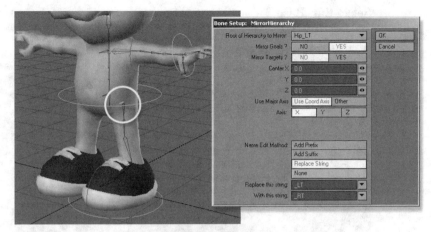

Figure 3.7-1. Mirror settings for the leg hierarchy.

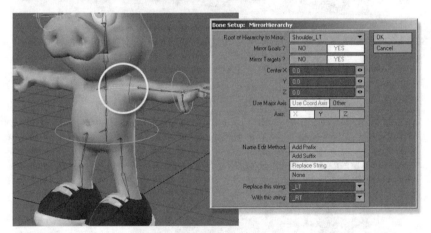

Figure 3.7-2. Mirror settings for the arm hierarchy.

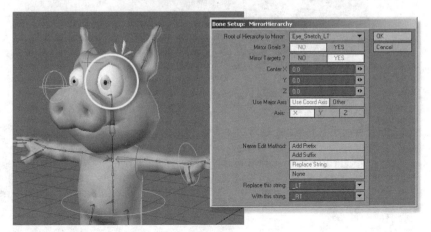

Figure 3.7-3. Mirror settings for the eye hierarchy.

5. Select **Ear_Base_LT** and **Mirror Hierarchy**. Change Mirror Goals to **NO** and Mirror Targets to **NO**, and replace _LT with **_RT**.

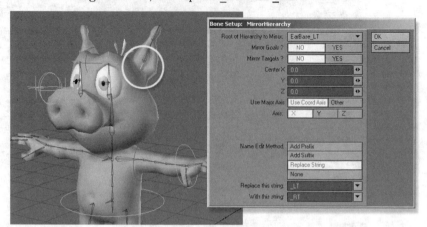

Figure 3.7-4. Mirror settings for the ear hierarchy.

Fixing the Right Controls

It's not perfect though; there is some fixing up needed after mirroring. If IK goals are nested, like the foot controls, the parent control isn't mirrored.

1. Select **Hamish_Foot_LT** and **Items▶Add▶Mirror**. Rename the mirrored item to **Hamish_Foot_RT**.

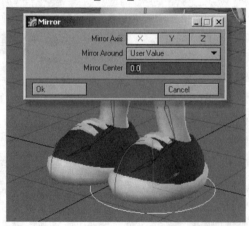

Figure 3.7-5. Mirror the foot control.

2. Open the Scene Editor and parent **Hamish_Ankle_RT** and **Hamish_Toe_RT** to **Hamish_Foot_RT**.

Figure 3.7-6. Parenting the right goals to the right foot.

Fixing the Right Eye

Mirroring hierarchies mirrors the bones as they're positioned on frame 0. Since we changed the rotation of the base eye bone to be different from its rest rotation, the rest rotation of the mirrored eye bones is incorrect.

1. Select **Eye_RT** and open Motion Options. Change the target to **(none)** and, using the numeric controls, set its rotation to **0, 0, 0**.

2. Select **Eye_Base_RT** and change to frame 1. Set the rotation to **0, –90, –180**, set the scale to **1, 1, 1**, and press **r** to rest the bone in that position.

3. Select **Eye_RT** and press **r** to rest it in its new position.

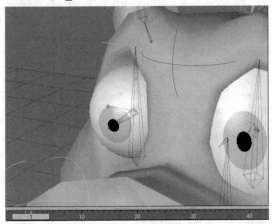

Figure 3.7-7. Setting the rest rotation.

4. Select **Eye_Base_RT** and **Delete Key (del)**, deleting the keyframe for frame 1.

5. Change back to frame 0. Notice the eyeball appears correctly shaped and aligned. Select **Eye_RT** and, in Motion Options, set its target back to **Hamish_EyeTarget_RT.**

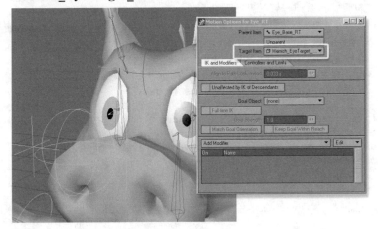

Figure 3.7-8. Right eye fixed.

175

Organizing the Rig

Items appear in the selection lists in the order that they're created. Because we haven't been very careful to create the items in a particular order, the bones and objects are all over the place in the item selection lists. If we leave it like this, it makes selecting items for animation very difficult. We really need to organize all the items so we can find things easily in the pull-down lists, and pressing the up or down arrows moves through the hierarchies in the right order.

We could have tried to create the items in order, but there would still be problem areas such as the bones that were split into two. Splitting each bone created the new bone at the bottom of the load order. We could have created each bone one by one and split before we created the next bone, but that would take a lot more time. Instead of wasting time worrying about load order during the creation process, we can fix the load order really quickly using a program called MSort, written by Scott Martindale.

Note: MSort is currently only available for PC. Scott is working on a new version that includes drag and drop editing, as well as much more functionality. Hopefully, the new version will be available for both PC and Mac. The updated version of MSort will be available from my web site.

1. Save the scene as **Scenes\Hamish_Rig01.lws**.
2. Load **\LWProjects\Manual Sort\MSortPurple.exe**.
3. Open **Hamish_Rig01.lws** and, when asked, press **Y** to sort bones as well.

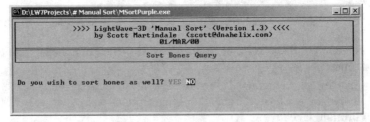

Figure 3.7-9. Select Yes to sort bones.

4. The objects and bones from the scene are listed in WordPad. **Cut** and **Paste** the bones and objects into your preferred selection order, leaving **Main Null** at the top of the list for now.

Figure 3.7-10. Initial load order listed.

Note: Instead of giving my suggested order here, I've included the MSort text file, including the items from the Hamish rig after sorting, in \LWProjects\LW8_ CartoonCreation\Hamish_Rig01_MSort.txt.

5. When you've organized the selection order, save the file and quit WordPad. MSort asks if you want to keep the Edit.Me file. (I rarely see a need to keep it.) Press **Y** to keep it or **N** if you don't want to keep it.

6. MSort tells you the name of the updated scene file, which is always the original scene name with **_MSort** appended to the end.

Figure 3.7-11. MSort confirms the reordered scene file name.

MSort correctly reorders the bones and objects in the scene, but any items using targeting lose their correct target due to the order change. We'll fix that before saving over the original scene file.

7. In Layout, load **Hamish_Rig01_MSort.lws**.

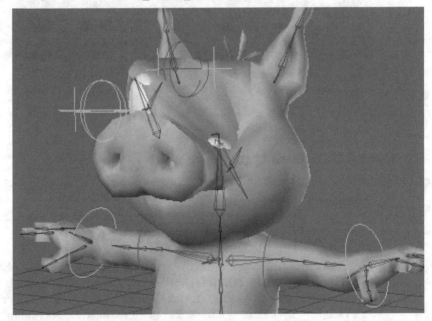

Figure 3.7-12. Targeted bones are targeting the wrong items.

8. Select the **Wrist_LT** bone and open Motion Options. Change Target Item to **Arm_Lower_LT**.

9. Change the target of Wrist_RT to **Arm_Lower_RT**.

10. Change the target of Eye_Stretch_LT to **Hamish_EyeStretch_LT**, and change the target of Eye_Stretch_RT to **Hamish_EyeStretch_RT**.

11. Change the target of Eye_LT to **Hamish_EyeTarget_LT**, and change the target of Eye_RT to **Hamish_EyeTarget_RT**.

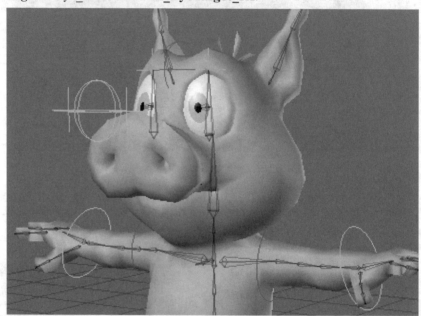

Figure 3.7-13. Fixed targeting.

12. Once all the targeting is fixed, save the scene as **Hamish_Rig01.lws**, saving over the previous rig scene.

Initial Control Configuration

Before testing the rig, it's useful to configure some of the controls so you don't accidentally move them incorrectly when posing the character.

1. Open the Scene Editor, right-click on **Hamish_Master**, and select **Expand child items (recursive)**. Click in the **Name** bar until it shows **ID ^**, so the items are displayed in the correct order.

2. Select all the default (cyan-colored) control items — Hamish_EyeStretch _LT, Hamish_EyeStretch_RT, Hamish_EyeTarget_LT, Hamish_Eye-Target_RT, Hamish_Ankle_LT, and Hamish_Ankle_RT — then click in the **Visibility** icon for one of the selected items and choose **Hidden**.

3. Lock the same items by clicking in the **Lock** column of the selected items.

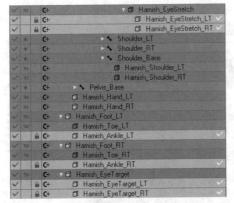

Figure 3.7-14. Locking items stops them from being selected in the selection lists, although you can still select them in the Scene Editor if you need to.

4. Select the **Property** tab and change the Property view to **Channels:Lock States.**

5. Select the values for **Lock H, Lock P,** and **Lock B** for the **Back01** bone. In the Adjust Properties panel, select **Check** and press **Apply.**

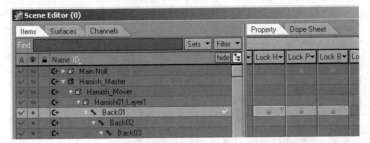

Figure 3.7-15. The first back bone is positioned using the Mover control.

6. Select and lock the HPB values for the following bones:
    EarBase_LT
    EarBase_RT
    Eye_Base_LT
    Eye_Base_RT
    EyeStretch_Base
    Pelvis

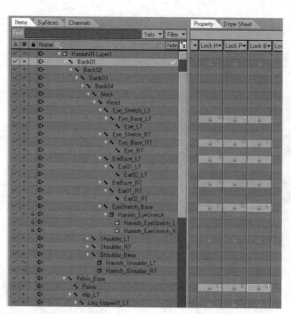

Figure 3.7-16. These bones are control bones that don't usually need to be rotated.

7. The right-side bones didn't inherit the locked values from the left side when they were mirrored, so check the Lock values of the right-side bones, copying the values from the left side.

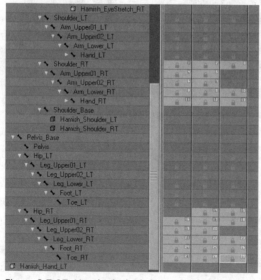

Figure 3.7-17. Use the locked channels of the left bones as reference for setting the right side.

8. Select and lock the **H** and **B** values for the second joint of the finger bones and third joint of the thumb bones.

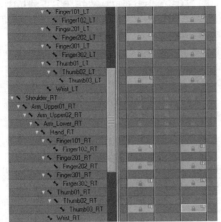

> **Note:** If your character has fingers with three joints, you should lock the H and B values of the second and third joints of each finger.

Figure 3.7-18. Lock joints.

9. Open the Object Properties for **Layer1** and set the Display SubPatch Level to **3**.

10. Make sure **Bone X-Ray** is turned on for the Perspective view so you can see the bones inside the shaded view of the character, and we're ready for testing.

Figure 3.7-19. Hamish rig ready for testing.

3.8 Testing the Rig

Now that the skeleton and controls are created and organized, it's time to test the rig. This lets you make sure that all the bones and controls are behaving correctly and see which joints need adjusting.

This can be one of the more tedious steps of rigging. The rig is more or less complete, and you're dying to start animating the character. It's important not to skip this step though. You'll appreciate the extra work you've done when you're animating or posing the character later on, and any other animators working with the character will thank you.

Controls and Posing

Testing the controls is important to make sure that all the bones and controls are doing what they're supposed to. It also gives you an opportunity to fine-tune the rig, hiding or locking controls, blocking channels from being manipulated, and setting rotation limits.

It's usually easiest to create three or four key poses for the character on different frames. It's important to space the poses out so you can see the transition from pose to pose, as often deformation or control problems only become apparent in the between poses. This also provides some good sample poses that you can render to show off the character to friends, colleagues, and clients.

You should also test the morphs, creating a different facial expression for each pose, making sure the morphs all work together nicely and seeing if any morph adjustments are necessary.

Creating Test Poses

I'll leave it up to you to create the poses, as this is where you can let your creativity run wild. You can also find a preprepared scene with some poses already in it in \Scenes\Chapters\Hamish_Rig01_v003.lws.

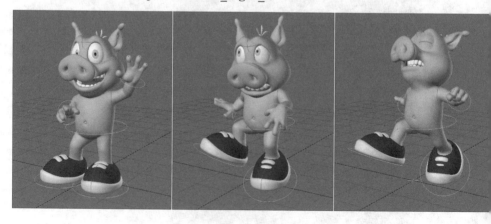

Make sure that you leave frame 0 in the default setup pose at all times. It's useful to create the poses on tens, for example, frame 10, frame 20, frame 30, etc. That way it's easy to remember what frames the poses are on, and it allows a decent number of frames to show the transition between poses.

Here's a little reminder of how to use the controls for posing Hamish. A more detailed description of the controls is included in Chapter 5, "Animation."

Main Controls

The Master control positions the character and its animation within a scene. You shouldn't need to adjust the Master at this stage. The Mover control positions the upper body independently of the feet.

FK Controls

The spine, pelvis, fingers, and ear bones are manually controlled using FK.

IK Controls

The legs are controlled using IK. The Foot control positions the foot. The Toe control bends the toes. The heading rotation of the Hip bone positions the knee. You can also use the bank of the Leg_Upper02 bone to tweak the knee position if the groin area deforms too much using just the Hip bone.

The arms are controlled using IK. The Hand control positions the hand. The Shoulder control positions each shoulder. The bank rotation of the Shoulder_Base bone positions both shoulders together. The bank rotation of the Arm_Upper02 bone positions the elbow. You can also adjust the bank of the Arm_Upper01 bone if the arm becomes too twisted using just the Arm_Upper02 bone.

The direction of the eyes is determined by the EyeTarget control. Don't worry about the EyeStetch control at this stage; it doesn't do anything yet. The eye stretching is set up in Chapter 4, "Advanced Rigging."

Morph Controls

The Eye morphs control the eyelids and eyebrows, and the Mouth morphs control the mouth and nose area.

Joints and Weight Maps

Once you've created some poses you can see if there are any areas of the object that are being influenced by other bones. Those areas need to be separated into their own weight maps. If you're using the basic weight maps, the most likely areas you need to do this are for the fingers and toes.

Once all the bones are affecting the correct areas you can check the deformation of the joints. A large amount of deformation adjustment can be done without touching the weight maps as there are a number of bone settings that can be used to adjust the deformation of a joint. It's best to try adjusting a joint using the bone settings before tweaking weight map values.

Bone Influence

The bone settings determine how each bone affects the object. Some settings apply to all the bones in an object, while others apply to individual bones.

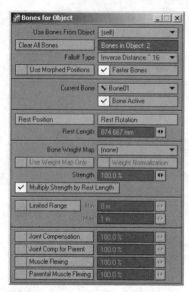

Figure 3.8-1. Bone properties.

Falloff Type

The Falloff Type setting applies to all the bones in an object and determines how competing bones affect the geometry. Falloff only comes into play when bones are sharing weight maps or weight maps aren't used.

You should experiment with the values to find the right one for your character. Higher values reduce the overlap in the bone influence, sharpening the joints. Lower values increase the overlap, making the joints more rubbery. A value of ^32 or ^64 is about right for most characters.

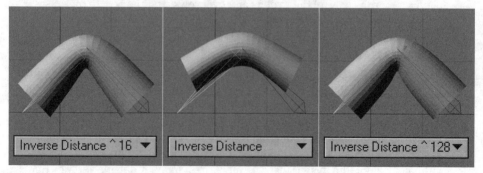

Figure 3.8-2. Adjusting falloff.

If you want loose joints for your character, for example where the arms and legs bend uniformly instead of firmly at the elbows and knees, you can accomplish this by using lower settings. You can also use lower settings so you don't need as many bones. A tail or tentacle can be posed smoothly using only a few bones with low falloff settings.

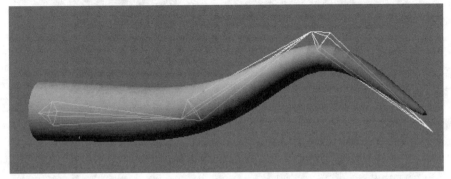

Figure 3.8-3. The geometry follows the bones more smoothly using lower falloff settings.

Faster Bones

For most characters, Faster Bones is a very useful function, as it reduces the control for each point to a maximum of four bones, speeding up the deformation calculation. You should only turn this off if you need to have more than four bones affecting any of the points in an object, which is fairly rare.

Rest Length

Rest Length determines the control area of a bone. Adjusting the rest length of bones sharing weight maps changes their area of influence, and when Multiply Strength by Rest Length is on it also changes the strength of the bone. Changing the rest length is a very useful way of adjusting joint deformation.

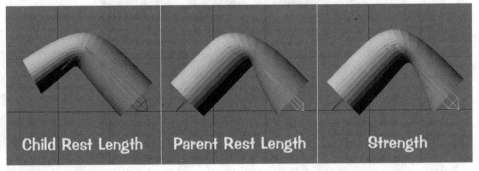

Figure 3.8-4. Bones sharing a weight map. Notice that changing the rest length produces a different result than just changing the strength.

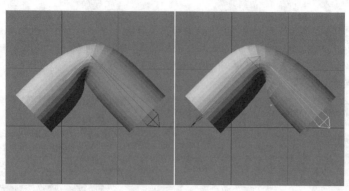

Figure 3.8-5. Separate weight maps.

Use Weight Map Only

Use Weight Map Only can only be used predictably where there are no bones sharing weight maps. Since it's useful to have bones sharing weight maps, I don't recommend using this option. Even without this setting on, bones will not affect areas with a different weight map.

Use Weight Map Only can be useful if you're creating a character for use in a game engine that requires every bone to have its own weight map. Use Weight Map Only will then simulate the effect of the bones in the game engine.

Bone Strength

Bone strength is a very useful setting. Bone strength is usually fine at the default 100% value, but you can use varying bone strengths to adjust the joint deformations, or set it to 0% to prevent control bones from affecting the geometry. You can also set it higher than 100% to give a bone greater hold over the surrounding geometry.

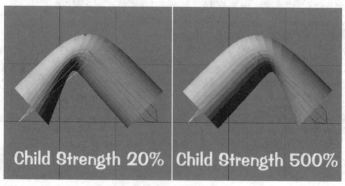

Figure 3.8-6. Sharing weight map.

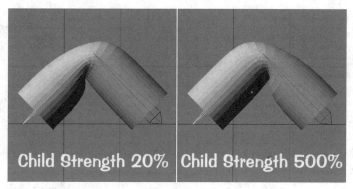

Figure 3.8-7. Separate weight maps.

It's usually easiest to leave Multiply Strength by Rest Length on, and adjust the Strength setting if necessary.

Bone Joint Settings

The bone joint settings give you control over how a joint reacts to being bent. The joint settings work on joints with or without weight maps, so they're useful for adjusting all the joints in a character.

Joint Compensation	100.0 %
Joint Comp for Parent	100.0 %
Muscle Flexing	100.0 %
Parental Muscle Flexing	100.0 %

Figure 3.8-8. Joint settings.

Joint settings have some limitations. They only work with the pitch rotation of a bone, which is one reason it's important to make the pitch of the bones the primary rotation axis. They don't work for bones using Match Goal Orientation, because when set to on, the rotation values of a bone aren't passed on to other areas of LightWave.

In many cases all you need is to have these settings on or off, but for extra control you can adjust the percentages. When you're adjusting the percentages, don't be afraid to push the values above 100%. Often, especially for muscle flexing, 100% is barely noticeable.

Make sure when you're setting these values that you're setting the right bone. The joint settings apply to the joint at the base of the bone. Setting Joint Compensation of a bone has no effect on the joint at its tip — only its base.

Joint Compensation

Joint Compensation prevents a joint from bending like a hose. It tries to retain the volume of the joint as it bends so the joint doesn't collapse. Joint Compensation only works in one direction, so it's often useful to use both Joint Compensation and Joint Comp for Parent on a joint.

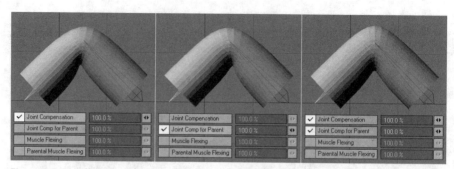

Figure 3.8-9. Different combinations of the two compensation settings.

Joint compensation for parent retains the volume of the joint as if it's the parent bone that is rotating instead of the child bone. It depends on where your bone joint is in relation to the geometry as to whether you need just Joint Compensation or just Joint Comp for Parent, or both.

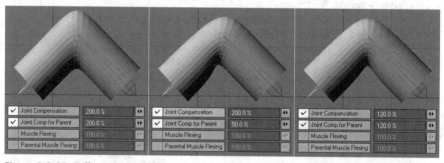

Figure 3.8-10. Different percentages of compensation.

Muscle Flexing

Muscle Flexing bulges the geometry under the joint to simulate the way the muscle flexes to bend a joint.

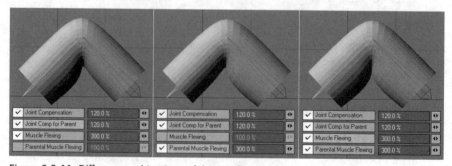

Figure 3.8-11. Different combinations of the two flexing settings.

Parental Muscle Flexing bulges the geometry above the joint, as if the parent bone is rotating instead of the child, to simulate the way the muscle flexes to bend a joint.

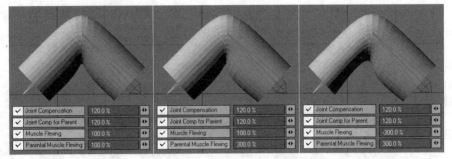

Figure 3.8-12. Different percentages of flexing. Notice negative values can be used.

Adjusting the Weight Maps

With the poses done you can check the areas where bones are sharing weight maps to see if any bones are affecting any geometry they shouldn't.

Adding New Weight Maps

By checking the poses I can see that some of the finger bones are affecting the wrong fingers. We'll fix that now.

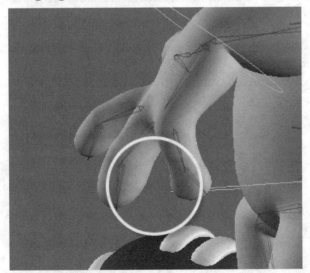

Figure 3.8-13. The middle finger is being affected by the pinky bone and the pinky is being affected by the middle finger bone.

1. Load your Hamish rig with poses into Layout (you can find a preprepared scene in \Scenes\Chapters\Hamish_Rig01_v003.lws).

2. Select the Hamish object or one of its bones and press **F12** to open or switch to Modeler.

3. Turn on **Symmetry**, select **Weight Shade** for the Perspective view, and zoom up on the hand.

4. Select the polygons of the first finger, from the knuckle to the tip.

5. Create a new weight map called **Finger1**, with an initial value of **50%**.

6. Contract the selection and Set Map Value to **100%**.

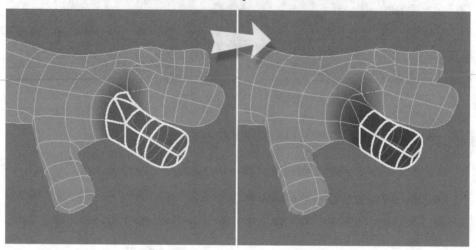

Figure 3.8-14. Weight map for Finger1.

7. Repeat steps 4-6 for each of the other fingers, calling the weight maps **Finger2** and **Finger3**.

8. Use **Combine Weightmaps** to subtract each of the three finger weights from the hand.

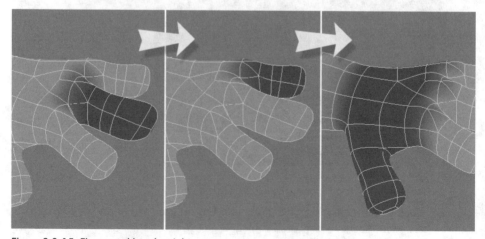

Figure 3.8-15. Finger and hand weight maps.

9. Press **F12** to switch back to Layout. Notice the fingers are being left behind in the poses now. Select the **Finger101_LT** bone and open the Bone properties. Change the weight map to **Finger1**.

10. Select each of the other finger bones and assign the appropriate weight map. Don't worry if you don't see any change right away; the weight map assignments aren't updated until you change frames.

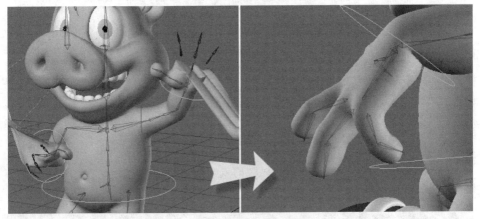

Figure 3.8-16. Updating the weight assignments. Notice the fingers are being affected only by the correct bones now.

Tweaking Weight Maps

I noticed when checking the poses that the top of the wrist wasn't deforming nicely when the hand was bent back. The bone joint settings don't work for the hands, as their rotation is controlled using Match Goal Orientation, so while we're working with the weight maps we'll adjust the wrist values.

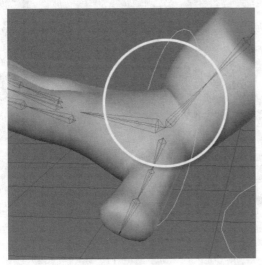

Figure 3.8-17. The top of the wrist is pushing into the forearm.

1. Switch back to Modeler and make sure the **Hands** weight map is still selected.
2. Select the three top points at the wrist and **Clear Map**.
3. Select the top three points at the base of the hand and Set Map Value to **25%**.
4. Select the **Arms** weight map, and with the points still selected Set Map Value to **75%**.
5. Select the top three points at the wrist and Set Map Value to **100%**.

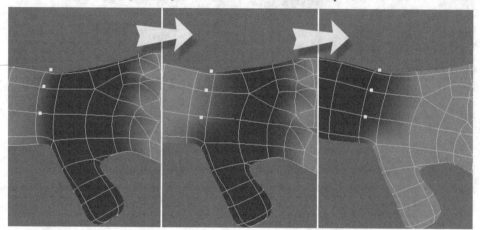

Figure 3.8-18. Adjusting the weight maps.

6. Switch to Layout and check the wrist deformation — it's much nicer now.

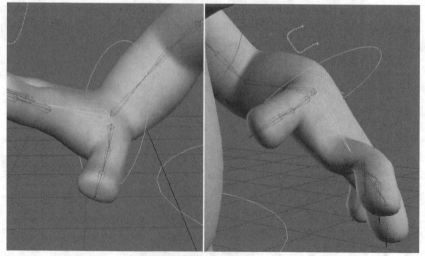

Figure 3.8-19. The wrist deforms nicely now.

7. With the weight map tweaking done for now, switch to Modeler and save the object.

Adjusting the Joints

Now we'll use the bone joint settings to adjust the rest of the joints. We'll start with the arms.

Adjusting the Arms

Checking through the poses, the shoulders look pretty good but the elbows are suffering a bit of the old bent hose syndrome, so we need to adjust their bone settings.

1. Select **Arm_Lower_RT** and center the Perspective view.
2. Open Bone properties and turn on **Joint Comp for Parent** and **Parental Muscle Flexing**.
3. The Parental Muscle Flexing isn't doing much at 100%, so set it to **200%**.
4. The area above the joint could still do with some beefing up, so select **Arm_Upper02_RT** and set its strength to **150%**.

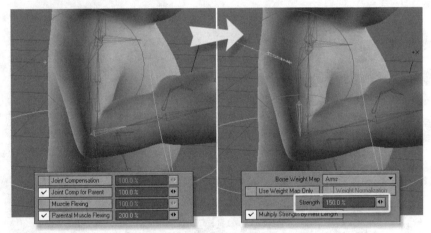

Figure 3.8-20. Muscle flexing can simulate the deformation of fat around a joint as well as muscle.

5. Repeat these settings for the arm bones on the left side.
6. Check all the poses to make sure the settings work well for all the arm positions, adjusting the settings if necessary to work best for all poses.

Adjusting the Legs

The groin area and knees need some adjusting.

1. Select **Leg_Lower_RT** and turn on all the bone joint settings: **Joint Compensation, Joint Comp for Parent, Muscle Flexing**, and **Parental Muscle Flexing**.

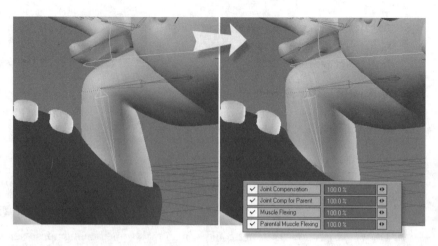

Figure 3.8-21. Adjusting the knee joint.

2. The groin area is deforming a bit too much with the legs, so select **Hip_RT** and set its strength to **50%**.

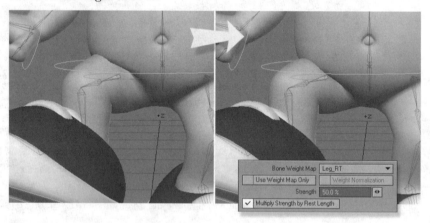

Figure 3.8-22. Adjusting the groin.

3. Repeat these settings for the leg bones on the left side and check all the poses.

Adjusting the Torso

Because the bone's strength is dependent on the size, you can see that the larger bones have a much larger effect on the geometry than the smaller bones. This is particularly evident in the torso where the shoulders are large and the back bones are small. We can fix this easily.

1. Set the strength of **Back01**, **Back02**, and **Back03** to **500%**.

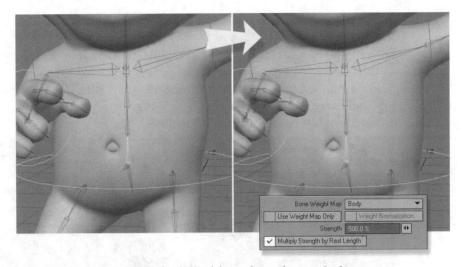

Figure 3.8-23. Higher strength for the back bones keeps the torso in shape.

We could set the strength of the shoulder bones to 20% to achieve the same thing, but that would adversely affect the shoulder joint, so increasing the strength of the back bones is the best solution.

Adjusting the Fingers

The fingers are pinching a bit when they're bent (fingers almost always do), so joint compensation is especially important here.

1. Select a pose with the fingers bent into a fist and select the **Finger101** bone for the appropriate hand. Turn on **Joint Compensation**.

2. Select **Finger102** and turn on **Joint Compensation, Joint Comp for Parent**, and **Parental Muscle Flexing**. Set Joint Compensation and Joint Comp for Parent to **50%**.

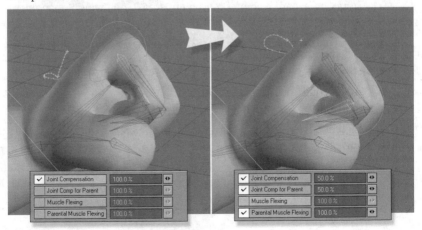

Figure 3.8-24. Adjusting the finger joints.

3. Repeat these settings for the joints of the other two fingers, then for the fingers of the opposite hand.
4. Select **Thumb02** and turn on **Joint Compensation** and **Joint Comp for Parent**.
5. Select **Thumb03** and turn on **Joint Compensation, Joint Comp for Parent**, and **Parental Muscle Flexing**.
6. Select **Thumb01** and set its strength to **50%**.

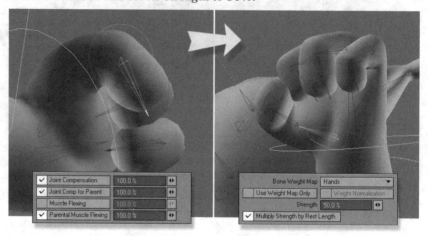

Figure 3.8-25. Adjusting the thumb joints.

7. Repeat these settings for the thumb of the opposite hand.
8. Scrub the timeline between poses with the fingers open and fingers closed into a fist to check that all the fingers retain their volume. Adjust the settings if necessary.

Adding Muscle Control Bones

The bum cheeks are a common problem area. Good weight mapping is important here, but weight maps alone can only do so much. The gluteus maximus, the bum cheek muscle, slides over the pelvis, so we need to simulate that by adding a muscle control bone.

1. Go to frame 0, select the **Hip_LT** bone, and center the view.
2. Add a child bone, calling it **Bum_LT**.
3. Set the Z position to **0** and the Pitch rotation to **160**.
4. Increase **Rest Length** until the tip of the bone is just almost touching the surface of the object.

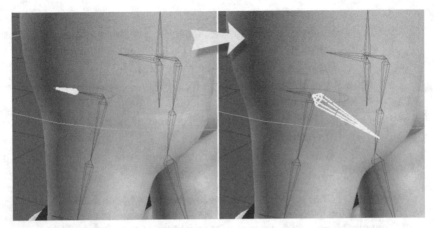

Figure 3.8-26. Creating a bum bone.

5. Making sure Parent in Place is on, open Motion Options and change Parent Item to **Pelvis_Base**. The rotation channels change when the parent changes, so set the rotation back to **0, 160, 0**.

6. Select **Add Modifier** and choose **Follower** from the list. Double-click the Follower entry to open its properties.

> **Note:** Follower and motion modifiers are explained in more detail in Chapter 4, "Advanced Rigging."

7. Set Item to Follow to **Leg_Upper01_LT**. Set all the Source references to **none** except for **Pitch Angle**. For Pitch Angle, set Multiply by to **0.5** and Add to **120**. Press **Continue** to close the properties.

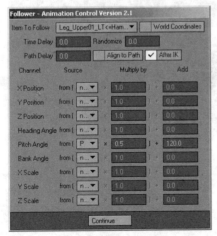

Figure 3.8-27. Follower settings.

8. Press **r** to rest the bone.

9. Run through the poses to see the bum bone in action. It should rotate a little with the leg but not too much. Go back to frame 0 to continue.

10. Clone **Bum_LT** and rename the clone **Bum_RT.**

11. With **Bum_RT** selected, set the **X** position to its negative value and press **r** to rest the bone in its new position.

12. Open the Follower properties and change Item to Follow to **Leg_Upper01_RT.**

13. Select **Bum_LT** and open the bone's properties. Set the weight map to **Body** and Strength to **1%.**

> **Note:** That's right, just 1%. We don't want the bum bone affecting too much of the lower torso, so setting the strength this low prevents it from affecting other areas while retaining control over the bum cheeks. Swap between values of 0% and 1% to see the difference.

14. Repeat the bone settings for **Bum_RT.**

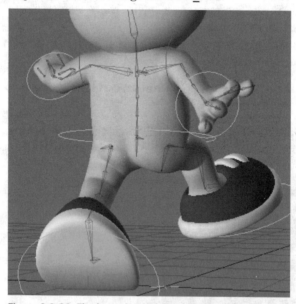

Figure 3.8-28. The bum cheeks hold their shape better now.

Further Adjustments

Continue adjusting the joints and weight maps until you're happy with all of them. You can further tweak the joints we've adjusted or just adjust the deformation of the joints that haven't been done yet.

You might notice the tops of the shoes are not deforming too well with the toes bent, but don't worry about that just yet; we'll fix that up in Chapter 4, "Advanced Rigging," as it involves some more advanced techniques.

Setting Rotation Limits

Now that the joints are deforming nicely we can determine the rotation limits each joint is capable of. The limits that are set for each joint depend on the mechanics of the joint and how far it can bend without breaking the joint or causing deformation problems.

If your poses don't include the extremes, choose a pose where they're close, and on the following frame, position each leg at the opposite extreme just before the deformation begins to break or the mechanical limits, whichever comes first. You can check the mechanical limits by bending your own joints to see how far each one can rotate before the joint above kicks in.

When setting limits, remember to set the lowest value for Min and the highest value for Max.

Upper Leg Limits

From its default position, the upper leg should rotate mainly forward, with some backward rotation.

1. Select each **Leg_Upper** bone and make a note of the pitch angle at the limits of its rotation.

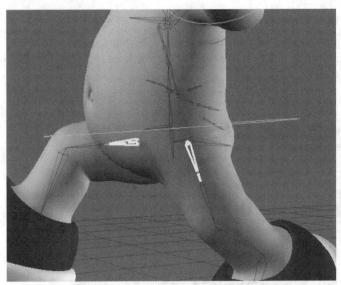

Figure 3.8-29. Each upper leg is at the opposite extreme, so the left leg gives me the backward limit and the right leg gives me the forward limit.

2. Open Motion Options and turn on **Pitch Limits**. Set Min to **0°** and Max to **100°**. Repeat for the opposite **Leg_Upper** bone.

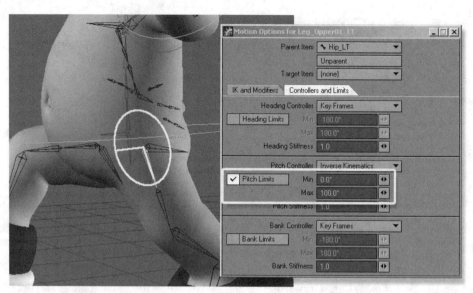

Figure 3.8-30. Upper leg limits.

Lower Leg Limits

From its default position, the lower leg should rotate mainly backward, with just enough forward rotation to fully straighten the knee, keeping the minimum rotation just above 0°.

1. Select each **Leg_Lower** bone and make a note of the pitch angle at the limits of its rotation.

Figure 3.8-31. I've positioned the lower leg at the backward extreme. The bone is at 24° in the default pose, so it can go a little closer to 0° for the forward extreme.

2. Turn on **Pitch Limits**. Set Min to **10** and Max to **120**. Repeat for the oppo-site **Leg_Lower** bone.

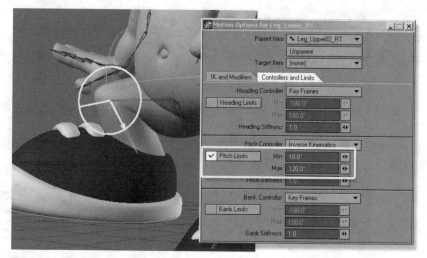

Figure 3.8-32. Lower leg limits.

Lower Arm Limits

From its default position, the lower arm should rotate mainly forward, with just enough backward rotation to fully straighten the elbow, keeping the minimum rotation just above 0°.

1. Select each **Arm_Lower** bone and make a note of the pitch angle at the lim-its of its rotation.

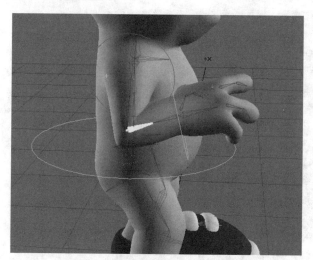

Figure 3.8-33. I've positioned the lower arm at the forward extreme. The bone is at 12° in the default pose, so it can go a little closer to 0° for the backward extreme.

2. Turn on **Pitch Limits**. Set Min to **5** and Max to **110**. Repeat for the opposite **Arm_Lower** bone.

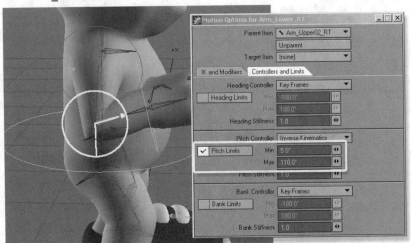

Figure 3.8-34. Lower arm limits.

Upper Arm Limits

The upper arm is a little trickier, as it has two rotation axes. On the pitch axis the upper arm should rotate mainly forward with a little backward rotation. On the heading axis, the upper arm should rotate mainly down with little or no upward rotation.

1. Select each **Arm_Upper01** bone and make a note of the heading angle at the limits of its rotation.

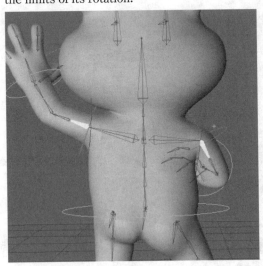

Figure 3.8-35. The upper arms are close to the heading extremes.

2. Select **Arm_Upper01_LT** and turn on **Heading Limits**. Set Min to **–80** and Max to **–2**. Because the heading values are opposite for the other side, for **Arm_Upper_RT** set the heading limits to Min **2** and Max **80**.

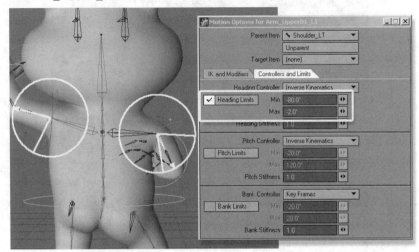

Figure 3.8-36. Notice the shoulder jumps up when the limit is set; this is what we want to provide realistic shoulder motion within the IK solution. I've allowed a little extra downward rotation, as the position of the elbow can offset the arm when it's close to the body.

3. Select each **Arm_Upper01** bone and make a note of the pitch angle at the limits of its rotation.

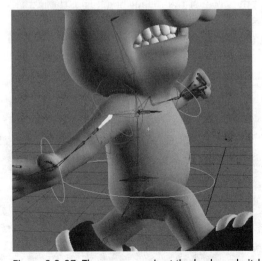

Figure 3.8-37. The upper arm is at the backward pitch extreme.

4. Turn on **Pitch Limits**. Set Min to **–20** and Max to **100**. Repeat for the opposite **Arm_Upper01** bone.

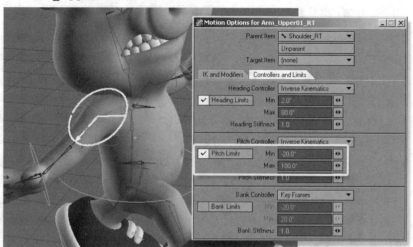

Figure 3.8-38. Upper arm pitch limits.

Knee and Elbow Helper Limits

Knee and elbow helper bones provide manual bank rotation to help position the knees and elbows without twisting the ball joints. Because these bones are just helpers (not the primary knee and elbow positioning controls) and create more twisting problems if they're rotated too far, we'll set limits for them. This also reminds the animator that they're just the helper bones, not the primary elbow or knee positioning bones.

1. Select each **Arm_Upper01** bone and turn on **Bank Limits**. Set Min to **–20** and Max to **20**.

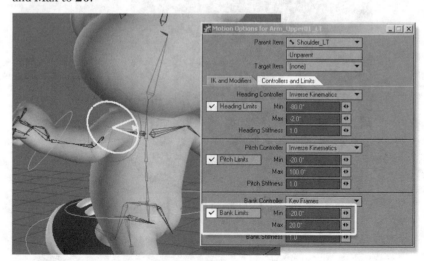

Figure 3.8-39. Upper arm helper bank limits.

2. Select each **Leg_Upper02** bone and turn on **Bank Limits**. Set Min to **–20** and Max to **20**.

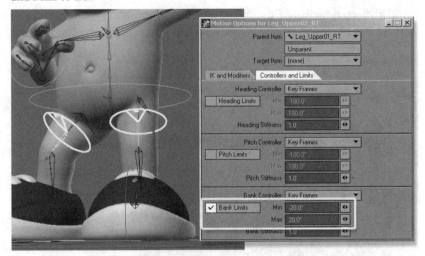

Figure 3.8-40. Knee helper bank limits.

These are the main joints that need limits. Setting limits for other joints can limit the posing ability of the character, but feel free to set limits for some other joints if you feel it's appropriate.

Unaffected by IK of Descendants

Unaffected by IK of Descendants is most useful when you have two or more IK chains sharing a common parent. This is quite common in a character rig, where the two leg chains share the pelvis parent and the two arm chains share the back bone parent. Even though neither of these parent bones has IK enabled, what

can happen is that the IK solution of one chain can be affected by the IK of the other chain, making the IK a little unstable. Unaffected by IK of Descendants stops the calculation of each IK chain at the item it's activated for.

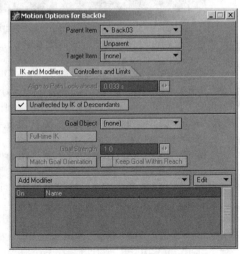

1. Select the **IK and Modifiers** tab in Motion Options and select the **Back04** bone. Turn on **Unaffected by IK of Descendants**.

Figure 3.8-41. Unaffected by IK.

2. Select the **Pelvis_Base** bone and turn on **Unaffected by IK of Descendants**.

Unaffected by IK of Descendants isn't always necessary, but if you're unsure whether you need it or not, it's better to turn it on for the parent of multiple IK chains.

3.9 Rigging Clothes

Rigging clothes can be simple or complex, depending on your needs. If the clothes have the same weight mapping as the body, you can just use the clothes in the existing rig and they'll deform with the character. For tight-fitting clothes this is fine, but it doesn't work so well for loose-fitting clothes. For loose-fitting clothes it's important to have a bit more control.

It's often easier to create the clothes after rigging. This makes it a bit easier to create the clothes, as the weight mapping is already done for the body, so you don't have to weight map the clothes again. This is especially useful when creating multiple sets of clothing, which are often required in a script where characters are wearing clothes.

In this case the clothes were created before rigging, so we need to copy the weight map values from the body to the clothes. The reason we didn't weight map the clothes at the same time as the body is so that any weight map adjustments done on the body during the testing of the rig can be accounted for in the clothing without doing extra work.

This chapter explains the process of rigging the clothing for manual animation. Animating clothing using dynamics is explained in Chapter 6, "Dynamics."

Weight Mapping

We can follow a similar process for weight mapping the clothing as for weight
mapping the body, since the geometry of the clothes is based on the geometry of
the body. You can check the weight values of the clothes compared to the body at
any time by switching between the body and clothing layers.

Mapping the Shirt

Weight mapping the shirt would be quite a tedious task if we had to weight map
both the inner and outer surfaces. To make it easier we'll delete the inner surface and weight map just the outer surface. When the inner surface is recreated
it will inherit the weight values from the outer surface, cutting down the
workload.

1. Load your Hamish object into Modeler (you can find a preprepared object in
    \Objects\Chapters\Hamish_Working_v007.lwo).
2. Select the clothes layer and change the Perspective view to **Weight Shade**.
    Make sure **Symmetry** is on.
3. Select the polygons of the **Shirt_Inner** surface and delete them. It's easier
    to weight the shirt as a single layer and recreate the inner surface after
    weight mapping.
4. Select the **Arms** weight map. Select the last band of the sleeves and **Set
    Map Value** to **100%**.

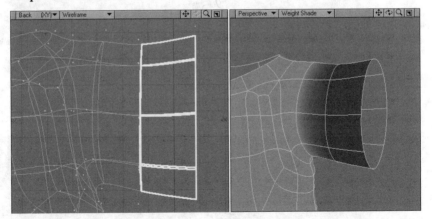

Figure 3.9-1. Initial weight values.

5. Select the top point at the peak of the shoulder and **Set Map Value** to **80%**.
    Following the row of points down from the Back view, select the two lower
    points and **Set Map Value** to **60%**. Give the middle points a value of **40%**,
    and the next two points a value of **20%**.

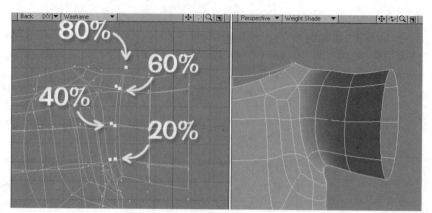

Figure 3.9-2. Adjusting weight values at the shoulder.

6. Select the top point of the row on the inside of the shoulder and **Set Map Value** to **30%**. Give the points under that a value of **20%** and the next two points a value of **10%**.

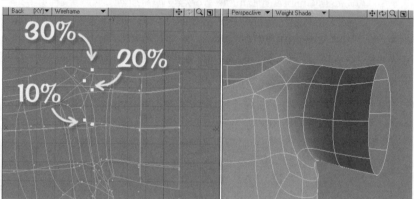

Figure 3.9-3. Smoothing the blended area.

7. Select the **Neck** weight map. Select the row of points at the top of the neck line and set their value to **50%**.

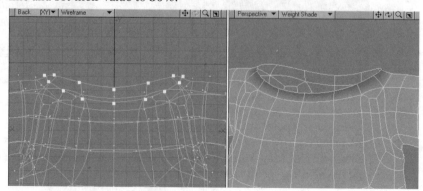

Figure 3.9-4. Weight values for the neck.

Mapping the Pants

Weight mapping the pants is just like mapping the legs.

1. Select the **Leg_LT** weight map. Select the bottom band of polygons of the pant legs and **Expand** the selection three times. **Set Map Value** to **50%**. **Contract** the selection and **Set Map Value** to **100%**.

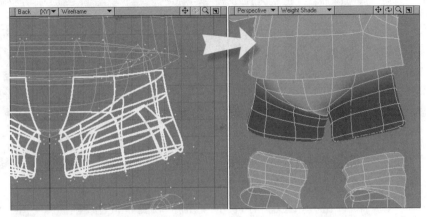

Figure 3.9-5. Initial weight values.

2. Select the four points at the base of the groin, as shown in Figure 3.9-6, and **Set Map Value** to **25%**.

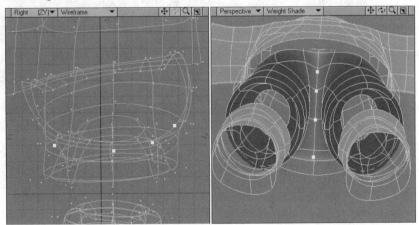

Figure 3.9-6. Adjusting the weights of the groin.

3. Select the inner point of the triangles at the front of each leg and the points of the bum cheeks shown in Figure 3.9-7, and set the value to **25%**.

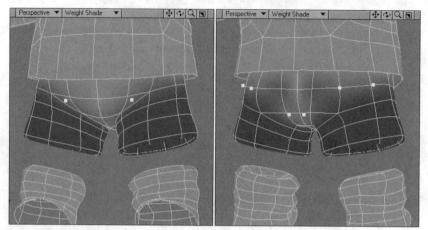

Figure 3.9-7. Smoothing the blended areas.

4. Select the three points at the bottom of the bum cheek and set the value to **50%**. Select the point at the inside top corner of the bum cheek and set the value to **10%**.

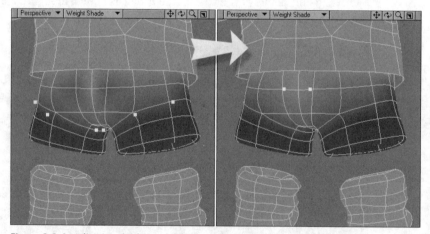

Figure 3.9-8. Adjusting the bum cheeks.

Mapping the Socks

Weight mapping the socks is a little different from mapping the legs, as there is additional geometry for the folds.

1. Select the polygons of the socks from the Right view and deselect the bottom band of polygons. **Set Map Value** to **50%**.

2. Contract the selection and set the value to **75%**. Contract the selection again and set the value to **100%**.

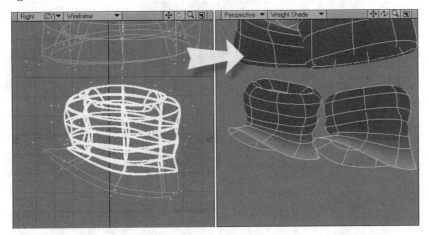

Figure 3.9-9. Weight values for the leg.

3. Select the **Foot_LT** weight map. Select the bottom two bands of polygons and set the value to **25%**. Contract the selection and set the value to **50%**.

4. Select the bottom row of points and set the value to **100%**.

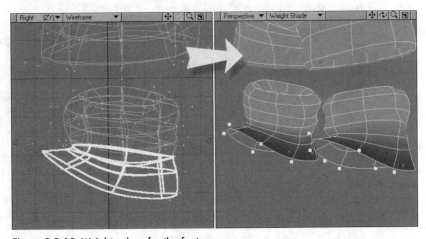

Figure 3.9-10. Weight values for the foot.

Separating Left and Right Sides

Now that the pants and socks are mapped we can separate the left and right sides the same way we did for the legs and feet.

1. Select the polygons of the right sock and the right side of the pants.

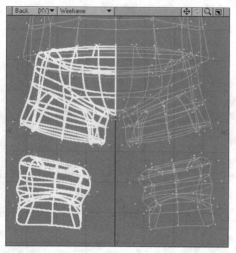

Figure 3.9-11. Be careful not to select any polygons of the left side.

2. Select the **Leg_LT** weight map and **Copy Vertex Map** to **Leg_RT**.
3. Copy the **Foot_LT** weight map to **Foot_RT**.
4. We want the values along the center line to be the same for each side, so before clearing the right side from the original weight maps, deselect the polygons along the center line (X=0) of the model. Now select the **Leg_LT** weight map and **Clear Map**. Do the same for **Foot_LT**.

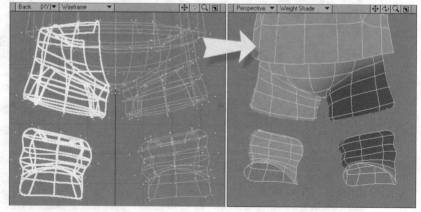

Figure 3.9-12. Deselect the middle polygons before clearing so the center values remain.

Body Weight Map

As we did earlier, instead of setting the body weight values manually we'll use the plug-in called Combine Weightmaps, written by Kevin Phillips, to subtract the arm and leg weight maps from the body.

1. Make sure just the clothes layer is in the foreground and select the **Body** weight map. Deselect all the polygons and **Set Map Value** to **100%**.

2. Select **Combine Weights** and subtract the **Arms** weight map from the **Body** weight map.

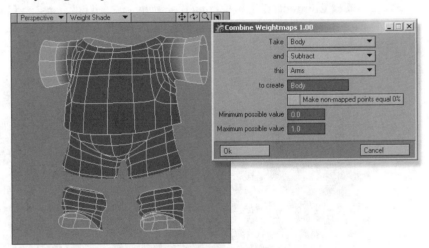

Figure 3.9-13. Subtracting the Arm weight values from the body.

3. Continue applying **Combine Weightmaps** until you've subtracted the **Neck**, **Leg_LT**, and **Leg_RT** weight maps from the body weight map.

4. Finally, select the socks and **Clear Map**.

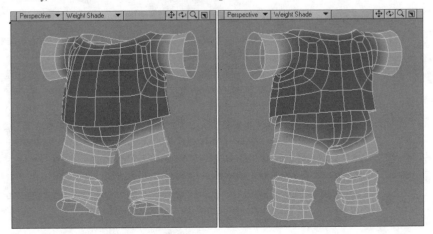

Figure 3.9-14. Final body weight map.

The initial weight mapping for the clothes is complete. If you made any adjustments to the original weight maps when testing the rig, remember to do the same adjustments to the clothes weight maps.

Finishing the Shirt

With the weight mapping done, the inner surface of the shirt can be recreated.

1. Select all the polygons of the shirt and **Copy** (**Ctrl+c**).
2. **Smooth Shift** with an offset of about **–10 mm**.
3. **Select Connected** (**]**), selecting the newly created polygons, and **Flip** (**f**).
4. With the polygons still selected, change the surface (**q**) to **Shirt_Inner**.
5. Deselect all, **Paste**, pasting the polygons copied in step 1, and **Merge Points**.

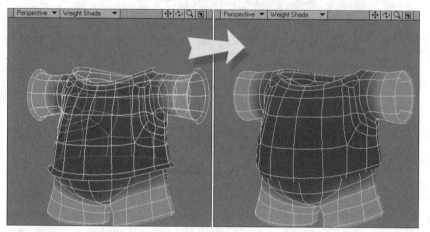

Figure 3.9-15. Recreating the inner surface of the shirt.

Testing the Weight Maps

If you choose to use the same bones as the body, the clothes are now ready. Let's see the result of the current weight maps in the rig.

1. Load your Hamish rig with poses into Layout (you can find a preprepared scene in \Scenes\Chapters\Hamish_Rig01_v004.lwo), or just switch to Layout if the rig is already loaded.
2. Open the Scene Editor and select **Layer3** of the Hamish object, the clothes layer. Set the visibility to **Textured Solid** and activate the object.
3. With **Layer3** still selected, press **Shift+b** for Bones mode. Open the Bone properties (**p**) and set Use Bones From Object to **Layer1**.
4. Check the clothes with the poses, making sure they're deforming properly and there isn't any skin poking through the clothing.

Figure 3.9-16. Clothes with default weight maps.

The clothes are deforming properly with the poses, but the edges of the shirt arms and pant legs are being deformed by the lower limb bones, distorting their shape. We can fix this and add independent control of the clothes at the same time.

Independent Clothing Controls

Independent clothing controls have two advantages: They ensure that the multiple bones of the body rig don't distort the clothing, and they give additional control over the clothes so they can be posed independently from the body of the character.

Independent control is especially important for loose clothing. It prevents the clothing from twisting with the elbow or wrist, and keeps it from distorting with the lower limbs. It also allows the sleeves and pants to be positioned more naturally on the arms and legs of the character, allowing for gravity and air resistance.

Creating New Weight Maps

The first step is to create new weight maps for the parts of the clothing that require additional controls. In this case since both the shirt and pants are quite loose, we'll create new weight maps for the limbs of both. Remember when doing this to clear the original (copied) weight maps from the affected areas or you'll end up with competing bones.

1. Press **F12** to switch back to Modeler.
2. Make sure just the clothes layer is in the foreground and select the polygons of the shirt and pants, leaving the socks unselected.

215

3. Select the **Leg_LT** weight map and Copy Vertex Map, calling the new map **Clothes_Leg_LT.** Select the **Leg_LT** weight map again and **Clear Map.** Repeat for the **Leg_RT** weight map.

4. Select the **Arms** weight map. **Copy Vertex Map** to **Clothes_Arms.** Select the **Arms** weight map again and **Clear Map.**

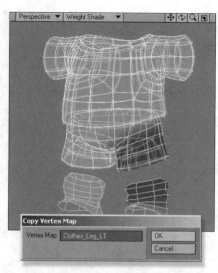

Figure 3.9-17. Duplicating the weight maps.

Creating Clothes Controls

With new weight maps for the clothes, new bones need to be added to the rig to affect those areas of the clothes.

1. Switch back to Layout and make sure you're on frame **0.**

2. Select the **Leg_Upper01_LT** bone. Create a child bone, calling it **Clothes_Leg_LT.**

3. Set the Z position to **0,** then select **Tip Move.** From the Back view, drag the tip closer to the bottom of the pants and out a bit from the leg bones.

4. Open the Bone properties, assign the **Clothes_Leg_LT** weight map, and press **r** to rest the bone.

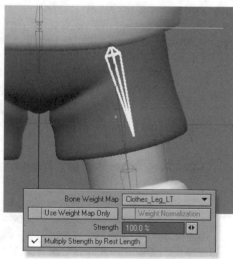

Figure 3.9-18. Pant leg control bone.

5. Select **Mirror Hierarchy**, replacing the string _LT with **_RT**.

6. Make sure **Parent in Place** is turned on and, in the Scene Editor, parent **Clothes_Leg_RT** to **Leg_Upper01_RT**. (See Figure 3.9-19.)

7. Turn on the **H** and **P** channel controls for both new bones.

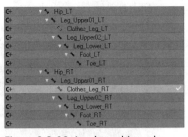

Figure 3.9-19. Leg bone hierarchy.

8. Select the **Arm_Upper01_LT** bone and create a child bone, calling it **Clothes_Arm_LT**.

9. Set the Z position to **0**, then select **Tip Move**. From the Back view, drag the tip closer to the edge of the shirt arm and up a bit from the arm bones.

10. Assign the **Clothes_Arms** weight map and press **r** to rest the bone.

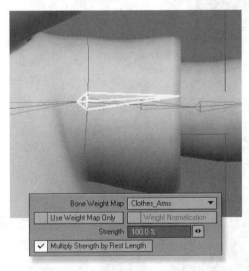

Figure 3.9-20. Shirt sleeve control bone.

11. Select **Mirror Hierarchy**, replacing the string _LT with **_RT**, and parent **Clothes_Arm_RT** to **Arm_Upper01_RT**.

12. Turn on the **H** and **P** channel controls and turn off the **B** channel control for both new arm bones.

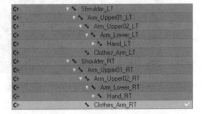

Figure 3.9-21. Arm bone hierarchy.

With the new control bones in place, check through the poses to make sure that the weight assignments are all correct.

Figure 3.9-22. Notice the arms and legs of the clothes are no longer being distorted by the lower limb bones.

Now you can adjust the rotation and scale of these control bones so the arms and legs of the loose-fitting clothes appear to hang off the body.

Figure 3.9-23. Poses with clothing adjustments.

Preparing the Final Object

The basic rig is almost complete. We just need to finalize the character object by making it a single layer and updating the rig appropriately.

1. Switch to Modeler, select **Layer2**, and delete the template eyeballs.
2. Select the clothes layer and **Cut** and **Paste** into Layer1.
3. Save the object as **Hamish01.lwo**.

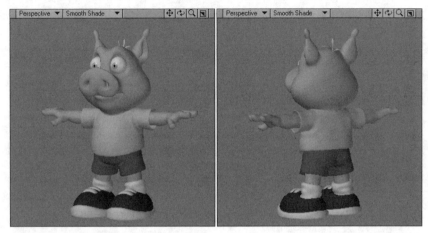

Figure 3.9-24. Hamish object as a single layer.

4. Switch to Layout, select **Layer3**, which now has nothing in it, and **Clear Selected Items** (–).
5. Select **Hamish01:Layer1**. Notice the layer suffix is still there even though there is only one layer in the object. Select **Items➤ Replace➤With Object** and press **OK**, leaving Hamish01.lwo as the chosen object. This forces Layout to update the object reference, removing the layer suffix.

Figure 3.9-25. Replace object.

6. Save the scene.

The basic rig is now complete and ready for the next stage. Establishing the final object name is an important step to prepare for adding expressions to the rig in the next chapter.

In this chapter you've learned the fundamentals of rigging that form the basis of every character rig. These techniques may be all you need for simple characters, but if you want extra control and to really make your characters shine, read on to learn some more advanced techniques.

Chapter 4

Advanced Rigging

Advanced character rigging largely deals with automating motion. Automating motion can be very valuable to character animation, as it allows the animator to concentrate on the important aspects of posing a character without worrying about the little things, resulting in higher quality animation in a shorter amount of time.

There is a danger to automating motion though. It's easy to get carried away with automating motion and end up handicapping the rig by taking away control that an animator needs to create the best performance for the character.

When automating motion you need to make sure the controls are intuitive and easy to use. Also make sure you don't get so excited about the possibilities of linking motions that you end up complicating the rig too much or make the controls so complex that using them becomes more work than animating the items manually. The basic rule for automating motion is: If it doesn't save any time, then don't complicate the rig.

Character rigging is mainly about problem solving. There is rarely just one solution to a problem, so it's important to understand a range of techniques so you can apply the best one for the job at hand. This chapter provides some methods for automating motion that complement the animation controls, rather than replacing them. It also provides alternate rigging techniques for different control methods, and shows how to apply existing rigs to different characters.

4.1 Expressions Made Easy

Expressions allow you to automate motion and to make the motion of one item dependent on another item. It's easy to be intimidated by expressions, but they can offer some really simple solutions to complex problems. Once you start using expressions, you'll wonder how you ever did without them. There are many possibilities for expressions within character rigging and animation, and the more comfortable you are with them, the more your character will be able to do.

At first glance, expressions seem like an innately unartistic tool, only useful for someone with a mathematics degree. It's true that having a good knowledge of mathematics helps you get the most out of expressions, but it's certainly not a requirement for using them.

Expressions can be very bewildering. There are multiple places to apply them, there are multiple types of syntax to reference items or channels, and there are dozens of possible commands, with little explanation of what each one does and when and how to use them. Fortunately once you understand a few simple guidelines, expressions become easy to use and fun to create.

Where to Apply Expressions

There are three places that an expression can be applied: as a motion modifier, in the Graph Editor as an integrated expression, and as a channel modifier. Each place has its own advantages and disadvantages.

Motion Modifier

Motion modifier expressions are usually the best ones to use for character rigging.

Motion modifier expressions are the only ones that allow the calculation to occur after IK, which is very useful since IK is used quite a lot in character rigs.

Motion modifier expressions allow you to place an expression on each channel of the item as well as giving you four scratch pads: A, B, C, and D. It's good to use these scratch pads as much as possible so the actual expressions on the channels refer to the scratch pad variables. This means you can see and adjust the useful information as soon as you open the expression properties, without having to search through the channels.

The disadvantage to motion modifier expressions is they can only be applied to items with motion options. This means that they can't be used to apply expressions to surfaces, textures, or morphs.

Graph Editor

Integrated expressions are limited to only working before IK. In most cases they should only be used when motion modifier expressions aren't available, such as for adding expressions to surfaces, textures, or morphs.

Integrated expressions are saved to the scene, not to an item within the scene, so having a single expression that is used by multiple items or objects can be more efficient. You can also save a library of integrated expressions that you can load into other scenes.

Integrated expressions don't have a scratch pad; instead they offer the ability to reference other integrated expressions as subexpressions by referencing the expression name. This doesn't really make up for the lack of a scratch pad though, as it's more difficult to find and edit the subexpressions being referenced.

The most important thing to remember when creating integrated expressions is to apply the character name as a prefix to the expression name, so integrated expressions for multiple characters in the same scene are kept separate. If the expression name is the same for each character, the expression will be replaced instead of added to when each character is loaded, and the expression will only apply to the most recently loaded character.

Channel Modifier

Channel modifier expressions are somewhere in between the other two. They are attached to a channel rather than an item, so they can be used for any channel with an envelope. They offer a scratch pad, but it isn't quite as useful as with motion modifier expressions since there is only one channel; however, it does save having very long expressions.

Syntax

There are two types of syntax for expressions: LScript syntax and bracketed syntax. In most cases these are interchangeable, so it doesn't really matter which you use.

The benefit to using both types of syntax is that bracketed syntax is evaluated before LScript syntax. This means you can have some control over the order in which expressions are calculated by using combinations of the two.

LScript Syntax

LScript syntax only works for channels that have translation data. For channels without translation data, such as surfaces, textures, and morphs, you need to use bracketed syntax.

Object.pos(Time).x references the X position of an object at the current time.

Object.Bone.rot(Frame).p references the pitch rotation of a bone in an object at the current frame.

> **Note:** You don't have to include the object name for a bone if the bone name is unique. It's best to get into the habit of including the object name though, so that you can have two or more characters in a scene with the same bone names, and the expression knows which character's bone you are referring to.

Object:Layer.pos(Time).x references the X position of a layer of an object at the current time.

Object.pos(Time - 1).x references the X position of an object one second before the current time.

Object.pos(Frame - 1).x references the X position of an object one frame before the current frame.

Bracketed Syntax

Bracketed syntax can reference channels that don't have translation data, such as surfaces, textures, and morphs, but can only reference channels that actually exist, so to find the world coordinates of an item you need to use LScript syntax.

Bracketed syntax references the current time or frame by default, so you don't need the additional time argument unless you want to specify a time or frame other than the current one.

[Object.Position.X] references the X position of an object at the current time.

[Object.Bone.Rotation.P] references the pitch rotation of a bone in an object at the current time.

[Object:Layer.Position.X] references the X position of a layer of an object at the current time.

[Object.Group.Morph] references the value of a morph in a group at the current frame.

[Object.Position.X, Time - 1] references the X position of an object one second before the current time.

[Object.Position.X, Frame - 1] references the X position of an object one frame before the current frame.

Expression Functions

This is where we start heading into mathematical land. Many of the functions available to expressions can only be understood if you have a solid understanding of mathematics. Fortunately there are only a few that are commonly used for character rigging, and they're fairly easy to remember.

I always find expressions easier to understand when they're explained in a practical sense. Instead of just explaining the functions by themselves, I'll show you some examples of where they're useful and how they work within the context of the task.

mapRange

The mapRange function remaps the range of an input to a defined output range. This allows you to easily set up complex relationships between items.

mapRange(Input, Input Min, Input Max, Output Min, Output Max)

You can tell one item to rotate from 20° to 65° when another item moves from point A to point B. You can scale a bone depending on the distance to a target, so the tip of the bone always touches its target. Any time you want a complex motion to occur based on the motion of another item, mapRange is probably what you'll use.

vmag

The vmag function can find the distance from an item to the origin (0, 0, 0). It can also find the distance between two items.

vmag(Input)

Vmag is very useful when combined with mapRange to create a muscle bone expression. Vmag finds the distance from the bone to the target, and mapRange remaps that distance to correctly scale the bone.

clamp

The clamp function limits the motion of an item to within a defined output range. This is similar to setting rotation limits for bones but can be used for any type of channel.

clamp(Input, Output Min, Output Max)

Clamp can stop a bone from moving or rotating too far, making sure it doesn't travel outside the deformation abilities of a character. It's also useful when combined with other functions to limit their output range.

center

The center function finds the central position between two item channels.

center(InputA, InputB)

Center is useful for all sorts of things but is commonly used for automatic hip movement.

Of course, instead of remembering expression functions, you can use the Expression Builder to create expressions for you, at least until you become more comfortable with the ones you use regularly.

Expression Builder

The Expression Builder can be found in the Graph Editor. It is a very useful utility that not only provides premade expressions but also offers explanations and examples of many of the provided expressions. The utility functions in the Expression Builder are particularly useful for character rigging.

Although it's in the Graph Editor, the expressions it creates can be used anywhere. When you've chosen the channels for the expression, instead of choosing Create Expression, you can copy the text and paste it in one of the other expression types. This is an easy way to get the expression you need, or at least a good starting point for building your own expression.

4.2 Applying Expressions

Now we'll look at some practical uses for expressions in character rigging.

Eye Stretch

We'll use muscle bone expressions on the eye stretch bones so the eye area can change scale with the position of the eye stretch control. We'll also link the scale of the eyeballs to the eye stretch control to enable the eyeballs to bulge out of the sockets for the classic cartoon double take.

Muscle Bone Expression

mapRange(vmag(<Bone>.wpos(Time) − <Target>.wpos(Time)),
    0, <Rest Length>, 0, 1)

Muscle bones have a large variety of uses in character rigs. The muscle bone expression consists of two functions: vmag and mapRange. Vmag finds the distance between the bone and the target, and mapRange remaps the distance to scale values for the bone. The names or values in <brackets> are placeholders that need to be replaced by items or values from your scene.

1. Load your Hamish rig into Layout (you can find a preprepared scene in \Scenes\Chapters\Hamish_Rig01_v005.lws).

2. Go to frame 0, select the **Eye_Stretch_LT** bone, and open the Bone properties. Make a note of the Rest Length of the bone; in my case it's **124.575 mm** or **0.124575**.

3. Open Motion Options and change Target Item to **(none)**. Select **Add Modifier**➤**Expression**, and open the expression properties.

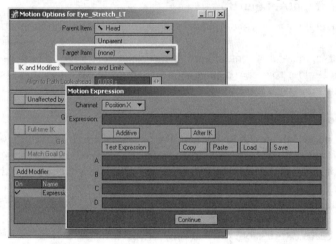

Figure 4.2-1. Set Target to (none).

4. Type the muscle bone expression in the A scratch pad, replacing the placeholders with the correct names and values:

    mapRange(vmag(Hamish01.Eye_Stretch_LT.wpos(Time) – Hamish_EyeStretch_LT.wpos(Time)), 0, 0.124575, 0, 1)

5. Select **Channel**➤**Scale.Z**, type **A** in the Expression field, and press **Continue**.

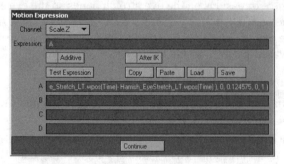

Figure 4.2-2. Eye_Stretch_LT expression.

6. Open the Scene Editor and expand child items if necessary. Find **Hamish_EyeStretch** and unlock it by clicking on the lock icon.

Now you can check to see if the muscle bone expression is working correctly. Go to one of the pose frames and move Eye_Stretch up and down. The left eye should stretch with the position of the eye stretch control.

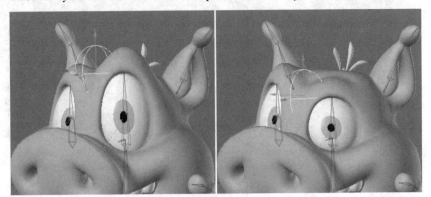

Figure 4.2-3. The muscle bone expression is stretching the left eye with the position of the eye stretch control.

When you've checked that it's working, go back to frame 0 to continue.

7. Select the **Eye_Stretch_LT** bone, open the expression properties, and select **Copy**. Close the expression.

8. Select **Eye_Stretch_RT** and change Target Item to **(none)**. **Add Modifier**➤**Expression**, open the expression properties, and select **Paste**.

9. In the expression, change all instances of _LT to _RT.

10. Select **Channel**➤**Scale.Z**, type **A** in the Expression field, and press **Continue**.

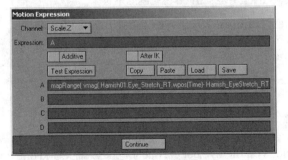

Figure 4.2-4. Eye_Stretch_RT expression.

Go to one of the pose frames and move Eye_Stretch up and down to check that both expressions are working correctly. Rotate the bank of Eye_Stretch to offset the stretch of each eye.

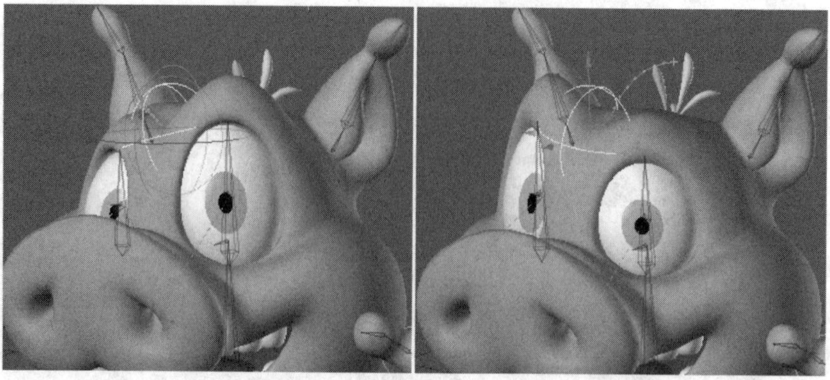

Figure 4.2-5. Both eyes stretching with the position and rotation of the eye stretch control.

Adjusting the scale of the character adversely affects the eye stretch expressions. If you perform minor scale adjustments, you can easily allow for the difference, but if you need to perform a significant scale adjustment, or you know that the character will be required to change scale often within the animation, it can be useful to allow for character scale adjustments in the eye stretch expressions for the character.

To allow for the Master scale, the eye stretch expression is:

mapRange(vmag(<Bone>.wpos(Time) – <Target>.wpos(Time)), 0, (<Rest Length> * <Master>.scale(Time).y), 0, 1)

In the Hamish rig, the left eye stretch expression is:

mapRange(vmag(Hamish01.Eye_Stretch_LT.wpos(Time) – Hamish_EyeStretch_LT.wpos(Time)), 0, (0.124575 * Hamish_Master.scale(Time).y), 0, 1)

Eyeball Bulging

The eyeball bulge is a simple link to the scale of Hamish_Eye_Stretch. We'll include two expressions on the eye bones: one for the Z scale and one for the Y scale. The Z scale follows the same scale of the eye stretch control but to make sure it isn't stretched too far we'll add a clamp function:

clamp(<Item>.scale(Time).z, 1, 3)

The clamp makes sure the Z scale can't shrink any smaller than its original size or stretch larger than three times its original size.

The equation for the Y scale gives the inverse scale of Hamish_Eye_ Stretch, so as the eye stretches larger in Z it stretches smaller in Y. So we have more control, we'll add a multiplier to determine how much inverse scale to apply.

A basic inverse equation is simple:

1 / <Input>

An inverse equation with a multiplier is a bit more complex:

1 / (1 – (1 - <Input>) * <Multiplier>)

You can experiment with different values for the multiplier until you find a value that works nicely.

1. Select the **Eye_ LT** bone, **Add Modifier**➤**Expression**, and open the expression properties.

2. Type the following expression in the A scratch pad:
   clamp(Hamish_EyeStretch.scale(Time).z, 1, 3)

3. Type the following equation in the B scratch pad:
   1 / (1 – (1 – A)) * 0.2)

4. Select **Channel**➤**Scale.Z** and in the Expression field, type **A**. Select **Channel**➤**Scale.Y** and in the Expression field, type **B**.

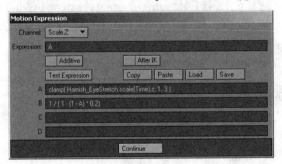

Figure 4.2-6. Eyeball expression.

5. Select **Copy** and press **Continue.**

6. Select the **Eye_RT** bone, **Add Modifier**➤**Expression**, open the expression properties, and select **Paste.**

7. Select **Channel**➤**Scale.Z** and in the Expression field, type **A**. Select **Channel**➤**Scale.Y** and in the Expression field, type **B**.

Go to one of the pose frames and adjust the Z scale of Eye_Stretch to check that both expressions are working correctly. You can adjust the multiplier for the inverse scale equation to suit the eyes and eye sockets of the character.

Figure 4.2-7. The eyeballs scale with the eye stretch control.

With the expressions done, we need to adjust the channel controls for the eye stretch control so the animator knows which channels can be adjusted.

8. Select **Hamish_EyeStretch**, press **t**, and turn off the X and Z Position channel controls, leaving only **Y**.

9. Press **y** and turn off the H and P Rotation channel controls, leaving only **B**.

10. Press **h** and turn off the X and Y Scale channel controls, leaving only **Z**.

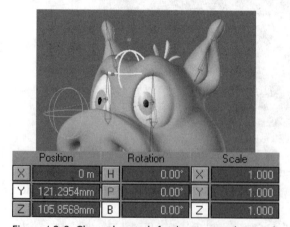

Position		Rotation		Scale	
X	0 m	H	0.00°	X	1.000
Y	121.2954mm	P	0.00°	Y	1.000
Z	105.8568mm	B	0.00°	Z	1.000

Figure 4.2-8. Channel controls for the eye stretch control.

Finally, now that you can see the effect of the eye stretching, feel free to adjust the Eyebrows weight map if necessary, remembering to also adjust the Head weight map to compensate for any changes.

Blink Morph Helper

The blink morph helper is an additional morph that's added as the blink occurs to help the eyelids travel over the curved surface of the eyeballs instead of in a straight line.

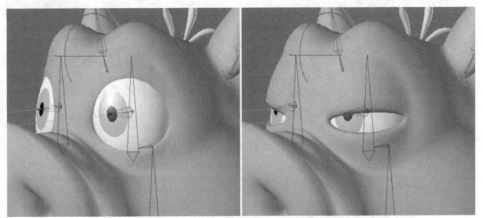

Figure 4.2-9. Currently the blink is linear, so the eyelids move in a straight line.

To do this we need to add a couple of new morphs, then tie the motion of the new morphs to the blink using an expression.

(1 – cos([Object.Group.Morph] * (2 * PI))) * 0.5

This expression creates a smooth curve from 0 to 100 and back to 0 for one morph as another morph travels from 0 to 100. This means that the helper morph will only kick in when the blink is in between its limits.

This expression is a highly mathematical one that is beyond my own abilities to create, so I asked expression guru Richard Brak to help me create an expression that would do this. To be honest I'm still not sure of the math behind the expression, or exactly why it works, but I'm happy just knowing that it does work.

Creating the Helper Morphs

We'll start by creating the helper morphs.

1. Switch to Modeler, and make sure **Symmetry** is turned on.
2. Create a new morph called **Control.BlinkHelp_LT**.
3. Select the middle polygons of the upper and lower eyelids.
4. Move the polygons a little way out from the eye socket.
5. Deselect the outside set of polygons and move the remaining selected polygons out again, about the same distance as before.

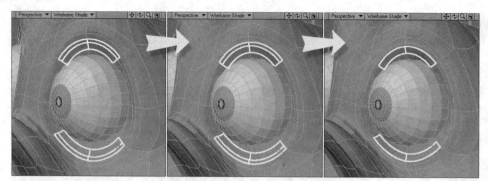

Figure 4.2-10. Creating the helper morphs.

6. Turn off **Symmetry** and select the polygons of the right eyelids.

7. **Copy Vertex Map**, calling the new morph **Control.BlinkHelp_RT**.

8. Select the **Control.BlinkHelp_LT** morph and **Clear Map**.

Adding Expressions

Now we can apply the helper morphs to the blinks.

1. Switch to Layout, open the Object properties for **Hamish01**, and select the **Deform** tab.

2. Remove **Morph Mixer**, then **Add Displacement**➤**Morph Mixer**. This forces Morph Mixer to update to include the new morphs.

3. Open the Morph Mixer panel, select the **Control** group, and press the **Graph Editor** button.

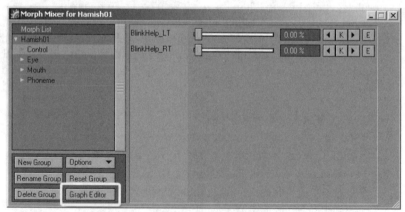

Figure 4.2-11. Morph Mixer.

4. Select the **Expressions** tab and select **New**. Change Name to **Hamish_Blink** and type the following expression for Value:
(1 − cos([Hamish01.Eye.Blink] * (2 * PI))) * 0.5

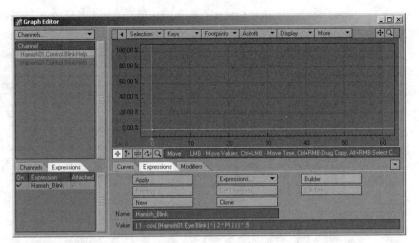

Figure 4.2-12. Blink expression.

5. Select **Clone**, change Name to **Hamish_Blink_LT**, and type the following expression for Value:

(1 – cos([Hamish01.Eye.Blink_LT] * (2 * PI))) * 0.5 +
    [Hamish_Blink]

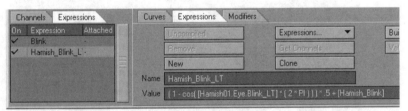

Figure 4.2-13. [Hamish_Blink] references the Blink expression. Adding [Hamish_Blink] to the expression means the helper morph will work for the left eye blink morph as well as the combined blink morph.

6. Select **Clone** again, change Name to **Hamish_Blink_RT**, and type the following expression for Value:

(1 – cos([Hamish01.Eye.Blink_RT] * (2 * PI))) * 0.5 +
    [Hamish_Blink]

Figure 4.2-14. Blink_RT expression.

233

7. Select the channel for **Control.BlinkHelp_LT** and the **Hamish_Blink_ LT** expression and press **Apply**.

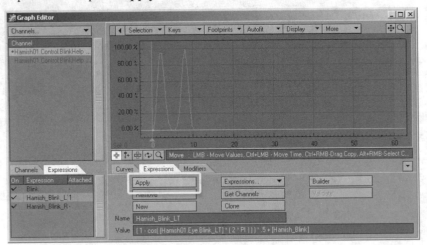

Figure 4.2-15. Applying the expression to the morph channel.

8. Select the channel for **Control.BlinkHelp_RT** and the **Hamish_Blink_ RT** expression and press **Apply**.

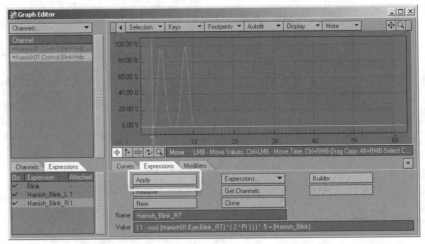

Figure 4.2-16. The modified curves appear because I've made Hamish blink at frame 5 to test the expressions.

Now check the transition between the open eyelids and the blink. You can adjust the multiplier in the expressions to make the effect more or less pronounced, and you can tweak the helper morphs themselves for even more control.

Figure 4.2-17. The eyelids travel more evenly over the eye surface now.

This section is a good introduction to expressions, but this is just the beginning of your learning. I hope this section has made you feel more comfortable with expressions, enabling you to experiment well beyond what's been shown here. There are many other functions to explore, and many other uses for expressions in character rigging, some of which are described in section 4.4, "Alternate Rigging Techniques." Some other uses of expressions are described in Chapter 5, "Animation," when creating morph joystick controls.

4.3 Modifiers

Motion modifiers modify the motion of an item, affecting the path that an item travels. Displacement modifiers modify the displacement of an item, affecting the points of an object.

Some modifiers are just easy-to-use expressions, putting an interface over a commonly used expression. Other modifiers do things beyond the abilities of expressions. When you have a choice between using a modifier and an expression, the decision is often determined by the requirements of the task. Sometimes it's easier to set up a motion modifier. Other times a motion modifier doesn't give enough control, so an expression is needed. It can also be useful to use a combination of expressions and modifiers for the same task.

Shoe Deformation

Hamish's shoes aren't deforming nicely when the toes are bent. This was more difficult to fix before, since joint compensation doesn't work with Match Goal Orientation.

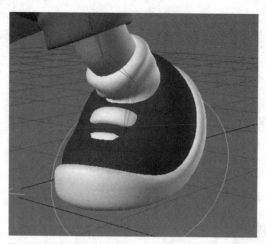

Figure 4.3-1. The top of the shoes aren't deforming nicely.

Follower

Follower allows an item to follow the motion of another item. You can choose which channels to follow as well as the percentage of motion inherited from the followed item. Although you can do the same thing using expressions, Follower is often easier to set up, so if it does what you require then you should use it instead of expressions.

We'll change the toe to rotate using the motion modifier Follower instead of Match Goal Orientation. This way we can use joint compensation on the toe joint.

1. Load your Hamish rig into Layout (you can find a preprepared scene in \Scenes\Chapters\Hamish_Rig01_v006.lws).
2. Select the **Toe_LT** bone and open the Motion Options.
3. Turn off Match Goal Orientation and set the Goal Object to **(none)**.

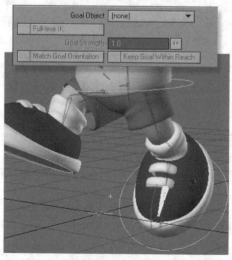

Figure 4.3-2. The toe loses its rotation when Match Goal Orientation is removed.

4.   **Add Modifier▷Follower** and open the Follower properties.

5.   Set Item To Follow to **Hamish_Toe_LT**, then set all the Source channels to none except for **Pitch Angle** and **Bank Angle** and uncheck **After IK**.

6.   Set Pitch Angle **Add** to **–15.88**, offsetting the rotation to include the toe bone's rest rotation. Press **Continue** and run through the poses to check that the toe is behaving properly.

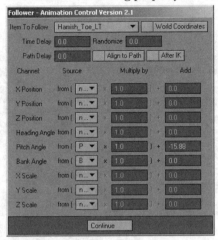

Figure 4.3-3. Follower settings for the left toe bone.

7.   Copy the Follower entry from **Toe_LT**, select the **Toe_RT** bone, and paste the modifier.

8.   For **Toe_RT**, turn off **Match Goal Orientation**, set the Goal Object to **(none)**, and open the Follower properties.

9.   Change Item To Follow to **Hamish_Toe_RT** and press **Continue**. Run through the poses again to check that both toes are behaving properly.

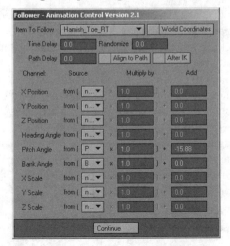

Figure 4.3-4. Follower settings for the right toe bone.

Adjusting the Toe Deformation

Now that the toes are using Follower, we can apply joint compensation to make the shoe deformation nicer.

1. Select the **Toe_LT** bone and open the Bone properties. Make sure you're on a pose where the toe is bent so you can see the results as you adjust the settings.
2. Turn on **Joint Comp for Parent**.

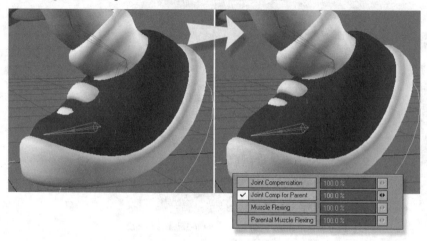

Figure 4.3-5. Joint Comp for Parent fixes the deformation of the shoe.

3. Select **Toe_RT** and turn on **Joint Comp for Parent**.

Well, that makes a big difference. The shoes are looking much better now, but there is still a problem with the shoelaces.

Joint Morph Plus

The displacement modifier Joint Morph Plus lets you apply morphs based on the rotation of a bone. You can also do this with expressions, but not after IK, so any bones rotated by IK won't affect the morph. Joint Morph Plus reads the bone rotation after IK, so it works for all bones.

Joint Morph Plus is often used to tweak the shape of joints when they're bent. This is useful for joints like elbows and knees that tend to change shape when they bend. There are many uses for Joint Morph Plus other than adjusting the joints of the body. We'll use Joint Morph Plus to adjust some deformations caused by bone rotation, starting with the shoelaces.

When the toes are bent, the front shoelace is being hidden by the front of the shoe. Notice how the back shoelace deforms as the toe bends. We'll get the front shoelace deforming the same way using Joint Morph Plus.

1. Switch to Modeler and zoom in on Hamish's shoes.
2. Create a new morph called **Control.Shoelace_LT**.

3. Select the front laces of both shoes and, from the Right view, move them up to just in front of the back laces. Rotate them a little closer to the rotation of the back laces.

4. **Stretch** the laces just a little bit wider, about **105%**.

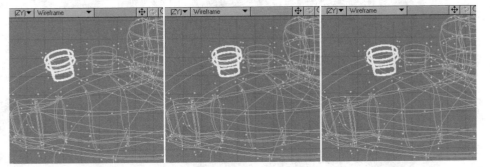

Figure 4.3-6. Creating the shoelace morph.

5. Switch back to Layout so we can test the morph before separating left- and right-sided morphs.

6. Open the Object Properties for Hamish01 and select the **Deform** tab.

7. **Add Displacement**>**JointMorphPlus** and open the Joint Morph Plus properties.

8. Set Control Bone to **Toe_LT**, change Axis to **Pitch**, and set Angle to **Min Morph** and **Max Morph**.

9. Activate **Value 1** and **Value 2**.

10. For Value 1, set Angle to **–15.88**, Morph to **Control.Shoelace_LT**, and Percentage to **0%**.

11. For Value 2, set Angle to **–62**, Morph to **Control.Shoelace_LT**, and Percentage to **100%**.

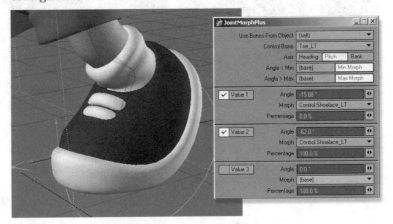

Figure 4.3-7. Joint Morph Plus settings for the left toe.

12. That looks pretty good, but I want the shoelace to be a little higher when the toe's bent, so switch back to Modeler and move the front laces up a touch. Switch back to Layout to check the results.

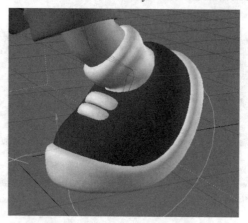

Figure 4.3-8. Shoelaces are looking good.

13. Switch back to Modeler and select just the right front shoelace.
14. **Copy Vertex Map**, calling the new morph **Control.Shoelace_RT**. Select **Control.Shoelace_LT** and **Clear Map**.

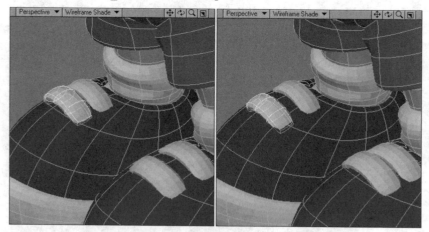

Figure 4.3-9. Left and right shoelace morphs.

15. Switch back to Layout and **Copy** and **Paste** the Joint Morph Plus entry.
16. Open the properties for the second Joint Morph Plus and change Control Bone to **Toe_RT** and the Value Morph entries to **Control.Shoelace_RT**.

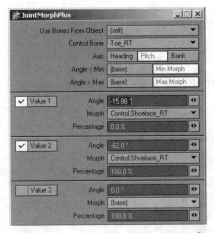

Figure 4.3-10. Joint Morph Plus settings for the right toe.

Shirt Deformation

You've probably noticed that the legs intersect the bottom of the shirt when they're raised. This can also be fixed using Joint Morph Plus. We'll also give the shirt some more detail at the bottom so we can create some wrinkles as it deforms.

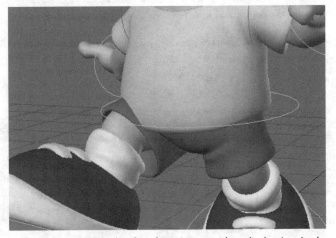

Figure 4.3-11. Notice the shirt doesn't move when the leg is raised.

1. Switch to Modeler and turn on **Symmetry**.
2. Select a couple of adjacent polygons on the bottom band of the shirt and select **BandSaw Pro**.
3. Create two segments at **50%** and **75%** (or 50% and 25%, whichever creates the segments closer to the top of the band).

> **Note:** Tools that cut polygon bands, such as BandSaw Pro and Cut, determine the direction of the bands by the order in which the polygons were selected. Selecting the polygons in the opposite order will reverse the percentages.

4. Adjust the points so the shirt maintains its original shape. It's often necessary to do this after cutting geometry, as the cuts follow the polygon cage, not the subpatched shape.

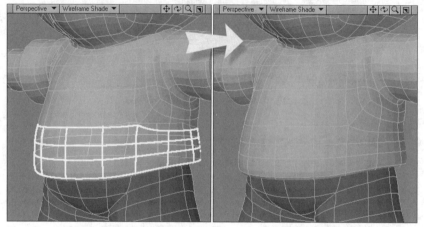

Figure 4.3-12. Adjust the points after BandSaw Pro to maintain the shape.

5. Create a new morph called **Control.Shirt_RT.** Because my poses have the right leg bent forward, I'll create and test the right morph first.

6. Select the polygons in the area that intersects with the leg and **Stretch** and adjust them, bending the bottom of the shirt.

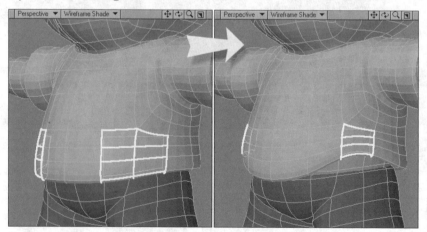

Figure 4.3-13. Raise the bottom of the shirt where the leg intersects.

7. Rotate the polygons, flaring out the area a little.

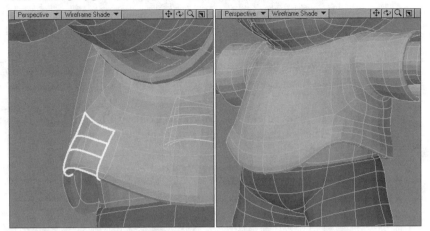

Figure 4.3-14. Flare the edges of the raised section.

8. That's a good starting point, so let's test the morph. Switch to Layout and select the **Leg_Upper01_RT** bone. To get the settings for Joint Morph Plus we need to find the point at which the leg starts to intersect the shirt. Find a frame where the leg is just touching the bottom of the shirt and make a note of the pitch rotation of the bone. In this case it's about **20°**. We know the forward limit of the bone is 0, which gives us both of the rotation values for Joint Morph Plus.

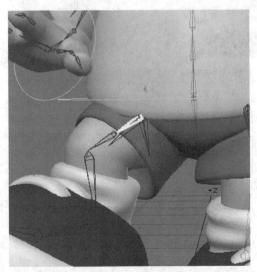

Figure 4.3-15. The upper leg at the first point of intersection.

9. Change to a frame with the leg rotated fully forward, select the **Hamish01** object, and open Object Properties.

10. In the Deform tab, **Add Displacement≻JointMorphPlus** and open the Joint Morph Plus properties.

11. Set Control Bone to **Leg_Upper01_RT**, change Axis to **Pitch**, and set Angle to **Min Morph** and **Max Morph**.

12. Activate **Value 1** and **Value 2**.

13. For Value 1, set Angle to **20**, Morph to **Control.Shirt_RT**, and Percentage to **0%**.

14. For Value 2, set Angle to **0**, Morph to **Control.Shirt_RT**, and Percentage to **100%**. The bottom of the shirt now moves up around the leg, but it still needs some adjusting.

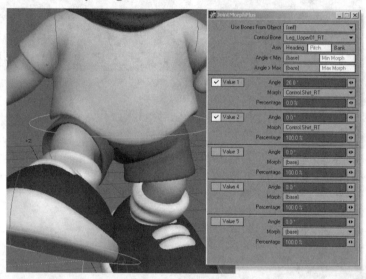

Figure 4.3-16. Joint Morph Plus settings for the right leg.

15. Switch back to Modeler and adjust the points so the shirt fits nicely around the leg, switching back to Layout to check the results.

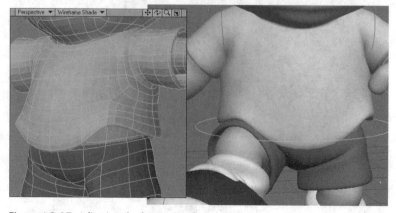

Figure 4.3-17. Adjusting the basic morph.

16. With the shirt conforming nicely to the leg, adjust the area around the bottom of the shirt to create some wrinkles, adjusting the points so the shirt behaves in the way you imagine a real shirt would in this situation. Remember to adjust the inside points of the shirt to compensate. You may find it useful to hide the body so you can select the inside of the shirt more easily.

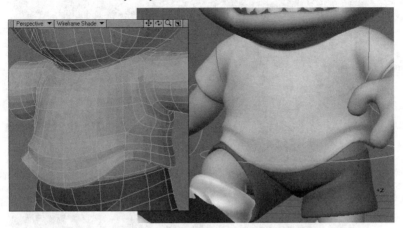

Figure 4.3-18. Finish the morph, creating wrinkles and detail.

17. Turn off Symmetry and select the polygons on the left side of the shirt. **Copy Vertex Map** and name the new morph **Control.Shirt_LT.**

18. Select **Control.Shirt_RT**, deselect the polygons along the center, and **Clear Map.**

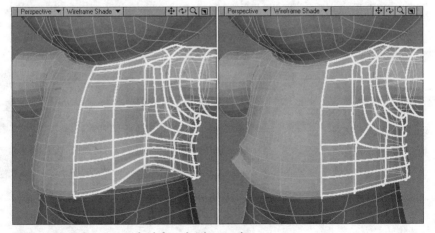

Figure 4.3-19. Separating the left and right morphs.

19. Switch back to Layout and **Copy** and **Paste** the Joint Morph Plus entry for **Leg_Upper01_RT.**

20. Open the properties for the new Joint Morph Plus entry and change the Control Bone to **Leg_Upper01_LT** and the Value Morph settings to **Control.Shirt_LT**.

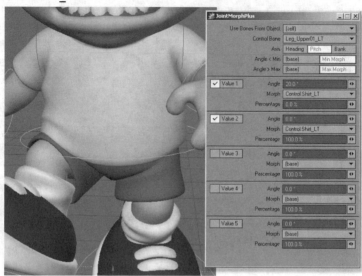

Figure 4.3-20. Joint Morph Plus settings for the left leg.

For even more control you can create morphs and use Joint Morph Plus again to adjust the shirt based on the H rotation of the hip bones. Keep in mind that the new morphs will be added to the existing ones, so don't include any upward motion — just sideways motion — to influence the existing shirt morphs.

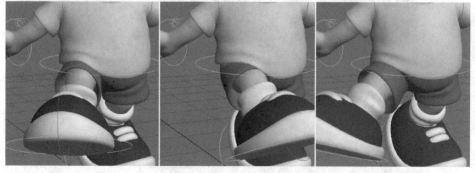

Figure 4.3-21. Additional morphs to adjust the shirt based on the hip rotation, or sideways motion, of the raised leg.

These morphs have been set up in the final Hamish rig so you can see how they're created. You can find the final Hamish rig in LWProjects\Scenes\Final\.

There are many other motion modifiers and deformation modifiers than have been covered here. Make sure you investigate all the modifiers available to you, as you never know when a modifier will come in handy for a specific character requirement. The next section describes some other uses of modifiers.

4.4 Alternate Rigging Techniques

Let's face it: All animators are individuals, and most have different preferences for animation controls. The basic control methods I've shown aren't necessarily the ideal ones for everyone. By understanding alternate control methods you have the ability to customize your rigs to your own animation style, but that's not the only reason to investigate alternate techniques.

It can be very difficult to create a character rig that covers all the possibilities of animating that character. While the default rig should handle most situations, if you were to include options for every possibility the rig would be very slow and unwieldy. It's far better to make specific alterations to a rig when they're needed for a specific shot.

When altering a rig, remember that control items should be kept to a minimum. Before adding a new control, first always see if an existing control can perform multiple duties. It's also very important when rigging to think outside the box. The less restricted you are by conventional thinking, the more flexibility and power you'll get from your rig.

You can find examples of the following techniques in Scenes\AlternateRigs\.

IK/FK Blending

If you want to use FK, it's best if you can use a single control method for each limb within each scene, either IK or FK. You can create multiple rigs for a character with different combinations of FK- and IK-controlled limbs for use in different scenes. There may be times though, where you want to switch control methods within a scene, or even use a combination of control methods at the same time. This is when multiple hierarchies come to the rescue.

The trickiest part of using multiple hierarchies for IK/FK blending is that the rotation of an item using Match Goal Orientation isn't recognized by expressions or modifiers. If your IK chain is using Match Goal Orientation, you need to do a couple of additional steps to work around this problem.

Multiple Hierarchies

When using multiple hierarchies, the primary hierarchy is animated using FK, and the secondary hierarchy uses IK or another control method.

This technique involves making a copy of the hierarchy or hierarchies for which you want to switch control methods. The original hierarchy uses FK and the copy's hierarchy uses IK. Once you have the two hierarchies set up, you need to add a control item to activate the blending, and link the rotation of the FK hierarchy to the IK hierarchy based on the position of the control item.

The arm hierarchy is a fairly complex IK chain due to the multiple IK goals: the FK elbow control and the wrist control. Applying IK/FK blending on simpler IK chains is a bit easier, but I'll show you how to apply IK/FK blending on the arm hierarchy so you can see how to accommodate these additional elements.

Copying the Hierarchy

The first step is to create the secondary hierarchy. The primary hierarchy is the original hierarchy. The secondary, copied hierarchy includes only the bones used in the IK solution, so once you've copied the hierarchy, you can remove the bones that aren't needed.

1. Load your Hamish rig into Layout (you can find a preprepared scene in \Scenes\Chapters\Hamish_Rig01_v007.lws). Save the scene under a different name, e.g., **Hamish_Rig01_IKBlend.lws.**

2. Select the **Shoulder_LT** bone and **Setup**▸**Edit**▸**Copy Hierarchy.**

3. In the CopyHierarchy panel, select **Yes** to copy targets, and choose **Add Suffix.** Enter **_IK** as the suffix name.

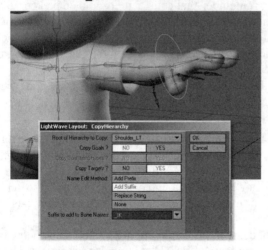

Figure 4.4-1. Copying the arm hierarchy.

4. The copied bones are the secondary hierarchy, so we don't need the entire hierarchy, just the IK bones. Open the Scene Editor, select all the bones under (children of) the **Hand_LT_IK** bone, and remove them (-).

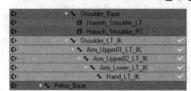

Figure 4.4-2. Remove the unnecessary bones.

5. Select the remaining bones of the new hierarchy and click in the **A** icon to deactivate them.

6. Select the **Shoulder_LT_IK** bone and, making sure Parent in Place is turned on, parent it to the **Shoulder_LT** bone.

7. Set the position to **0, 0, 0,** then reparent it to the **Back04** bone.

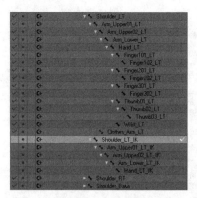

Figure 4.4-3. Final hierarchy.

8. Select the **Shoulder_LT** (not the IK bone) bone and open Motion Options to the Controllers and Limits tab. Set all the controllers to **Key Frames**.

9. Continue down the left arm bones to the hand, setting all the controllers to **Key Frames**.

10. When you reach the **Hand_LT** bone, switch to the IK and Modifiers tab. Turn off Full-time IK and Match Goal Orientation, and set Goal Object to **(none)**.

11. Select the **Arm_Upper01_LT** bone, turn off Full-time IK, and set Goal Object to **(none)**.

12. Select the **Arm_Upper01_LT_IK** bone and set Goal Object to **Hamish_Shoulder_LT** and turn on Full-time IK. Set Goal Strength to **100**.

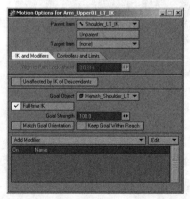

Figure 4.4-4. We need to change IK settings for both arm hierarches, changing the original hierarchy to FK and the new hierarchy to IK.

13. Select the **Hand_LT_IK** bone and set Goal Object to **Hamish_Hand_LT**, turn on Full-time IK and Match Goal Orientation, and set Goal Strength to **100**.

Figure 4.4-5. IK hand settings.

14. Select **Setup**➤**General**➤**Enable IK** (**Shift+F8**) and go to frame 10 or the first pose in the scene.

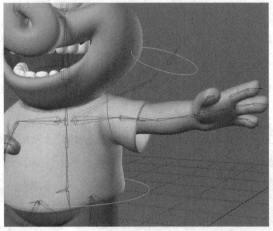

Figure 4.4-6. Notice the new arm hierarchy moves with the IK goals and the original arm hierarchy stays in place.

IK/FK Blending Expression

Let's take a look at the blending expression.

   (<Object.FK Bone>.rot(Time).<channel> * (1 – A)) +
      (<Object.IK Bone>.rot(Time).<channel> * A)

A is the position of the FK/IK blend control.

The expression is telling the item to follow the rotation of the FK bone when the IK/FK blend control (A) is at 0 and to follow the rotation of the IK bone when the IK/FK blend control is at 1. When the IK/FK blend control is between 0 and 1, the two rotations will be blended together.

Applying Modifiers

We want the bones in the FK hierarchy to follow their counterparts in the IK hierarchy based on the position of the IK/FK blend control. The exception to this is the elbow control. The elbow control bone of the IK hierarchy needs to inherit the rotation of its counterpart in the FK hierarchy.

1. Add a null (**Ctrl+n**) called **Hamish_IKArms** and turn off the X and Z channel controls. This is the IK/FK blend control.

2. Parent **Hamish_IKArms** to **Hamish_Master**.

3. Select the **Arm_Upper02_LT_IK** bone and **Add Modifier**➤**Follower**.

4. Set just the bank channel to follow the bank of **Arm_Upper02_LT**, and turn off After IK.

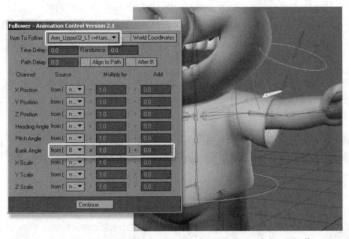

Figure 4.4-7. The IK now calculates with the rotation of the FK elbow control.

5. Select the **Shoulder_LT** bone and **Add Modifier**➤**Expression**.

6. Turn on **After IK** and enter the following expressions:

Scratch pad A:
   clamp(Hamish_IKArms.pos(Time).y, 0, 1)

Scratch pad B:
   (Hamish01.Shoulder_LT.rot(Time).h * (1 − A)) +
   (Hamish01.Shoulder_LT_IK.rot(Time).h * A)

Scratch pad C:
   (Hamish01.Shoulder_LT.rot(Time).p * (1 − A)) +
   (Hamish01.Shoulder_LT_IK.rot(Time).p * A)

Scratch pad D:
   (Hamish01.Shoulder_LT.rot(Time).b * (1 − A)) +
   (Hamish01.Shoulder_LT_IK.rot(Time).b * A)

Rotation.H: **B**, Rotation.P: **C**, Rotation.B: **D**

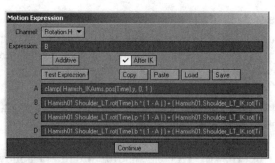

Figure 4.4-8. Expressions for Shoulder_LT.

7.   Close the Expression panel and **Copy** the expression entry.

8.   Select **Arm_Upper01_LT, Paste** the expression entry, and open its panel. Go through each scratch pad, changing Shoulder_LT to **Arm_Upper01_LT**, and Shoulder_LT_IK to **Arm_Upper01_LT_IK**.

> **Tip:**   A quick way to change the expressions is to change the first shoulder to Arm_Upper01. Select Arm_Upper01 and copy. Select each shoulder and Paste until they're all replaced.

9.   Select **Arm_Lower_LT, Paste** the expression entry, and edit each scratch pad, changing Shoulder_LT to **Arm_Lower_LT**, and Shoulder_LT_IK to **Arm_Lower_LT_IK**.

Now this may seem like a lot of work just for one arm, but once you get the hang of it, it only takes a couple of minutes. You can definitely see the benefit of using the scratch pads now. Changing the names for those expressions was much quicker since we used the scratch pads. Now let's see the results so far.

10.   Turn on the appropriate rotation channel controls for the FK hierarchy to allow posing.

11.   On frame 10, pose the arm using the FK hierarchy.

12.   Select **Hamish_IKArms** and press **Enter** twice to create a keyframe at frame 10.

13.   Go to frame 20 and set the Y position to **1**. Notice the arm switches to the IK position. Scrub the frames between 10 and 20 and see the arms blend from the FK rotation to the IK rotation.

This is all you need to do for some simple IK chains or if you're happy using FK control for the hand bone all the time. If you want the IK goal to determine the orientation of the hand bone when IK is active, there's a bit more work to do.

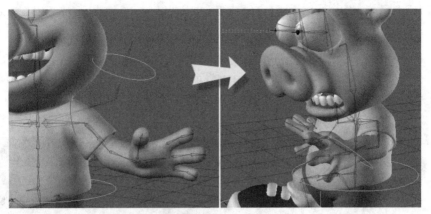

Figure 4.4-9. Left: FK control. Right: IK control.

Simple Orient Constraints

We'll use constraints to simulate Match Goal Orientation for the hand bone. While Match Goal Orientation is a better choice for full-time IK, the benefit of constraints is that they can be enveloped, so the modifier can be linked to the position of the IK blend control.

1. Select the **Hand_LT** bone and, in the Motion Options, **Add Modifier**➤ **SimpleOrientConstraints**.
2. Open the properties for the Orient Constraint and select **Add**, bringing up the control panel for the constraint.
3. Change the target item for H, P, and B to the **Hamish_Hand_LT** object.

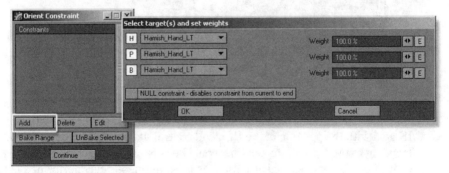

Figure 4.4-10. Adding a constraint to the hand bone.

4. Click the envelope icon (**E**) for H, which opens the Graph Editor. Click the envelope icons for P and B. Notice new channels have been created for the hand bone: Target1_Weight1, Target1_Weight2, and Target1_Weight3. Select **OK** on the constraint panel, closing it to enable working in the Graph Editor.

253

5. Select the three new channels for the hand bone and drag them up to the channel bin.

6. In the Expressions tab, create a new expression called **Hamish_IKArmBlend**. Enter the following expression for Value:
clamp (Hamish_IKArms.pos(Time).y, 0, 1)

7. Apply the expression to all three Target channels.

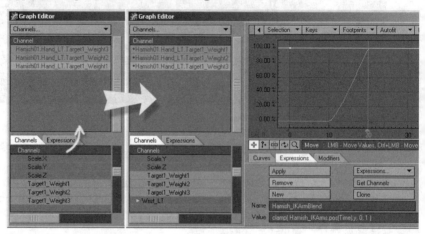

Figure 4.4-11. Applying the blend expression.

8. Close the Graph Editor and select **Edit** on the constraint properties to open the control panel. Make sure the Frame slider is set to **0** and close the panels.

Figure 4.4-12. The Frame slider tells the constraint when to come into effect.

The hand bone is now blending between its own rotation and the rotation of the IK goal with the position of the IK blend control. If you were applying IK/FK blending to the leg hierarchies this would be all you need to do, but the wrist control needs some special attention, as its targeting is being performed before the hand constraint.

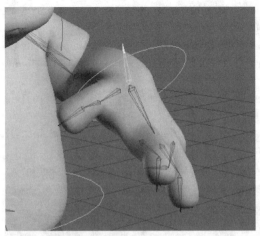

Figure 4.4-13. The hand is oriented to the IK goal, but the wrist targeting is incorrect.

Adjusting the Wrist Control

The current wrist control method doesn't work with constraints on the hand bone, so we'll set up a new wrist bone with some additional modifiers.

1. Select the **Wrist_LT** bone and **Clear Selected Items** (-), removing it from the scene.
2. Select the **Arm_Lower_LT** bone and create a child bone (=). Rename the new bone to **Wrist_LT**.
3. Open the Bone properties and set Bone Weight Map to **Arms** and turn off joint compensation settings. Turn off all the rotation channel controls.
4. Open the Motion Options and **Add Modifier➤Expression**, then enter the following expressions:

Scratch pad A:
   clamp(Hamish_IKArms.pos(Time).y, 0, 1)

Scratch pad B:
   Hamish01.Hand_LT.rot(Time).b * (1 – A)

Rotation.B:
   D

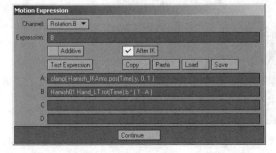

Figure 4.4-14. This expression tells the wrist to follow the bank of the hand bone when the IK/FK blend control is at 0, and to be at a value of 0 when the IK/FK blend control is at 1.

255

This sets up the condition for the FK control, but for the IK control we need to add another constraint.

5. **Add Modifier▷SimpleOrientConstraints** and open the properties.

6. Open the properties for the Orient Constraint and select **Add**, bringing up the control panel for the constraint.

7. Turn off the H and P settings, and change the target item for B to the **Hamish_Hand_LT** object.

8. Click the envelope icon (**E**) for B, opening the Graph Editor. Select **OK** on the constraint panel, closing it to enable working in the Graph Editor.

9. Apply the **Hamish_IKArmBlend** expression to the Target channel.

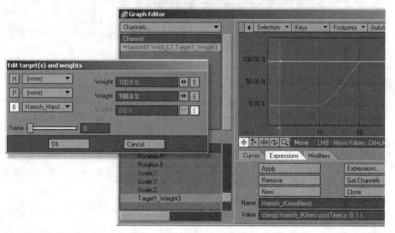

Figure 4.4-15. Applying the blended constraint to the wrist bone.

10. Close the Graph Editor and select **Edit** on the constraint properties to open the control panel. Make sure the Frame slider is set to **0** and close the panels.

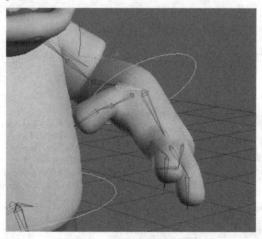

Figure 4.4-16. The wrist now rotates along with the hand.

Use the channels of the finger control so the controls are intuitive. I've offset the rotation of each finger using the bank of the control, and set it up so the fingers offset in the same direction as the control rotates.

You can use the scale channels of the control for even more variety. I don't recommend using the position channels, as it's best to keep the finger control in the same place so it's easily selected, and item moving has issues with the grid size that rotation and scale don't have. I've included the Y scale to independently adjust the rotation of the second finger joints.

Clamp the expressions for joints that are likely to rotate too far.

Using the example setup, you can pose the fingers in all sorts of ways by adjusting the four channels of the finger control.

Figure 4.4-23. These poses and many more are possible using the single finger control.

The pitch controls the bending of the fingers.

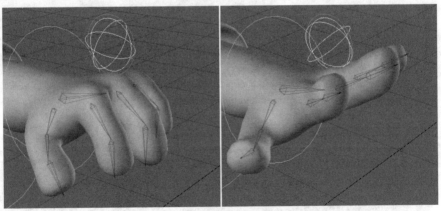

Figure 4.4-24. The second finger joints are clamped so they don't rotate backward with the first finger joints.

The heading controls the splay of the fingers.

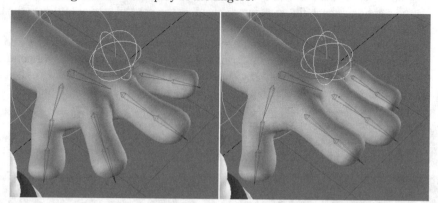

Figure 4.4-25. The heading of the control directs the heading of the fingers. Nice and intuitive.

The bank offsets the bend of each finger.

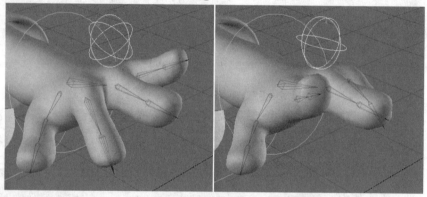

Figure 4.4-26. The bank is nice and intuitive too, rotating the fingers in the same direction.

The Y scale bends just the second finger joints.

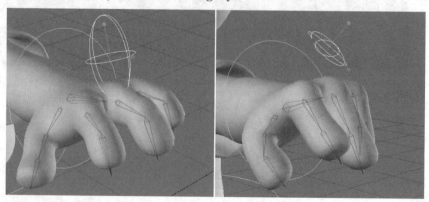

Figure 4.4-27. Scale gives you extra control of the second finger joints.

Taking It Further

It's easiest to include only four control channels, as that fills up the scratch pads. You can, however, add other channels; you just need to include the full channel name in the expression. Try adding the other two scale channels of the finger control into the mix to add more control and variety to the poses.

Sliders

Another way to control the fingers is by using sliders. You could attach the four control channels to sliders instead of rotating and scaling the control item itself.

Instead of controlling all the fingers at the same time, you could add separate controls for each finger. You can also attach these to sliders so you have slider control of each finger individually.

Remember to keep the scene efficient when using sliders. Don't add a separate item for every slider. Use all the channels available to you so you don't clutter up the scene. When you use a null object for slider control, you have nine channels available to you — three rotation, three position, and three scale. That means you can get nine different sliders out of each control null.

Hip Centering

Automatic hip centering should rarely, if ever, be used for character animation. The hip position has too many variables to control using simple calculations. The hips move in relation to the feet to maintain the center of gravity, but the center of gravity changes depending on whether the character is moving or posing in one spot. There is also the matter of height. There is no easy way to determine why a character is moving a foot up or down, and why they're doing it determines where the center of gravity is. This means that the intentions of the character largely determine the rules for the hip position, and you can't easily calculate a character's intentions using a mathematical equation.

One of the most common mistakes in 3D character animation is when hip centering has been used without offsetting it to maintain the center of gravity, resulting in unrealistic animation. If you choose to use hip centering for your character, it's vitally important to adjust the hip position to maintain the proper center of gravity.

There are two ways to use hip centering for your character: as a temporary guide for the hip position or for permanent automated hip positioning.

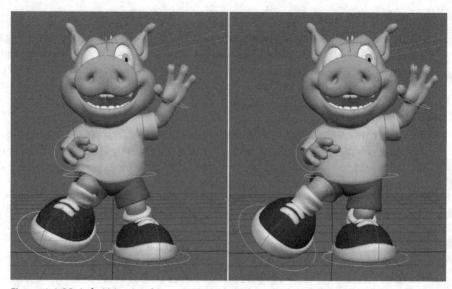

Figure 4.4-28. Left: Using just hip centering, Hamish is about to fall over. Right: Adjusted hip position to maintain the center of gravity.

Temporary Hip Centering

Hip centering as a temporary guide for positioning is the simplest application of hip centering, and the one I most recommend using. Doing this involves centering the Mover control between the feet using an expression, but having the expression turned off as a default. You can turn on the expression to quickly keyframe the basic hip positions for certain actions, then turn it off again to adjust the position of the hips. This is useful when the character needs to perform an action such as walking. You can turn on the expression so the hips stay between the moving feet, keyframe the hips, then turn the expression off to adjust the hip positions to where they should be.

Permanent Hip Centering

Permanent automated hip positioning is a bit more complex. You need to include an extra control for the hip centering, and parent the Mover control to it. You can then use the Mover control as an offset for the automated hip position to maintain the correct center of gravity. I don't recommend using this method of hip centering, because it requires just as much work to position the hips accurately as if you didn't use it and you still have to adjust the Mover control either way.

Hip Centering Expression

The expressions for hip centering are fairly simple. They merely position the hips halfway between the ankles. This is done with the following expressions:

Position.X channel:

> **center (<Left Ankle Control>.wpos(Time).x, <Right Ankle Control>.wpos(Time).x) – <Master Control>.pos(Time).x**

Position.Z channel:
> center (<Left Ankle Control>.wpos(Time).z, <Right Ankle
> Control>.wpos(Time).z) – <Master Control>.pos(Time).z

Rotation.H channel:
> center (<Left Foot Control>.rot(Time).h, <Right Foot
> Control>.rot(Time).h)

Foot Controls

The foot controls used for Hamish are intuitive and easy to use. They are also quite different from the reverse foot setup that many people recommend. The reverse foot setup has become somewhat of a standard when it comes to setting up the IK for the legs and feet, but that doesn't mean it's the best technique for controlling the feet. In fact, there's a fatal flaw in many implementations of the reverse foot setup. The reverse foot setup features the primary control — the pivot point for the foot — at the heel. There is usually a control that allows rotation at the ball of the foot, but in many cases it only allows for pitch, or up and down rotation, meaning the foot can't pivot sideways from the ball at all.

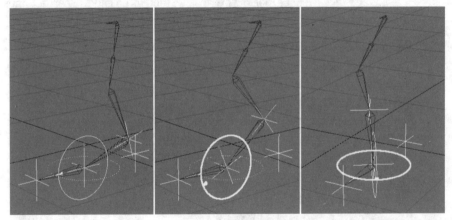

Figure 4.4-29. The classic reverse foot setup causes the toes to bend sideways when you pivot on the ball of the foot. Ouch!

The fact is that all creatures with feet pivot on the ball of the foot 99% of the time. That means that the primary pivot point for the foot controls should be at the ball of the foot, not at the heel as it is in the reverse foot setup. If you don't believe me, stand up and do a little waltz. Go on, humor me. Okay, now do the same dance, but only allow yourself to pivot on your heels. Feels awkward doesn't it? When you pivot on your heels your movements become almost robotic.

So why would you want the primary foot control at the heel of the foot, when it only makes it difficult, or impossible, to pivot on the ball of the foot? The reason is for animating a walk. When we walk, the foot lands on the heel and rotates from the heel to become flat on the ground. Animating a walk cycle is one of the only times that having control from the heel of the foot is useful, which is why I recommend the reverse foot setup as an alternative technique.

It's a control method that should only be used when required, not as a default, since even a walk cycle can easily be animated using my standard foot setup.

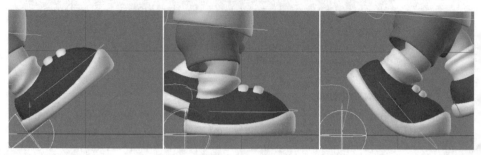

Figure 4.4-30. Walk cycle using the reverse foot setup.

The trouble is that having the primary foot control at the heel can restrict the ability to rotate on the ball of the foot, unless you set it up right. Even when it is set up right, animating the feet usually involves a lot more work when you use the reverse foot setup.

So let's take a closer look at the reverse foot setup and the correct, most efficient way to set it up so it provides the necessary control.

Reverse Foot Setup

The reverse foot setup involves four foot controls: the heel, the ball, the toe, and the ankle.

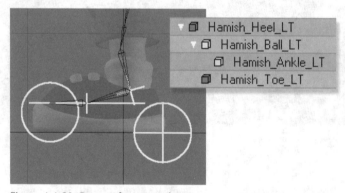

Figure 4.4-31. Reverse foot controls.

The heel control is placed at the point where the character's heel touches the floor. The ball control is placed at the base of the toe bone, where the foot and toe bones meet. The ankle control is placed at the base of the foot, where the foot and lower leg bones meet. The toe control is placed toward the front of the foot.

The heel is the master foot control. The ball and toe are parented to the heel, and the ankle is parented to the ball.

The toe bone requires an expression so it follows the rotation of the toe control. You should not use Match Goal Orientation or targeting for the toe bone, because it should only be allowed to rotate on the pitch axis, and Match Goal Orientation and targeting will cause it to rotate on all axes. Also, as we've discovered, Match Goal Orientation doesn't allow full control of the deformation of the toe joint. So to simulate Match Goal Orientation for just the pitch axis, the following expression should be applied to the pitch axis of the toe bone:

<Toe Control>.rot(Time).p – <Ball Control>.rot(Time).p +
<Pitch Rest Rotation>

This expression means the toe bone will retain its rotation as you rotate the pitch of the ball control, but the toe will follow with the heading rotation of the ball control. You could do a similar offset expression for the bank so the ball of the foot can rotate on its bank without affecting the toe rotation.

The heel control is used to position and rotate the foot.

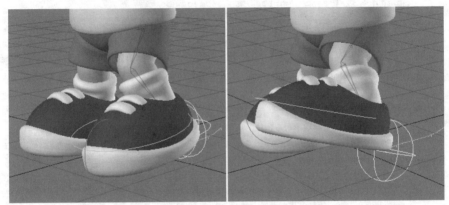

Figure 4.4-32. The heel is the primary foot mover.

The ball control is used to offset the rotation of the foot from the heel rotation, leaving the toe in place when rotated on its pitch.

Figure 4.4-33. The ball control pivots from the ball of the foot, allowing up, down, and sideways rotation.

The toe control is used to tweak or offset the toe from the heel rotation.

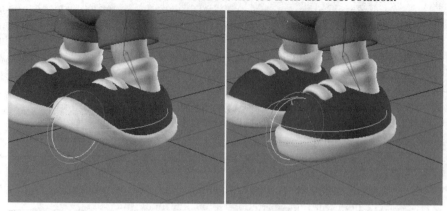

Figure 4.4-34. The toe control adjusts the toe rotation.

The ankle control is only used for IK, so it should be locked and hidden.

The heading rotation of the ball control can be used to pivot sideways on the ball of the foot, but when you change the position of the foot using the heel control you should reset the heading of the ball control at the new pose or position.

Spine Controls

The spine is usually best left to manual control. You can select all the spine bones and rotate them in unison or rotate individual spine bones to create more complex poses.

The chest control allows you to pose all the spine bones at once using a single control, but doesn't easily allow bones to be individually rotated for more complex poses. The chest control can simplify the animation process for simple characters or be used to quickly rough in the basic spine poses.

Chest Control

The chest control involves an animation control for the chest and expressions for the spine bones.

Figure 4.4-35. Rotating the chest control bends the entire spine.

The chest control is parented to the Mover control. The second back bone follows the rotation of the chest control, with some notable adjustments. Because the back bones and the chest control have different orientations, the bone channels must follow different chest control channels. Let's look at the expressions for the second back bone:

Rotation.H channel:

<Chest Control>.rot(Time).b / 3

Rotation.P channel:

<Chest Control>.rot(Time).p / 3

Rotation.B channel:

<Chest Control>.rot(Time).h / 3

You will also need to adjust for any offset rotation of the chest bone to make sure the bone rotates in the same direction as the chest control. This might mean negating some of the expressions or even adjusting some plus or minus 180°, depending on the rotation of the back bone in relation to the chest control. Experiment with the rotations to see if the expressions need adjusting.

To make the bone rotate in the opposite direction, divide by –3 instead of 3, e.g.:

<Chest Control>.rot(Time).b / –3

If the bone flips around 180°, add –180 to the expression before the division, e.g.:

(<Chest Control>.rot(Time).h – 180) / 3

The division by 3 is so the three upper back bones add up to the same rotation as the chest control. If you have more or less than four back bones, change this number to the number of back bones minus one.

The third and fourth back bones can use an expression or follower to inherit the rotation of the second back bone.

You can also parent the hand controls to the chest instead of the Mover so the hands follow the position of the chest as it rotates the spine.

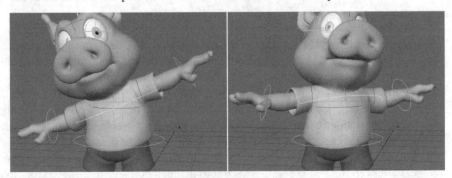

Figure 4.4-36. The hands follow the chest position when the hand controls are parented to the chest control.

Head Control

Because the head is at the top of the spine, it moves and rotates with the spine. If the spine twists or rotates, the head needs to counter-rotate to keep it pointed in the same direction. This means that in reality, head rotation is never absolutely steady, so to maintain maximum believability in our animation it's best to animate the rotation of the head manually. This is quite easy to do, especially since you only have to rotate one animation control — the head bone.

The alternative is to have the head point toward a target. Although it can result in less believable animation, there are times when having the head point toward a target can be useful, especially for cartoon animation. The other disadvantage to targeting the head is that you need to animate two controls instead of one, as targeting only works on two axes. You need to move the head target control, which rotates the head on the heading and the pitch axes, and rotate the bank of the head bone manually for the third axis of rotation.

Targeting the Head

To target the head you need to slightly modify the bone setup and include a target control for the head.

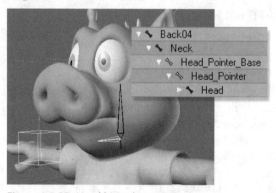

Figure 4.4-37. Head hierachy.

The base head bone is parented to the neck and rotated to point forward. The base bone orients the rotation of the pointer bone so that targeting works predictably. The pointer bone is parented to the base head bone and performs the targeting. The head bone is parented to the pointer, so it inherits the targeted rotation.

Some targeted head setups don't have a separate head bone, instead only using the pointer bone or equivalent. This is restricting because you can't adjust the automated rotation without moving the head target control. It's best to include or keep the additional head bone. Apart from making it easy to add to the existing rig, the head bone allows you to manually offset the targeted rotation if you need to, so you're not restricted to only pointing the head toward the target.

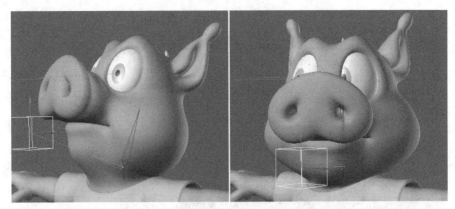

Figure 4.4-38. The head follows the target.

Figure 4.4-39. The additional head bone allows you to offset the head position from the target.

4.5 Quadruped Rigging

Rigging quadrupeds isn't very different from rigging bipeds. There are some differences in the bone structure and control methods, but the basic principles are the same.

Once you've done your research and studied the anatomy and other characteristics of the animal, you're ready to start rigging. This chapter explains the basics of rigging a quadruped using Hamish's rig as a starting point. This will help demonstrate the differences between bipeds and quadrupeds while also showing you how to use the character setup tools to convert and adjust an existing rig for a different character.

LightWave 8's rig files make it easy to apply and adjust a rig for different characters. You can save an entire rig or individual hierarchies in the rig format, along with bone settings, IK settings, IK goals, and targets. Before mirroring the rig for Hamish we saved the rig file. We'll use that rig file now to apply the rig to a quadruped.

The character we're rigging is Jack the dog. The model of Jack was created, and kindly donated, by William "Proton" Vaughan.

Importing a Rig

The first step is to import and adjust an existing rig. If your character is similar to the one the rig file was created from, adjusting the rig is very simple. Since we're converting the rig to a quadruped rig, there are a few more steps involved.

I've preprepared some files for you: a scene with the Jack model ready to be rigged and a rig file ready to be converted.

1. Load **\Scenes\Chapters\ProtonJack.lws**.
2. Select **Setup≻Edit≻Import RIG, Browse Rig File** and find **\Scenes\Chapters\ProtonJack.rig**. Select **YES** to all options, and **Replace String**, replacing **Hamish** with **Jack**.

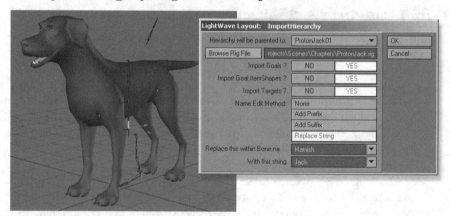

Figure 4.5-1. The imported rig is the Hamish rig without arms or eye bones. To save some steps I removed them from the rig file, as they won't be needed.

3. Select the **ProtonJack01** object and select **Setup**≻**Modify**≻**Scale Hierarchy**, selecting **Yes** to the requester.

4. Scale the rig up until the pelvis is just under the top of the back and press **Spacebar** to confirm the scale.

5. Select the **Back01** and **Pelvis_Base** bones and move them in Z to the pivot of the pelvis, or just at the front of the back leg.

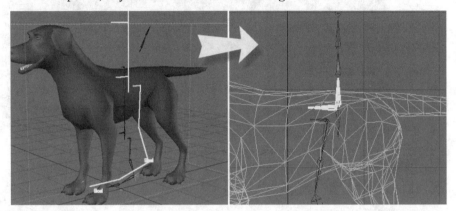

Figure 4.5-2. Selecting the object allows you to scale the entire rig. Selecting a bone will just scale its hierarchy.

6. We need to rotate the pelvis 180°, but that will adversely affect the leg bones, so open Scene Editor and parent **Hip_LT** to the **ProtonJack01** object, then set the heading of **Pelvis_Base** to **0**.

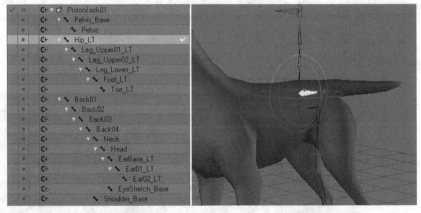

Figure 4.5-3. Adjusting the pelvis.

7. Move **Hip_LT** to the pivot point of the back leg, as shown in Figure 4.5-4.

8. Set the Bank rotation of Hip_LT to **0**, then go down the leg hierarchy, setting the heading and bank channels of each bone to **0** and aligning the bones in a straight line.

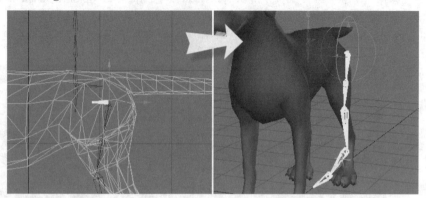

Figure 4.5-4. Preparing the leg hierarchy.

9. Select **Object** mode and select **Setup➤Modify➤Tip Move (Ctrl+t)**. In the Right view, use RMB to drag the knee joint just inside the leg. Use LMB to drag the ankle and foot joints into place. When you get to the tip of the toe, use RMB to drag it just inside the toe geometry, keeping its angle.

> **Tip:** Tip Move moves the tip and all the bones under the tip, just like moving skelegons. This is a quick way to reposition bones without affecting the orientation of bones lower in the hierarchy. Joint Move moves the joints without moving the bones lower in the hierarchy, like dragging skelegons. You can use both tools to adjust the bones. It's good to start by doing the major bone positioning with Tip Move, then tweak the joint positions using Joint Move.

10. Drag the joints of the back and head into the positions shown in Figure 4.5-5. Press **Spacebar** to confirm when you're finished.

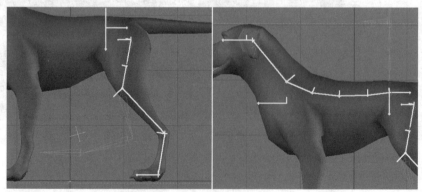

Figure 4.5-5. Adjusting the bone positions.

11. Notice after the bones are repositioned that Foot_LT is on the wrong pitch angle. Open Motion Options and turn off **Match Goal Orientation** to fix it.

12. Select **Hip_LT** and move it in X so the leg bones are in the center of the leg.

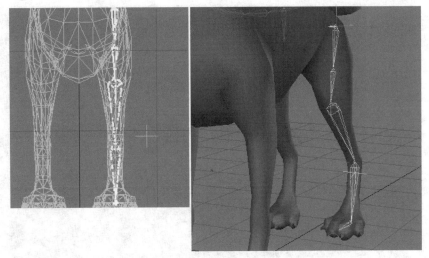

Figure 4.5-6. Positioning the leg hierarchy.

Creating the Arm Bones

We need to copy the leg bones and reposition them for the arm (foreleg). It's easier to do this than adjust Hamish's original arm hierarchy, as the leg hierarchy already has the correct controls set up.

1. Select **Leg_Upper01_LT** and **Setup➤Edit➤Copy Hierarchy**. Choose **YES** to Goals and Item Shapes and **Replace String**, replacing **Leg** with **Arm**.

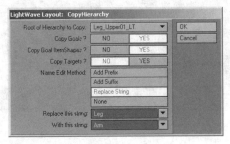

Figure 4.5-7. Copy Hierarchy settings.

2. From the Right view, move **Arm_Upper01_LT** to the top of the shoulder. Use **Tip Move** on the object and move the arm bones into place. Notice the positions are quite different. Also, drag the tip of **Shoulder_Base** to the same angle as the first arm bone.

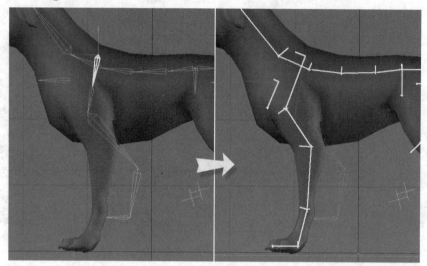

Figure 4.5-8. Adjusting the arm bones.

3. Move **Shoulder_Base** up to **Back04**, then move **Arm_Upper01_LT** in X so its base is just inside the shoulder.

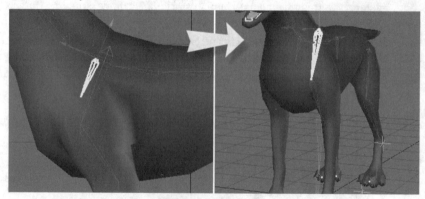

Figure 4.5-9. Adjusting the shoulder bones.

4. Select **Tip Move** and, from the Back view, move the first joint of the arm so the lower bones are centered in the leg.

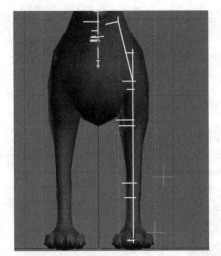

Figure 4.5-10. Positioning the arm hierarchy.

5. Adjust the ear bones to fit the ear.

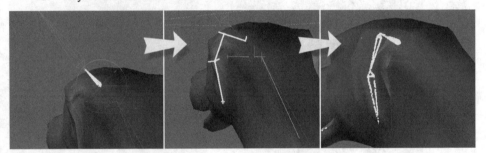

Figure 4.5-11. Positioning the ear bones.

6. Select **EyeStretch_Base** and set its position to **0, 0, 0.**

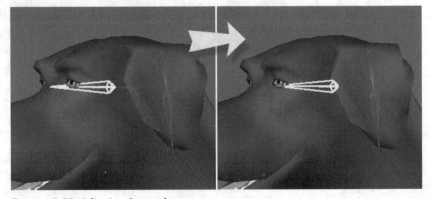

Figure 4.5-12. Adjusting the eye bone.

Adjusting the Rig

With the bones in place, we need to do some organizing. Most of these steps are concerned with converting the biped rig to a quadruped rig.

Renaming

We'll rename some of the bones and controls so they make more sense for a four-legged character.

1. Open Scene Editor and expand **ProtonJack01**. Notice there are some bones and controls with duplicate names. Change the control and bone names to those shown in Figure 4.5-13.

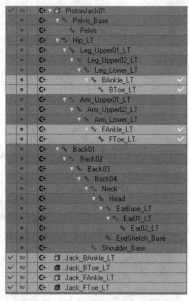

Figure 4.5-13. Rename duplicate items.

2. Rename Head to **Head_Base** and rename EyeStretch_Base to **Head**.

Figure 4.5-14. Rename the head bones.

278

Positioning Controls

First we need to position the controls that were imported with the rig.

1. We need to parent the goals to the bones to position them, but that won't work while the bones are using the controls as goal objects. Set Goal Object to **(none)** for all the ankle and toe bones, then parent each control object to the same named bone.

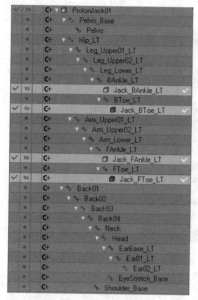

Figure 4.5-15. Parenting to set the initial control position.

2. Select all the control objects, select **Move (t)** and **Modify⟩General⟩ Reset**, then select **Rotate (y)** and **Reset**. This is a quick way to set the position and rotation of each item to 0, 0, 0.

Figure 4.5-16. Reset position and rotation.

Additional Controls

Now we need to create the additional controls that weren't imported with the rig.

1. Add two nulls, calling them **Jack_Master** and **Jack_Mover**.
2. Clone **Jack_BAnkle_LT** and **Jack_FAnkle_LT**. Rename the clones **Jack_BFoot_LT** and **Jack_FFoot_LT**.
3. Turn off **Parent in Place** and parent **Jack_Mover** to **Pelvis_Base**.

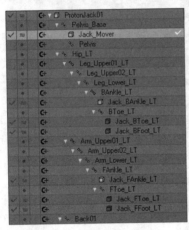

Figure 4.5-17. Adding controls.

Final Hierarchies

Now let's set up the final hierarchies. Turn Parent in Place back on for the following steps.

1. Parent **Jack_Mover, Jack_BFoot_LT,** and **Jack_FFoot_LT** to **Jack_Master**.
2. Parent **ProtonJack01** to **Jack_Mover**.
3. Parent **Jack_BAnkle_LT** and **Jack_BToe_LT** to **Jack_BFoot_LT**, and parent **Jack_FAnkle_LT** and **Jack_FToe_LT** to **Jack_FFoot_LT**.

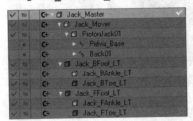

Figure 4.5-18. Final control hierarchy.

4. Parent **Hip_LT** to **Pelvis_Base**.
5. Parent **Arm_Upper01_LT** to **Shoulder_Base**.

2. Select **Shoulder_LT** and **Mirror Hierarchy** using the same settings.

3. Select **Ear_Base_LT** and **Mirror Hierarchy**. Choose **YES** to Mirror Goals and Item Shapes, and replace _LT with **_RT**.

4. Select **Jack_BFoot_LT** and **Jack_FFoot_LT** and **Items**≻**Add**≻**Mirror** (**Shift+v**). Rename the mirrored items from _LT to **_RT**.

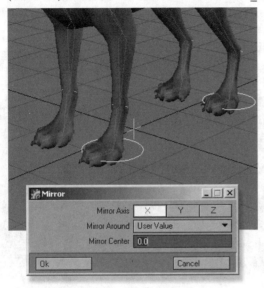

Figure 4.5-30. Mirror foot controls.

5. Parent the right ankle and toe controls to the appropriate right foot controls.

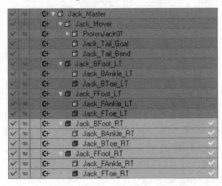

Figure 4.5-31. Reparent the right ankle and toe controls.

6. Check that the item shapes are the same for the controls on both sides.

Creating the Tail

We'll create a simple IK chain for the tail. We can use the bone tools to create this quickly and easily.

Creating the Bones

By using Bone Split we can quickly create a chain of bones for the tail that all inherit the settings of the original bone.

1. Select **Pelvis_Base** and create a child bone called **Tail**.
2. Move the tail bone to the base of the tail, then **Tip Move** and use the RMB to drag the tip to the end of the tail.

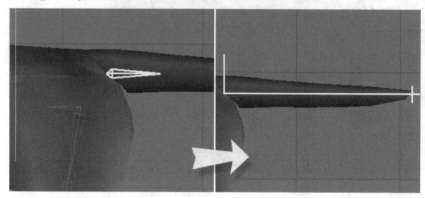

Figure 4.5-32. Creating the initial tail bone.

3. Open the Bone properties. Assign the **Tail** weight map and set the strength to **100**.
4. Open Motion Options and set the Heading and Pitch controllers to **Inverse Kinematics**.
5. Select **Bone Split** and create six collinear bones. Rename the tail bones **Tail01** to **Tail06** to maintain the naming convention.

C+	⌄ ⚲ Tail01	✓
C+	⌄ ⚲ Tail02	✓
C+	⚲ Tail03	✓
C+	⚲ Tail04	✓
C+	⚲ Tail05	✓
C+	⚲ Tail06	✓

Figure 4.5-33. Notice the new tail bones retain the properties and the IK settings of the original bone. This makes it nice and quick to set up simple IK chains.

6. Select **Tail06** and add a child bone called **Tail07**.

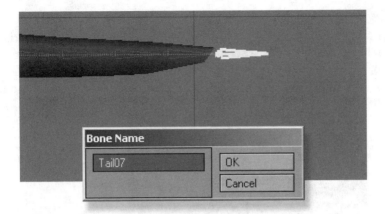

Figure 4.5-34. This bone is the IK goal for the tail.

7. Add two nulls called **Jack_Tail_Goal** and **Jack_Tail_Bend**.

8. Turn **Parent in Place** off and parent **Jack_Tail_Goal** to the **Tail07** bone, and parent **Jack_Tail_Bend** to the **Tail04** bone.

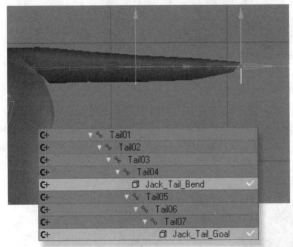

Figure 4.5-35. Adding the IK controls.

9. Turn **Parent in Place** on and parent both tail controls to **Jack_Mover**.

Figure 4.5-36. Final tail control hierarchy.

IK Settings

There isn't much to do here, as many of the IK settings have been inherited from the original bone. We'll set up some stiffness so the joints in the tail rotate nicely, and we need to give the tail some IK goals.

1. Select **Tail01** and open Motion Options. Set the Heading and Pitch stiffness to **100**.

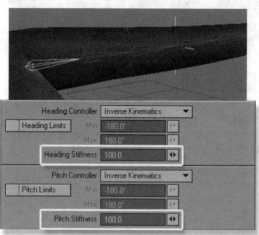

Figure 4.5-37. Setting stiffness values.

2. Select **Tail02** and set the stiffness for both Heading and Pitch to **30**.
3. Select **Tail04** and set the stiffness for both Heading and Pitch to **20**.
4. Select **Tail05** and set the stiffness for both Heading and Pitch to **10**.
5. Select **Tail07** and set Goal Object to **Jack_Tail_Goal** with Full-time IK on and Goal Strength of **100**.

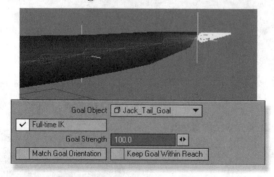

Figure 4.5-38. IK settings for the tip.

6. Select **Tail04** and set Goal Object to **Jack_Tail_Bend** with Full-time IK on and Goal Strength of **50**.

1. On frame **0**, select the **Hamish_Mover** object and press **Enter**. Deselect all the scale channels by pressing the **Scale** heading, and press **OK**.

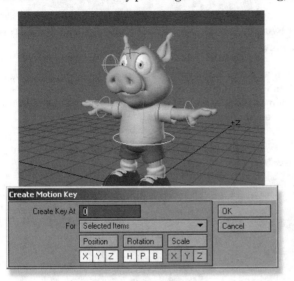

Figure 5.1-4. Set just the position and rotation keyframe channels for Hamish_Mover.

2. Create a keyframe on frame 0 for each of the active (non-locked) animation controls, deselecting the appropriate channels (the channels that aren't regularly used) for each item.

3. Do the same for all of the manually adjustable bones, basically replicating the channel control settings.

Preparing the Final Rig

The rig is now complete. The final step is to prepare the rig for loading into animation scenes. This is another very important step, for which the animators will thank you.

The first step is to delete all the extra keyframes. If you include any poses or extraneous keyframes in the final rig, each time it's loaded into an animation scene, the animator needs to delete those poses or keyframes, which becomes very frustrating.

The exception is when the rig needs some extra keyframes, if Cyclist (a motion modifier) is being used, or there are other keyframed events, such as envelopes on textures or other areas. If this is the case, delete all the keyframes *except* the required ones.

The next step is to delete any extra items in the scene so the only objects in the scene are the character master control and its children. If your character has lights attached, then you also need to delete all the other lights in the scene so you can load the lights with the character when you select Load From Scene. If the character doesn't include any lights, you can leave the lights in the scene and choose not to import the lights with the character.

1. Save the scene as **Hamish_Rig01_Poses.lws** so you don't lose the poses you've created already.

2. Select **Plugs➤Additional➤Motify** and change Delete Mode to **Delete Keys Within Range**, deleting keys from **1** through **60** for **All Items** and all channels, including **All Other Channels**.

> **Note:** Choosing All Other Channels also deletes the keyframes for Morph Mixer, so you don't have to delete those manually. If you have keyframed enve- lopes for automated motion or effects, don't choose All Other Channels; instead delete the additional keyframes for Morph Mixer manually.

3. Clear **Main Null** from the scene. Since there are no lights attached to Hamish, choose **NO** to clearing descendants.

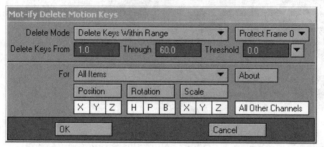

Figure 5.1-5. Mot-ify Delete settings.

4. Select the **Hamish01** object and open the Object Properties panel.

5. Change Display SubPatch Level to **2** and Render SubPatch Level to **4**.

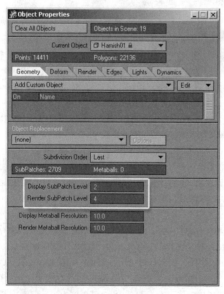

Figure 5.1-6. Create a few test renders of the character at different render subpatch levels to determine the optimum default value. The default value should be just high enough so no individual polygons are visible and there is no stepping around the edge of the character when rendered in a full body view at the final resolution. The render subpatch level can be adjusted for different shots, increasing it for close-ups or decreasing it for distant shots.

6. Save the scene as **Hamish_Rig01.lws**. This is the final rig scene used for loading into animation scenes.

7. If you've used preprepared scenes up to this point, select **Hamish01** and save current object, saving as **\Objects\Hamish01.lwo**.

Congratulations! The primary rig is now complete and ready for animation. These final steps are never fun, but the extra work definitely pays off in the end. I call this the primary rig because there are still some additions you can make to the rig described in the following chapters, but I usually create alternate versions of the primary rig for those additions.

5.2 Body Animation

It's best to start with the body animation when animating a character. The body attitude, poses, and motion convey a great deal about the intent of the character. The aim is for the body to tell the story as much as possible. You should be able to watch the body animation without any facial animation at all and know exactly what the character is feeling. Once that's accomplished, the facial animation is the icing on the cake.

> **Note:** Whether you're animating for yourself or a director, it's important to observe the order in which each animation pass is created. The director or lead animator usually reviews the animation after each pass. The order outlined in the following chapters makes sure that any changes that may be required after each review have the least impact on the existing animation, making it relatively quick and easy to implement the changes without having to redo too much work.

A common mistake is to leave too much acting to the facial animation, creating ambiguous body animation that really doesn't reflect the emotion or intent of the character. We notice the body language of a character before noticing the facial expressions, so if the body language doesn't reflect the intent or emotion of the character the audience can be left confused as to what the character is doing. If you can tell what the character is doing and feeling just by watching the body animation, then you can be confident that you're telling the story well.

I nearly always act out a scene before I start animating, and quite a few times while I'm animating. While the neighbors think I'm a bit crazy, jumping around the backyard talking or singing to myself, it's the best way to work out the poses and motions, the timing for the motions, and how the body weight shifts between and during those poses.

If you can record yourself acting out the scene, that's even better. When acting out the scene over and over, there's a risk that the motions and timing might lose their spontaneity. If you have a video camera and record yourself acting out the scene, you can play it back as many times as you need, so the performance doesn't become too rehearsed.

Posing the Character

You've already played with the controls when creating the poses for testing the rig and deformations, so you should have a pretty good idea of what they all do. Here's a detailed explanation of the controls, together with some tips on how to use them to make the animation process quick and efficient.

Positioning the Character

The Master control positions the entire character and its animation within a scene. In most cases you only need to position this once when you first import the character into a scene.

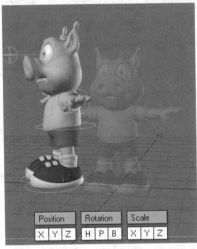

Figure 5.2-1. The Master control can move, rotate, and scale.

The other benefit to the Master control is that it allows easy organization of the objects in the Scene Editor. Because the character and all its controls are parented to the Master control, you can collapse the Master control for all the characters in a scene when they're not being animated, and just expand the Master control for each character while you're animating it. This means you can easily see and access the entire scene in the Scene Editor even if you have many characters in a scene.

The Master control is also used to adjust the size or scale of a character. If you've created the character at the correct scale, then you should rarely need to adjust the scale of the character during animation, but it can be useful to enhance a shot. Remember to use the alternate eye stretch expression (see Chapter 4, "Advanced Rigging") if the character needs to adjust scale often.

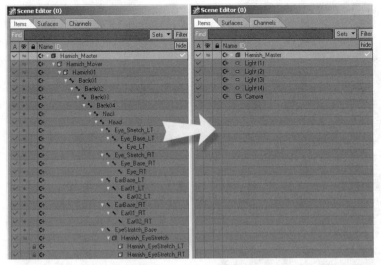

Figure 5.2-2. Collapse the Master control when you're not using the character to keep the items managable in the Scene Editor.

Positioning the Torso

The Mover control positions the torso by moving the character object. The foot and eye target controls are parented to the Master control, so the Mover control moves the torso independently of the feet and eye direction.

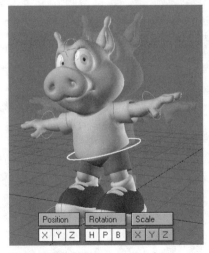

Figure 5.2-3. The Mover control can move and rotate.

You can also parent the hand controls to the Master control so the Mover control moves the torso independently of the feet, eyes, and hands.

Figure 5.2-4. With the hand controls parented to the Master control, the hands stay in place as the body moves.

Note: You can move the entire character without affecting the existing animation by selecting the Mover and foot controls and moving them together.

Posing the Torso

The back bones pose the torso. The first back bone, Back01, is positioned by the Mover control, so only Back02, Back03, and Back04 should be rotated.

Figure 5.2-5. The back bones can rotate on all axes.

You can select all the back bones to pose them together, or pose each one individually to create more complex poses.

Posing the Head

The neck and head bones pose the head. Keep in mind when posing the head that it can't rotate without the neck also rotating, so it's a good idea to rotate the neck and head bones together to rough out the pose, then adjust each one individually if necessary.

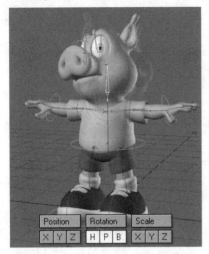

Figure 5.2-6. The neck and head bones can rotate on all axes.

Since the rotation channels of the neck and head match the spine, you can also rotate the spine, neck, and head together to rough out the pose.

Posing the Pelvis

The Pelvis_Base bone poses the pelvis. You can rotate it in any direction to offset the hips from the torso.

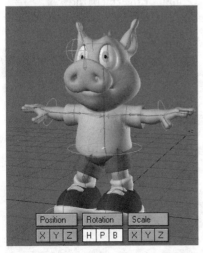

Figure 5.2-7. The Pelvis_Base bone usually rotates in bank but can also rotate on the other axes.

Using the pelvis is very important when posing a character. It's fairly rare that the pelvis stays straight in any pose or animation. It's especially important to use the pelvis when a character walks. A walking motion without the pelvis rotating appears mechanical and lifeless.

Posing the Legs and Feet

The foot controls position the feet. The legs are controlled using IK, so positioning the foot moves the leg to match the foot position. Try not to place the foot in a position that the leg finds it difficult or impossible to reach, or you may have problems with the IK solution.

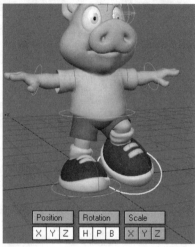

Figure 5.2-8. The foot controls can move and rotate.

The toe controls bend the toes. The toe controls mainly rotate on the pitch axis, but can also rotate on the bank axis to account for the roll of the foot.

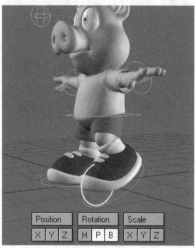

Figure 5.2-9. The toe control usually rotates in pitch but can also rotate in bank.

The heading rotation of the hip bones positions the knees. The hip bones can be the trickiest of all the bones to select in the viewport. When using the viewport for selection, it can be easier to select an upper leg bone, then press the Up Arrow key to cycle up the bone list to the hip. Otherwise, the Scene Editor or a character picker provides quick access to the hip bones.

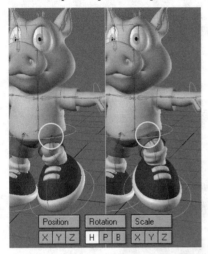

Figure 5.2-10. The hip bones manually rotate in heading only.

Use the bank of the Leg_Upper02 bone to tweak the knee position in extreme poses where the groin area deforms too much using just the hip bone.

Posing the Arms and Hands

The hand controls position the hands. The arms are controlled using IK, so positioning the hand moves the arm to match the hand position. Try not to place the hand in a position that the arm finds it difficult or impossible to reach, or you may have problems with the IK solution.

Figure 5.2-11. The hand controls can move and rotate.

Because of the range of motion of the hands, it is difficult to use the hand controls without running into gimbal lock or resorting to local coordinates. This is a good example of using the rotation axis hierarchy to our benefit. If you follow these steps, you'll have predictable hand motion no matter how it's posed:

1. Move the hand control into place.
2. Rotate the **heading** until the control is aligned with the forearm, so the arrow on the heading rotation handle points in the same direction as the forearm.
3. Rotate the **pitch** to determine the vertical rotation of the hand.
4. Rotate the **bank** to determine the roll of the hand.

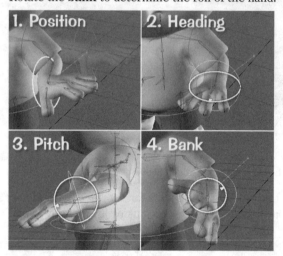

Figure 5.2-12. Position the hand controls in the right order to maintain predictable motion.

The bank rotation of the Arm_Upper02 bone positions the elbow.

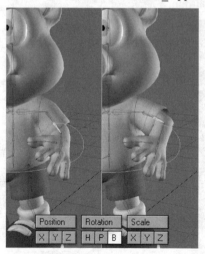

Figure 5.2-13. The Arm_Upper02 bone rotates in bank only.

You can also adjust the bank of the Arm_Upper01 bone if the upper arm becomes too twisted using just the Arm_Upper02 bone.

Posing the Shoulders

The shoulder controls position the shoulders.

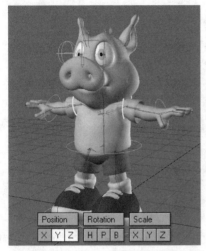

Figure 5.2-14. The shoulder controls can move in Y and Z.

The bank rotation of the Shoulder_Base bone moves both shoulders at the same time so the shoulder bones maintain a straight line.

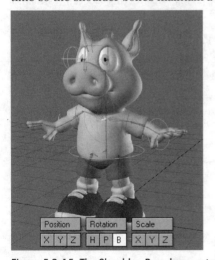

Figure 5.2-15. The Shoulder_Base bone rotates in bank only.

Posing the Fingers

The finger and thumb bones pose the fingers. It's often useful to select multiple finger bones and rotate them together before tweaking the rotation of each bone individually. Just remember that when making a fist, the finger joints don't all rotate by the same amount.

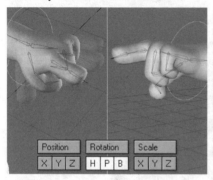

Figure 5.2-16. The finger bones rotate only. Different finger bones can rotate on different axes.

Once you have a few poses for the fingers, or even just an open hand and a fist, you can quickly rough out the other finger poses by moving to a frame that has the fingers posed closest to how you want them (this can be a frame where the fingers have keyframes or in-betweens) and creating a keyframe for the hand bone, choosing the frame for the new pose and selecting Current Item and Descendants.

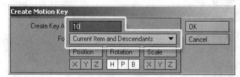

Figure 5.2-17. Creating a keyframe for current item and descendants creates a keyframe for the selected item and all its children.

An easy way to select the finger bones is to select the hand bone, then use the arrow keys to cycle through the finger bones.

Posing the Eyes

The position of the EyeTarget control determines the rotation of the eyes. The position of the eyes is independent of the body and head motion, so the character can keep looking at something while moving.

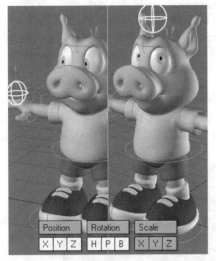

Figure 5.2-18. The EyeTarget control can move and rotate.

You can also target the EyeTarget control to the EyeStretch_Base bone, so the distance between the individual left and right eye targets is maintained as the EyeTarget control moves around the head.

Note: You may need to swap the X position of the left and right eye targets when you do this, depending on the orientation of the EyeTarget control.

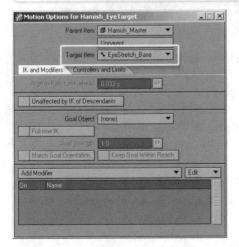

Figure 5.2-19. Targeting the EyeTarget.

Stretching the Character

When working with any animated character, especially cartoon characters, it's important to be able to stretch the body. Stretching the body can be used to create *Squash and Stretch*, the first of Disney's 12 fundamental principles of animation, or just to help the character to reach something.

You may think it's really easy to stretch the character in 3D — after all we have Squash and Stretch tools — but it's not quite that simple. The scale of an item is inherited by all its children. This means that if you change the scale of an item, in most cases you should only adjust the scale of the parent item, not every item in the hierarchy. This can be used to your advantage to achieve effects such as stretching the eyes flat while still allowing them to rotate within their flattened shape. The disadvantages to scaling items is that the children aren't always oriented the same way as the parent, and items that have IK goals don't inherit the scale of their parents but inherit the scale of their IK goal.

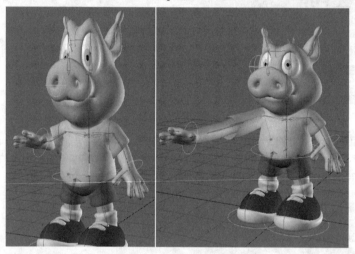

Figure 5.2-20. Scaling bones to stretch.

Instead of scaling bones to stretch the character, it's often better to move the bones along their Z axis. If you move a chain of bones, it stretches that part of the character without any of the disadvantages of scaling bones. You can stretch any part of the character this way, and have full control of where the stretching occurs as the child bones retain their relative position and scale.

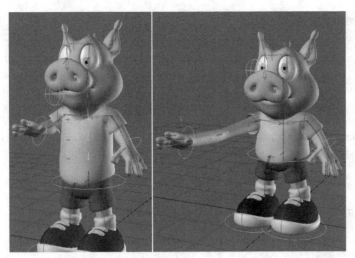

Figure 5.2-21. Moving bones to stretch.

Display Speed

When animating a character, the last thing you want is to be waiting for the software to catch up with your train of thought. It's important to have the character respond as fast as you can manipulate it. It's rarely an issue when you have a single character in a scene, but when you have location geometry and multiple characters, the display updates can slow down quite dramatically.

We've already done the first step for keeping display updates fast by making sure only the rendered objects are geometrical objects, and all non-rendered objects, such as animation controls, are null objects. Null objects update much faster, as the software doesn't have to calculate any polygons.

You can enhance the update speed by adjusting the Display SubPatch Level setting of the objects. Decrease the display level for the character and other associated geometrical objects until you have acceptable response time. You might adjust the display subpatch level a few times during animation, reducing it while posing the character, then increasing it once the animation is done to check that the deformations and other aspects of the character are working well with the motion.

Hiding all non-essential objects keeps the display speed high. Hide any areas of the location or environment that the character doesn't interact with. Hide all the characters except the one being animated, unless the current character is interacting with another character.

There are a number of display options that can be turned off or reduced to help increase OpenGL speed. The fewer display options that are active, the faster the update speed.

Animating with IK

Animating with inverse kinematics is quite different from animating with forward kinematics. It can take a little practice to feel comfortable animating with IK. If you're inexperienced with using IK, there are some common problems that you might come across, such as the inability to pose a character properly, the way the software handles the motion between keyframes or in-betweens, and the inability to successively break joints in a limb. These are often the reasons that animators prefer to use FK for certain hierarchies or limbs, but all of these have solutions when using IK, allowing you to keep all the other benefits of IK.

> **Note:** Another alternative that combines the power of IK and FK is part-time IK. Part-time IK lets you pose a hierarchy using a goal but then manipulate each item in the hierarchy after that without the IK-controlled channels being locked off. Because you still have to keyframe each item in the hierarchy, the in-betweens are calculated differently than full-time IK.
>
> Unfortunately, there are a few limitations to part-time IK that make it a less useful option than it could be. Part-time IK doesn't work with multiple goal items or controls, and at the time of publication, it doesn't work with nested controls when the goal item is parented to another item that is being moved.

Character Posing

Many problems with posing an IK chain, especially the limbs of a character, are the result of trying to place the IK goal in an impossible position. Common symptoms of this are joint flipping, where a joint moves radically between keyframes, and deformation problems, where the model twists out of shape around a joint. These problems are usually caused by not understanding the mechanics of the joints involved, the limits of the skeleton, or the rules of the particular rig being used.

The software does its best to make the IK chain rotate to meet the goal, but can only work within its own limitations and those set on the limb by the IK settings. If you try to place a hand goal in a position it can't possibly reach within the limitations of the rig, the bones of the arm often don't know what to do. By keeping the goals within reach of the IK chain you won't get any flipping of joints.

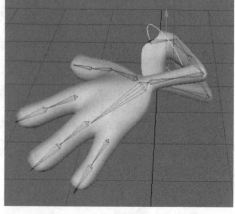

> **Note:** By keeping the goals within reach of the IK chain, I mean purposely placing the goals in such a position, not the IK option Keep Goal Within Reach, which should rarely if ever be used as it causes more problems than it solves.

Figure 5.2-22. The hand goal is not able to be reached, causing flipping of the elbow joint.

Joint deformation problems (not counting existing joint deformation problems due to poor character creation) can be caused by not understanding the rules of the rig. Because we have some bones that emulate the skeleton and others that emulate muscles and flesh, each rig has specific ways to reach certain poses. Understanding the relationships of these bones to each other and to the surrounding bones is important to being able to pose them correctly, thus minimizing joint problems. Even though this problem occurs with both FK and IK, it's often IK that gets the blame.

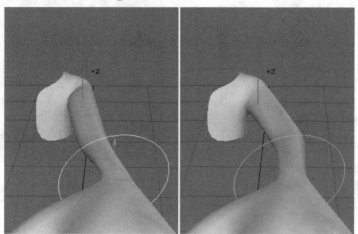

Figure 5.2-23. Left: Bad shoulder pose. Right: Good shoulder pose.

It's your job as a character creator to make sure the animators understand how to use the rig so these problems don't occur.

In-betweens

When we move, each body part moves between poses in an arc due to the rotation of the bones required to move the body part from point A to point B. Creating *Arcs* in motion is another of Disney's 12 fundamental principles of animation.

When a body part is animated using FK, the arcs of motion are automatically created by the rotation of the bones higher up in the hierarchy. The problems occur when IK is used, as it's the software that decides the path of the body part, or IK goal, rather than the rotation of the bones, and the software doesn't always move the IK goals between poses or keyframes in the correct arc.

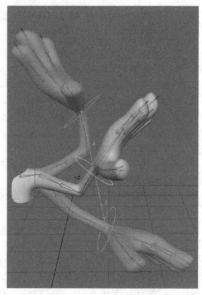

Figure 5.2-24. IK goal moving in a straight line between poses doesn't create a natural motion for the arm.

The software determines the motion of an item between keyframes (in-betweens) through spline interpolation. Unfortunately, this isn't always the correct motion for the item. One way to overcome this is to adjust the type of spline used and the various attributes for how the spline enters and leaves a keyframe. If an IK goal is suffering from incorrect arcing between poses, the easiest way to fix the problem is to create a keyframe for the goal item or animation control between each pose, forcing the item to move in an arc.

A side effect of bad arcs is that sometimes the incorrect motion between keyframes causes the goal item to move through a position that's impossible for the hierarchy to reach, causing the same flipping or joint deformation problems discussed earlier. Making the IK goals move in arcs plays a big part in solving this issue and is the first thing you should look at if you find flipping or deformation problems between keyframed poses.

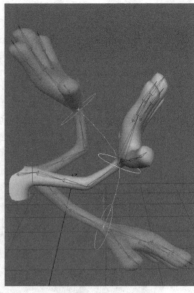

Figure 5.2-25. An extra keyframe between main poses creates a nice motion arc.

Fixing an IK Goal in Place

The other disadvantage to spline interpolated in-betweens is when you want to fix an item or IK goal in place over a series of frames. Fixing an item in place is useful in all sorts of ways when animating characters, but the most regular use is for the foot controls. To make sure the feet don't slide around on the ground, it's important to fix them in place between keyframes when they're not moving.

One way to fix an item in place between keyframes is to set the incoming curve to linear using the Graph Editor, but that isn't always a good option for character animation. Setting the curve to linear makes the item come to a sudden stop, which usually results in a more mechanical motion than you want for a character.

In most cases a part of a character will slow down slightly as it comes to a stop, then when it moves again it starts slowly and builds up speed. This behavior is commonly known as *Slow In and Slow Out,* another of Disney's 12 fundamental principles of animation. The easiest way to achieve slow in and slow out, or ease in and out, is to leave the curve as TCB and adjust the tension of the keyframes at the beginning and end of the fixed range. To fix the item absolutely in place, set the tension to 1. You can also reduce the amount of spline overshoot of the keyframes by setting the tension to between 0 and 1, or increase the spline overshoot by setting the tension to a negative value.

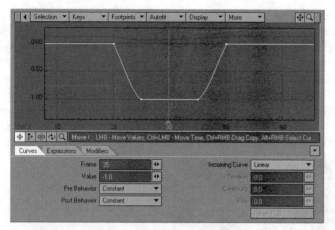

Figure 5.2-26. Setting Incoming Curve to Linear.

> **Tip:** You can adjust the TCB settings without opening the Graph Editor by selecting Modify≻Tools≻Move TCB (Ctrl+g).

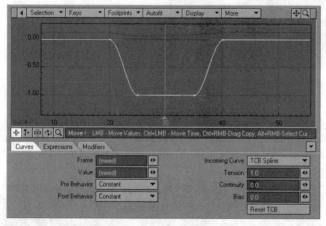

Figure 5.2-27. Adjusting the tension creates more natural motion.

Successive Joint Breaking

Successive breaking of joints is a subtle effect that occurs in many motions but is especially noticeable in the limbs. It's perhaps more commonly known as *Follow Through*, another one of Disney's 12 fundamental principles of animation. It describes the motion between poses. For example, on leaving a pose, the upper arm starts moving a fraction before the forearm, which in turn moves a fraction before the hand. The same thing happens in reverse as the character reaches a new pose — the upper arm stops just before the forearm, which stops just before the hand.

It's commonly believed that successive breaking of joints isn't possible using IK, but that's certainly not the case. It actually relates to motion arcs, so it is really an extension of the previous issue. Let's look at it a little more closely.

A human limb has three joints — beginning (hip or shoulder), middle (knee or elbow), and end (ankle or wrist). Since the first joint is fixed to the body whether we're using IK or FK, it's not an issue; what we need to look at are the middle and end joints. Excluding the potential for stretching the limbs in cartoon characters and sideways motion of the middle joint, basic physics says there is only one place that the middle joint can be for any given position of the end joint.

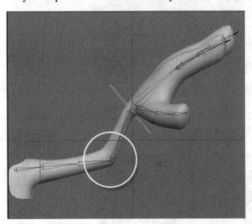

Figure 5.2-28. There is only one place the elbow can be when the hand is in this position.

This means that when using IK, as long as the end joint or the IK goal moves in the same arc as a joint animated using FK and featuring successive joint breaking, the upper arm and forearm will break in exactly the same way using either animation method.

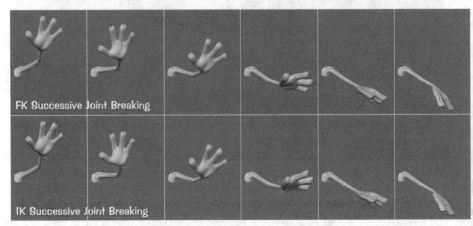

FK Successive Joint Breaking

IK Successive Joint Breaking

Figure 5.2-29. The IK-controlled arm follows the same motion as the FK-controlled arm with successive joint breaking as long as the IK goal follows the same path as the hand of the FK-controlled arm.

This sometimes requires a couple of extra keyframes for the IK goal, but those keyframes are often necessary to create a nice arc, and it's still less effort than doing the same thing using FK.

Trying to visualize the correct motion path for the IK goal might seem a little daunting at first, but it doesn't take long before moving the IK goals in the right way to create follow-through becomes second nature.

Item Selection

There are a few ways to simplify item selection when you're working with characters. The animation controls are easy to select by clicking on them in the viewports, and you can usually select bones in the viewports pretty easily, but some of the bones aren't always easy to get to.

The easiest way to select the bones of a character is by using the Scene Editor. If you keep the Scene Editor open all the time and the character you're working on expanded, you can easily find and select the bone you need. Having Scene Editor open all the time is only practical if you have multiple monitors; otherwise it obscures the viewports too much. What other options are available?

There is the Schematic view, which shows all the items in the scene. Personally I'm not a fan of the Schematic view because it takes up a viewport, it takes quite a while to set up in a usable fashion, and it can become quite unwieldy when you have more than one character.

> **Note:** See the LightWave manual for tips on setting up the Schematic view for item selection.

Another method of item selection has emerged recently that is especially useful for characters: using a character picker. A character picker provides a panel where you can click to select various items in the scene. You can create your own background and choose where the nodes or buttons appear and which items are selected when you click on each node. Using a character picker to select the most commonly used bones can make animating a character much easier.

Character Picker Setup

We'll set up a character picker for the Hamish rig. The character picker we'll use for Hamish is called Custom Character Picker, written by Jacobo Barreiro.

There are a number of ways to use a character picker. You can set up just the controls that are difficult to reach, leaving other selections to clicking on the item in the viewports, or you can set up all the controls in the character picker so you don't have to select anything in the viewport, or somewhere in between. If you set up all the controls you may also choose to hide all the controls so you only see the character object and the currently selected animation control. This can work for simple scenes, but when a scene becomes more complex with multiple characters, it's useful to be able to see the controls and bones in the characters, so I recommend leaving the animation controls visible as a default. The benefit to only setting up the difficult controls is that it keeps the character picker simple and easy to use, with fewer nodes or buttons.

We'll set up the difficult-to-reach controls in the picker for the Hamish rig. You can continue setting up the other controls afterward if you wish to.

1. Load your Hamish rig into Layout (you can find a preprepared scene in \Scenes\Chapters\Hamish_Rig01.lws). Save the scene as **Hamish_Rig01_CCP.lws**. Select **Bone X-Ray** for the Perspective view.

2. Select the **Hamish01** object and select **Plugs≻Additional≻[CCP]**.

> **Note:**   Custom Character Picker is applied as a Custom Object to the selected object, so it's important to select the character object before running CCP.

Figure 5.2-30. The initial CCP interface.

3. Select the **Background** tab and **Add Pic**. Choose **Images\Chapters\CCP_ Hamish.tga**. Click the **CCP_Hamish.tga** entry to enable the background image.

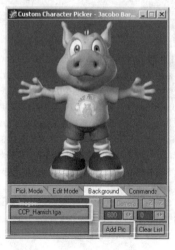

Figure 5.2-31. Setting the background image. You can render an image or take a screen shot from Modeler or Layout to create the image for your character. Just make sure the final image is 300 x 295 pixels.

4. Select the **Edit Mode** tab and click to create nodes for the head, back, pel-
    vis, knees, elbows, and hands. You can also create nodes next to the elbows
    and knees for the clothes controls.

5. Change the selection mode to **Rotate**, as we're selecting bones that can
    only rotate.

Figure 5.2-32. Create the nodes for the bone controls and select Rotate mode.

6. Select the **neck** and **head** bones and click on the head node with the MMB
    to assign the selected bones to the button.

> **Note:**   As you assign items to the nodes, they appear in the text box so you
> can double-check that you've assigned the correct items. You can also move the
> mouse over the nodes in Edit mode and the text box shows which items are
> selected to each node.

Figure 5.2-33. In Edit mode, select the item(s), then MMB-click on the appropriate node to assign those items.

7. Select **Back02**, **Back03**, and **Back04** and assign them to the back node.

8. Select **Pelvis_Base** and assign it to the pelvis node.

9. Assign **Hip_LT** to the left knee node (the right-hand knee node in the interface as you're looking at the character). Assign **Hip_RT** to the right knee node.

10. Assign **Arm_Upper02_LT** to the left elbow node (the right hand node as you're looking at the character) and assign **Arm_Upper02_RT** to the right elbow node.

11. Assign the **Hand_LT** bone to the left hand node and the **Hand_RT** bone to the right hand node.

12. Assign the clothes bones to the appropriate nodes.

13. Move the mouse over each node to double-check that they all have the correct assigned items, then change to the **Pick Mode** tab.

14. Now you can click on each node and the appropriate bones are selected. Save the scene to save the Custom Character Picker setup.

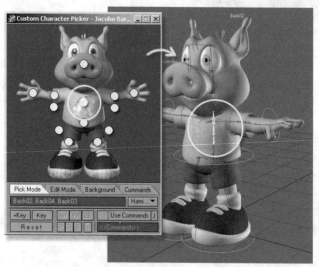

Figure 5.2-34. In Pick mode, click on the node to select the appropriate item(s).

You can continue creating more nodes if you wish. You can assign other animation controls to those nodes or use the Commands tab to assign almost any tool or scene option to the nodes. This can make the character picker a very powerful and useful tool for animation.

To use the Custom Character Picker when animating the character, import the character into the scene (using Load From Scene...) using the [CCP] version of the rig.

5.3 Facial Animation

Facial animation can be one of the most challenging aspects of character animation, especially animating speech, commonly referred to as lip sync animation. I highly recommend learning more about facial animation (and animation in general) from the animation masters. *The Illusion of Life* by Frank Thomas and Ollie Johnston is required reading for any animator, and one of the most valuable books on my shelf.

While the techniques for creating facial animation are quite different between 2D and 3D animation, the theories behind it are very similar. Where and how to use different expressions and phonemes are the same; the major difference is how the expressions and phonemes are created. Instead of drawing individual facial poses for every expression or mouth shape, you mix different morphs together to create the same effect.

As with the body animation, I often act out the scene, noting the movement of my face. I make a point of noticing not just the main expressions, but also when I blink, and when and how the expressions change. While I'm animating the face I tend to act out the scene less, but when watching the animation previews I often act it out in front of a mirror, just moving my face and head along with the character's body movement and the audio track.

Facial Expressions

The body animation provides the broad strokes for the character's intent and emotion, but it's the facial animation that provides the more subtle and complex emotions.

Facial expression is very important to character animation. It's through facial animation that the audience believes that the character is not only alive, but is a thinking, feeling being. The broad thoughts and feelings can be communicated through the body language and motion, but until facial animation is included, the character is little more than a puppet.

It's the character's thought process that really drives any animation. If a character is not thinking, it is not truly alive. While cartoon animation is usually quite broad, it can be much more convincing when the facial expressions are subtle. Often just a slight movement of the eyebrows or change in the intensity of a smile is enough to indicate a change in the thought process.

The Eyes

The eyes are the most expressive and honest part of a character. The body and mouth can be deceptive in their expression, but the eyes almost always indicate a character's true feelings. In most cases the eyes complement the body language and mouth expression, but they can also be used to great effect by contradicting the main expression. The eyes can also contradict each other for even more variety of expression.

Figure 5.3-1. The eyes and mouth can contradict each other.

The eyes include expressive and functional morphs, although the combination of the two creates even more expressions. The eyebrows are expressive morphs, and tend to show the most emotion. The eyelids are functional morphs, but can enhance the emotion of the eyebrows. They also have unique capabilities, such as indicating tiredness, which the eyebrows alone can't convey.

Figure 5.3-2. The eyelids show that Hamish is sleepy.

Blinking

There are two types of blinking: directional blinking and emotive blinking.

Directional blinking is the easiest to implement, indicating and strengthening a shift in the direction of the eyes. In most cases a character will blink as it changes the direction of its gaze, but be careful not to overdo it. If the character is changing the direction of gaze rapidly, you might want to blink at the beginning and the end, but not for every change in direction.

Figure 5.3-3. Directional blinking.

Emotive blinking is much more subtle and challenging to perform well. An emotive blink can indicate a change in the thought process or emotion of a character, or can just be to moisten the eyeballs. If there isn't an obvious action between emotions, a blink can clue the audience in that the change is occurring. If there's a period of less movement, such as holding a pose or gaze, a blink can help maintain the believability of the character by creating just that little movement in the otherwise still pose.

Very few, if any, blinks should be random. Every blink should have a purpose. In most cases a character should only blink to emphasize an action or emotion, or to break up a long pause in action. If your character has large eyes, blinking is far more obvious than in humans, so you can't use exactly the same rules. Certainly act out the scene and replicate your blinks, but once you've done that check the animation. If the character seems to be blinking too often, decide which blinks are least important and remove them.

The speed of a blink is important. A fast blink occurs over four to six frames, while a long blink can last as long as you need it to. The speed of a blink indicates many things. Fast blinking can indicate alertness or is useful for breaking up a holding pose. Slower blinking can indicate tiredness or deep thought. It's useful to vary the speed of the blinks in a scene. It gives you another option for showing the character's thought process as well as making sure the character doesn't appear too mechanical.

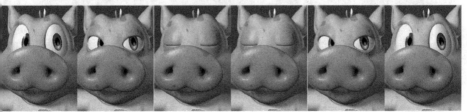

Figure 5.3-4. A fast blink occurs over four to six frames.

The Mouth

The mouth tends to show basic emotions, but is also capable of more subtle emotion. The left and right sides of the mouth can also contradict each other for even more variety.

Figure 5.3-5. Two sides of the mouth contradicting each other.

The mouth has the same complexities as the eyes, with the combination of expressive morphs and functional morphs. The mouth and lips opening are functional morphs, and the others are expressive morphs. As with the eyes, the combination of expressive and functional morphs creates even more expressions.

Figure 5.3-6. Left: Happy. Right: Really happy.

Lip Sync

Lip sync is one of my favorite aspects of character animation. It can take a while to get the hang of it, but once you have you can create great lip sync very quickly.

Many people suggest creating a breakdown or exposure sheet before creating the lip sync animation, but that's really only necessary for 2D animation, where the animator doesn't have direct access to the audio track. In 3D animation, you can see the audio track in the timeline and watch the animation play with the dialogue as you scrub through the timeline, which makes creating an exposure sheet unnecessary for timing lip sync.

> **Note:** An exposure sheet is useful for determining the timing of other aspects though. I often create an exposure sheet when animating to music so I know on what frames the beats and major musical features fall.

Words vs. Sounds

The very first step to creating convincing lip sync is to forget about what the written words look like or how they're spelled. Concentrate on what the words and phrases sound like, and what mouth shapes are required to create those sounds.

It's difficult to explain exactly what words sound like. It's often suggested to analyze the words phonetically, but that isn't always accurate, as the sound of the words and phrases largely depends on the voice artist. The accent and type of character can dramatically change the sound of the words, and therefore the mouth shapes needed to create those words. It's usually easier just to listen to the dialogue and decide as you go which mouth shapes you need.

There are 58 phonemes in the International Phonetic Alphabet and over 40 phonemes in the English language, but many phonemes involve multiple sounds. If you break all the phonemes down into individual sounds, there are only 15 mouth shapes necessary for creating those sounds.

Sound	Examples
AH, U	Part, half, laugh, other, cup, some, tough
A	Hat, man, cash
E	Pet, many, meant
EE, I	Sit, finish, mystic, eat, see, unique
O	Cot, what, mop
OR	Short, bought, talk, caught
ER	Hurt, bird, word, serve
R	Ring, wrist, remember
W, OO	When, always, book, could, put, spoon, blue, you
S, T, Z	See, assist, goose, time, fatal, zoo, easy, has
SH, CH, J	Sheep, mission, cheese, much, genre, measure, beige, age
M, B, P	Meat, lamb, beat, rubber, pig, top
F, V	Fine, left, vain, give, tough
L, D, N	Dog, admit, low, feel, nice, inside
TH	Thank, lethal, cloth

Notice the omission of some sounds from the list: G, NG, K, and H. These sounds are made mostly with the tongue and throat and are rarely represented by a unique mouth shape, instead taking the form of the preceding or following sound.

Other mouth shapes can also be dependent on the sounds that come before and after, especially the sounds that are made predominantly with the tongue. For example the mouth shape for the "L" sound in "always" is very different from "allosaurus." This makes it even more important to watch yourself saying the phrase in a mirror or feel yourself saying the phrase if you don't have a mirror.

The sounds that have combined mouth shapes, or no mouth shapes, can be individually represented by different tongue positions or the throat shapes, but cartoon characters rarely need that level of detail.

Note: Adding to the basic mouth shapes by including different throat shapes and tongue positions in the morphs adds a great deal of believability to lip sync animation for human characters.

Using Phoneme Morphs

You will have realized by now that the phoneme morphs don't really represent true phonemes at all. I only call the lip sync morphs phonemes because it's a name that's traditionally used and that everyone associates with syncing mouth shapes to dialogue.

All of the 15 mouth shapes necessary for creating any sound can be made by mixing different combinations of the nine phoneme morphs. Let's look at the mouth shapes again, this time looking at what combination of morphs can achieve each shape.

Note: Keep in mind this is just a rough guide for how you can use the phoneme morphs to create a variety of mouth shapes, rather than a definitive explanation for what each sound looks like.

AH, U

Examples: **P**art, half, la**u**gh, **o**ther, **c**up, s**o**me, t**ou**gh

The long "A" sound or short "U" sound consists of just Phoneme.A.

The long "A" sound involves the mouth opening as much as needed. This is one of the most basic and easiest sounds to sync.

A

Examples: Hat, man, cash

The short "A" sound consists of mostly Phoneme.A with some Phoneme.E.

The average short "A" sound involves the mouth opening as much as needed and widening just a little bit. You can open and/or widen the mouth even more if there's an emphasis on the sound, as in "fan-**tas**-tic."

E

Examples: Pet, many, meant

The short "E" sound consists of mostly Phoneme.E and some Phoneme.A.

The average short "E" sound involves the mouth opening and widening a little. The mouth opens a little less than for the short "A", but widens a little more. As with the short "A", you can open and/or widen the mouth for emphasis, as in "what-**ev**-er." You can also include some sneer or grimace to really emphasize the sound.

EE, I

Examples: Sit, finish, mystic, eat, see, unique

The long "E" or short "I" sound consists of just Phoneme.E.

The "EE" sound is more pronounced than the "I" sound, so sometimes the "I" sound can also be made using Phoneme.A or a smaller percentage of Phoneme.E than the "EE" sound.

O

Examples: Cot, what, mop

The short "O" sound consists of Phoneme.O with as much Phoneme.A as necessary.

The short "O" sound involves the mouth narrowing evenly and opening as much as the sound requires.

OR

Examples: Short, bought, talk, caught

The "OR" sound consists of mostly Phoneme.O with a little Phoneme.W and as much Phoneme.A as necessary.

The "OR" sound involves the mouth narrowing, the lips puckering a little, and the mouth opening as much as the sound requires.

ER

Examples: Hurt, bird, word, serve

The "ER" sound consists of Phoneme.W and as much Phoneme.A as necessary.

The "ER" sound involves the lips puckering and the mouth opening as much as the sound requires. You can also narrow the mouth a little if necessary.

R

Examples: **R**ing, **wr**ist, **r**emember
The "R" sound consists of mostly
Phoneme.W with as much Phoneme.A
as necessary.
The "R" sound involves the lips
puckering and the mouth opening just a
little. Often the "R" mouth shape is
blurred or lost during the course of dialogue. You should use it only when the
sound is emphasized.

W, OO

Examples: **W**hen, al**w**ays, b**oo**k, c**ou**ld,
p**u**t, sp**oo**n, bl**ue**, y**ou**
The "W" or "OO" sound consists of
Phoneme.W.
The "W" sound involves the lips
puckering. You can also mix a little
mouth opening and narrowing depending on the exact sound.

S, T, Z (D, N)

Examples: **S**ee, a**ss**i**s**t, goo**s**e, **t**ime,
fa**t**al, **z**oo, ea**s**y, ha**s**
The "S", "T", and "Z" sounds consist of Phoneme.S.
The "S" sounds involve the lips
opening with the teeth together. How
much the lips open and the shape of the
mouth depend on the sounds before and
after. As long as the teeth are together
the mouth can be almost any shape. The
main difference between the individual
sounds is the position of the tongue,
which isn't noticeable with the teeth
closed.

SH, CH, J

Examples: **Sh**eep, mi**ss**ion, **ch**eese, mu**ch**, **g**enre, mea**s**ure, bei**g**e, a**ge**

The "SH", "CH", and "J" sounds consist of Phoneme.S with as much Phoneme.W as necessary.

The "SH" sounds involve the lips opening with the teeth together and the lips puckering. How much the lips pucker depends on the sounds before and after and the emphasis on the sound. The main difference between the individual sounds is the position of the tongue, which isn't noticeable with the teeth closed.

M, B, P

Examples: **M**eat, la**mb**, **b**eat, ru**bb**er, **p**ig, to**p**

The "M", "B", and "P" sounds consist of Phoneme.M.

The "M" sounds involve the lips closing. Since the default position of the mouth is closed, you can use the default position for the "M" sounds, only making the lips press harder together for emphasis.

F, V

Examples: **F**ine, le**f**t, **v**ain, gi**v**e, tou**gh**

The "F" sound consists of Phoneme.F.

The "F" sound involves the lower lip pressing against or tucking under the top teeth. The exact position of the lower lip differs from person to person, as well as how emphatic the "F" sound is. For greater variety you can separate these sounds into two morphs: Phoneme.F with the lower lip tucked under the top teeth and Phoneme.V with the lower lip just touching the top teeth.

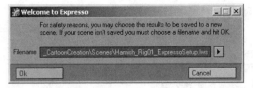

Figure 5.4-2. Choosing a new scene name.

4. You're presented with the main setup interface. Here you can choose which controls are active, and which morphs are assigned to each control. Assign the morphs as shown in Figure 5.4-3.

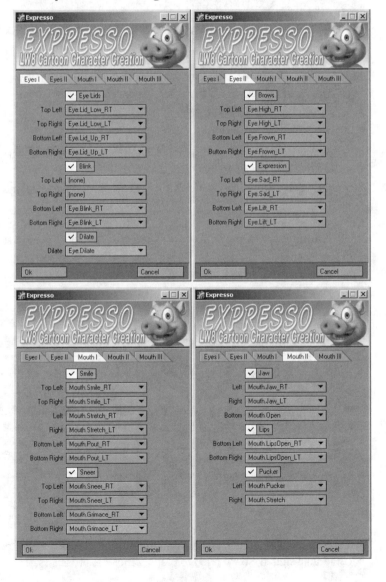

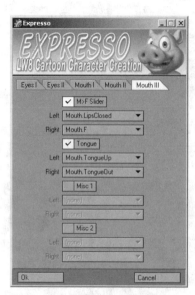

Figure 5.4-3. Morph assignments.

5. When you press **OK** the new scene is loaded with the joystick controls. Choose **No** when it asks to load lights.

6. Open the Scene Editor and select **Name_Expresso**, the control interface object.

7. Change the working viewport to **Back**, **Textured Shaded Solid**. Scale and move **Name_Expresso** so the controls are sized and positioned how you want.

8. Center the selected object, zoom until the joystick interface fits nicely, then turn off centering.

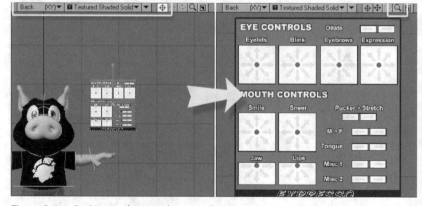

Figure 5.4-4. Position and center the controls.

When Expresso is applied, any existing integrated expressions in the scene become unassigned, so we need to reapply those expressions.

9. Open the Graph Editor. In the Channels list, find **Hamish**▷**Control**▷
   BlinkHelp_LT and **Hamish01**▷**Control**▷**BlinkHelp_RT**, and drag them
   into the channel bin.

10. In the Expressions list, find and select the **Hamish_Blink_LT** expression
    and apply it to **Hamish01.Control.BlinkHelp_LT**. Apply the
    Hamish_Blink_RT expression to **Hamish01.Control.BlinkHelp_RT**.

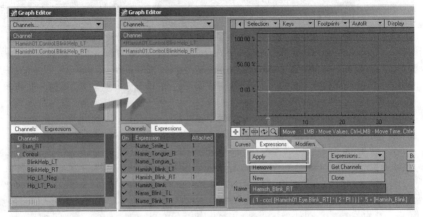

Figure 5.4-5. Reapply all the integrated expressions from the original rig.

11. Move to frame 10 and try out the controls to make sure it's all set up cor-
    rectly. Delete all keyframes at frame 10 and save the scene.

Renaming the Controls

Now, although Expresso is set up, the controls need to be renamed so there can
be more than one character using Expresso in the same scene.

Renaming can be done within native Layout, but doing mass name changes
is very time consuming. One of the benefits of LightWave scene files is that
they're saved as plaintext format, so you can perform global name changes very
easily by doing a find and replace in a text editor. Instead of doing this we'll use
the very useful Renamer plug-in, also by Samuel Kvaalen. Renamer does the
same find and replace as a text editor, but you don't have to leave LightWave.

1. Select the **Name_Expresso** object using the Scene Editor. Select
   File▷**Save**▷**Save Current Object**. Find the Objects directory in the content directory, and save as **Hamish_Expresso.lwo**.

2. Save the scene to store the new object name in the scene file.

3. Select **Plugs**▷**Additional**▷**Renamer JG** and change Find to **Name_** and
   Replace to **Hamish_**. Change the scene to be saved (the bottom scene) to
   Hamish_Rig01_Expresso.lws.

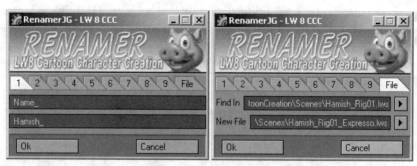

Figure 5.4-6. The Expresso controls and expressions have the same naming convention so the one find and replace operation updates the control names and expression names.

4. The new scene will load with the name changes. Check that everything is working correctly after the name change.

The controls are now customized for Hamish. By doing this every time you set up Expresso for a character you ensure that the joystick controls will remain separate when more than one character is in a scene.

To use Expresso when animating the character, import the character into the scene (using Load From Scene...) using the Expresso version of the rig.

Figure 5.4-7. The correctly named controls.

Custom Joysticks

The advantage of the custom joystick setup is that you have the flexibility to design and create your own set of joystick controls for any character or any combination of morphs.

Custom joystick setup can involve fairly advanced expressions (LightWave and facial). You can create custom joystick interfaces without creating or editing any expressions, using the templates that I've provided, but if you're comfortable with expressions, be sure and read on so you can make the most of the joystick controls.

There are two aspects of designing a joystick setup. The first is choosing the right combination of morphs for each joystick control. The second is determining the best behavior for the morphs within each joystick control. Choosing the right morphs and the best behavior for those morphs is important to ensure you have as much control as possible over every morph. You need to make sure the joysticks allow mixing as many complementary morphs as possible, and as few conflicting morphs as possible.

Joystick Types

There are four basic types of joystick controls, but each type of control can work in many different ways when combined with the different transition behaviors.

One-way Joystick/Slider

A slider replicates the behavior of a normal morph slider, providing control of a single morph.

Two-way Joystick

The two-way joystick is an enhanced slider, providing control of one to three separate morphs.

Five-way Joystick

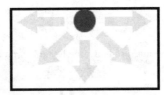

The five-way joystick is basically half of an eight-way joystick, providing control of two to five separate morphs.

Eight-way Joystick

The eight-way joystick offers the most flexibility, providing control of four to eight separate morphs.

These are the most common joystick controls but not the only ones. You can also have a three-way joystick or, if you're feeling brave, a 16-way joystick. You could even add a third dimension to an eight-way joystick, controlling up to 26 separate morphs (although this would likely be a nightmare to control). What I'm really trying to say is don't limit the possibilities of your joystick design by conventional thinking. If you have a use for a different type of joystick than I've included here, feel free to use it. It's only through creative thinking that techniques like this are developed and advanced.

Transition Behavior

When it comes down to it, the different types of joystick controls are very similar. They all control the transition from no effect to a morph, and most control transitions from one morph to another. It's the combination of different transition behaviors that makes each joystick control different.

If we look at joysticks in the simplest terms, each one is a combination of two-way sliders. In a two-way slider there are three basic types of behavior for the transition between morphs.

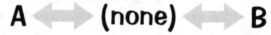

Figure 5.4-8. This transition is used for conflicting morphs.

Figure 5.4-9. This transition is used for complementary morphs.

Figure 5.4-10. This transition gives extra control between morphs by including a third morph.

Keep in mind these aren't the only possible transitions, just the primary ones. By delving further into the expressions, a slider could feature A – A + B + C – B where C is a corrective morph or enhances A + B, or could feature A + C – C – C + B. The possibilities are endless.

Joystick Templates

I've included the most common joystick controls as templates for you to design and create your own joystick interfaces. All you need to do is to load the template, which includes the controls and expressions, and apply the expressions to the appropriate morphs.

8way8

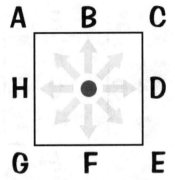

This eight-way joystick controls up to eight morphs, allowing a separate morph for each direction. This is useful if your left- and right-sided morphs, when added together, aren't the same as the symmetrical morphs.

You can leave any expression unassigned if you don't want a morph in that position. You can control four morphs without any mixing by assigning only the four corner or four side expressions.

8way6_V

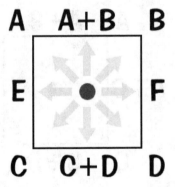

This eight-way joystick controls six morphs. This is useful if your left- and right-sided morphs, when added together, are the same as the symmetrical morphs, but you want additional morphs between the top and bottom morphs. The Smile control in Expresso is an 8way6_V joystick.

By leaving the side (L and R) expressions unassigned you can use this joystick to control four morphs with no mixing between the morphs at the top and bottom. The Blink control in Expresso is a four-morph version of this joystick with the side expressions unassigned.

8way6_H

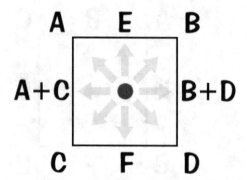

This eight-way joystick controls six morphs. This is useful if your left- and right-sided morphs, when added together, aren't the same as the symmetrical morphs, but you want to mix the top and bottom morphs.

By leaving the top and bottom (T and B) expressions unassigned you can use this joystick to control four morphs with no mixing between the morphs on each side.

8way4

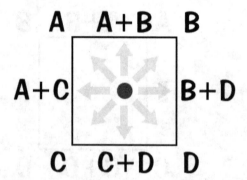

This eight-way joystick controls four morphs. This mixes each pair of morphs on each side of the joystick. The Eyelids control in Expresso is an 8way4 joystick.

5way5

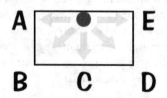

Top Right

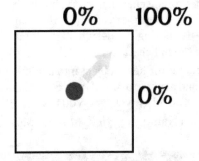

clamp (max([<Control>.Position.Y], 0) * [<Control>.Position.X], 0, 1)

This expression tells the morph to increase as the joystick moves up and right to the corner, but decrease as the joystick moves toward the center of each side.

Right

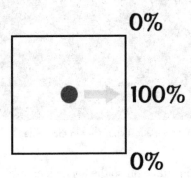

clamp ([<Control>.Position.X] – abs([<Control>.Position.Y]), 0, 1)

This expression tells the morph to increase as the joystick moves right, but decrease as the joystick moves up or down.

The other directions are variations on these basic expressions. Check out the expressions included in the joystick templates for more ideas.

Custom Joystick Setup

Creating custom joystick controls involves two stages: designing the joystick setup and applying the joystick setup to your characters.

Setting the Scene

It's best to design the joystick controls separate from the character rig. This makes it easier to set up as it ensures that only the joystick expressions are in the scene, so it doesn't become confusing if you have other integrated expressions in your rig. It also makes it easier to create a stand-alone joystick scene that you can import for any character. You can still build on it after importing, to customize it further for specific characters, but it gives you the default setup.

It's useful to save a separate version of the character object with just the head geometry to use during the design stage. It takes up less room and updates more quickly than the full character.

1. Load the character (or head) object into a new scene. Set the subdivision order to **last** and apply **Morph Mixer**. Save the scene, naming it something meaningful such as **MyJoysticks_v001.lws**.

2. Add a null called **Name_Joystick_Master**. Move it in **Z** so it's behind the character.

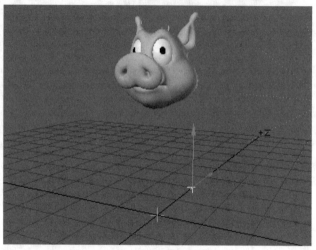

Figure 5.4-11. Set up the test character in the scene.

3. Turn **Parent in Place** off so the joystick controls inherit the position and scale of the master null when they're parented.

4. Open the Graph Editor and turn off the **Track Item Selections** option so the channels remain as the other items are worked on.

5. Remove the existing channels from the bin, select the **Eye** and **Mouth** morph groups (and any other morph groups you wish to assign to joystick control) of the character from the channel list, and drag them into the channel bin.

6. Move the Graph Editor out of the way or minimize it. Don't close it or you'll have to place the morphs in the channel bin again.

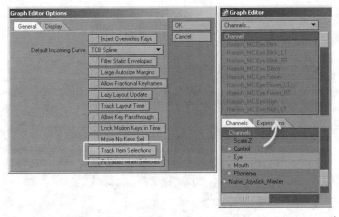

Figure 5.4-12. Setup Graph Editor, ready to assign expressions to morphs.

Creating the First Joystick

It's easy to design the joystick controls using the templates provided. You can play around with the layout and functionality quickly and easily. If a joystick isn't doing what you want you can just remove it and try another one without redoing the whole thing.

The first joystick involves positioning and scaling the master control so the joystick controls are manageable.

1. Select **Load From Scene...**, choosing one of the joystick templates from the **\Scenes\JoystickTemplates** directory.

2. Open the Scene Editor and parent the joystick box object to **Name_Joystick_Master**.

3. Position and scale **Name_Joystick_Master** so that it's out of the way and a manageable size, then change the working viewport to the Back view and center the view on the object.

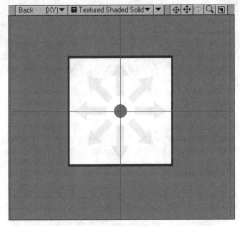

Figure 5.4-13. Set up the Back view for the joystick control.

4. In the Graph Editor, assign the appropriate morphs to the expressions for the joystick control, remembering that left morphs go on right control expressions and vice versa.

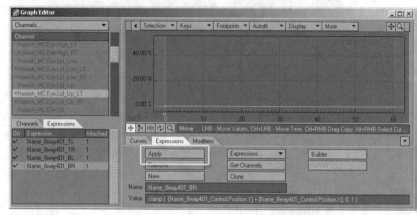

Figure 5.4-14. I've set up the first joystick the same as the Eyelids joystick in my Expresso design.

5. On frame 10, test that the joystick control is working correctly. When it's correct, delete the keyframe on frame 10 for the joystick control and move back to frame 0.

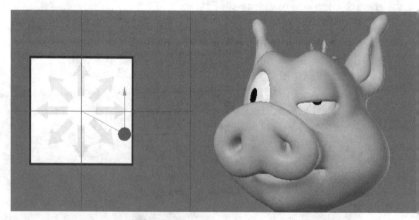

Figure 5.4-15. Testing the joystick control.

> **Note:** As you create each joystick control, make a note of which morphs each joystick controls. This comes in handy later for renaming the controls so they're intuitive.

Applying the Joysticks

With the joystick setup saved separately, it can easily be applied to any character. With this method you don't have to stick with the default joysticks. Once you've imported your default joystick setup, you can continue to customize the joystick setup further if the character has unique requirements.

1. Load your Hamish rig into Layout (you can find a preprepared scene in \Scenes\Chapters\Hamish_Rig01.lws).

2. **Load From Scene...** choosing your custom joystick scene.

3. Position and scale **Name_Joystick_Master** to where you want it.

4. Apply the joystick expressions to the appropriate morphs and save the rig scene with **Joysticks** appended to the name, e.g., Hamish_Rig01_Joysticks.lws.

5. Select **Renamer JG** and replace Name_ with **Hamish_**.

You now have a version of the Hamish rig with custom joysticks, ready to load into a scene for animating.

> **Note:** Load From Scene... doesn't retain the locked status of the items. When you load the character with the custom joysticks into an animation scene, it's useful to lock the joystick master and box objects so only the joystick control items can be selected in the viewports.

Using this method you can apply the same custom joystick setup to any character, or create a number of custom joystick setups to use for different characters. Instead of designing a joystick setup from scratch you could also use this method to add to the Expresso joystick setup, combining the quick and simple setup of Expresso with the flexibility and power of the custom setup.

5.5 Creating a Test Animation

Whether you're creating a character for yourself or another animator, it's useful to create a test animation. Sometimes problems with the rig or other areas only become apparent during animation, and it saves a lot of time if you can pick up on those things before the character is in production. A test animation also provides a good showcase for the character and what it's capable of doing.

A test animation can be as simple or as complex as you have time for. You can import the character into a scene with a location or just use the standard setup scene. It really depends on how much time you want to dedicate to the animation and how much variety you want the animation to demonstrate.

Body Animation

The test animation can give the animators important information about how the character can and should move, whether the character walks with a limp, runs on all fours when in a hurry, is confident, clumsy, carefree, or paranoid — any type of character trait can be demonstrated in the test animation. It's useful to show a decent range of motion in the test animation, not just to show what the character is capable of, but also to continue testing the rig, controls, and deformations. The initial body animation doesn't have to be long though; a few seconds is usually all that's necessary.

I've included Hamish jumping in the test animation so I can use the same scene later to test how the dynamics behave with the more extreme motion.

1.   Load **Hamish_Setup.lws** (or feel free to load or create another scene with different lighting or including a location or scenic elements), then **Load Items From Scene...** , choosing your Hamish rig (or the preprepared rig \Scenes\Chapters\Hamish_Rig01.lws). Save the scene as **Hamish_TestAnim_v001.lws**.

> **Note:**   Feel free to import any of the alternative rigs instead of the primary rig, including one or more of the alternate or additional control methods we've covered.

2.   Create a short animation of Hamish using what you've learned in this chapter. At this stage only animate the body and eye target, although as you animate think about what facial animation you can include to enhance the scene. Bring Hamish up to the camera (or move the camera toward Hamish) toward the end of the animation so you end up with a bust view of Hamish (ready to show off the facial animation).

> **Tip:**   Use the Dope Sheet and Dope Track to quickly adjust animation timing.

You can find my initial body animation scene for Hamish in \Scenes\ Chapters\Hamish_TestAnim_v001.lws or see the rendered version in \Movies\Hamish_TestAnim_v001.mov.

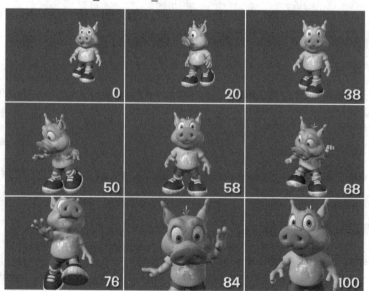

Figure 5.5-1. Some frames from my initial body animation pass.

Adding Audio

The next step is to add an audio file and create body animation appropriate for what Hamish is saying. The audio section of the test animation is mainly to demonstrate the facial expressions and lip sync, but first we need to create the body animation to the audio.

Adding the audio after the initial animation means you're not restricted to a specific length of time for the initial body animation. This way you can start the audio at the time frame where the existing animation finishes. It's a little different from production animation where every action is carefully timed out before you start, but it's nice to have the extra freedom in this case.

1. Open the Scene Editor and select **Audio≻Load Audio**. Choose **Sound\HamishTest_22k.wav.**

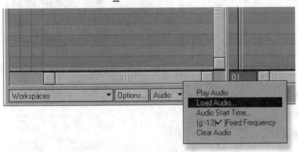

Figure 5.5-2. Load Audio.

2. The start time for an audio file defaults to the beginning of the scene. We don't want it starting until after the existing animation, so select **Audio≻Audio Start Time** and set it to a few frames after the existing animation finishes. I've set it to frame **105**, five frames after my existing animation finishes.

> **Note:** The audio start time is different in the two Scene Editors. The Classic Scene Editor start time is in seconds, and the new Scene Editor start time is in frames. For my scene, the audio start time in the Classic Scene Editor is 3.5 (Start frame/Scene FPS) since we're working at 30 frames per second.

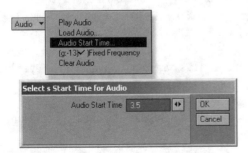

Figure 5.5-3. Setting Audio Start Time.

3. Save the scene incrementally as **Hamish_TestAnim_v002.lws**.

4. Continue creating body animation for Hamish to the audio. Be as creative as you like, but still only animate the body, making sure the body language tells the audience what Hamish is doing and thinking.

You can find my body animation scene including audio in \Scenes\Chapters\ Hamish_TestAnim_v002.lws or see the rendered version in \Movies\Hamish_TestAnim_v002.mov.

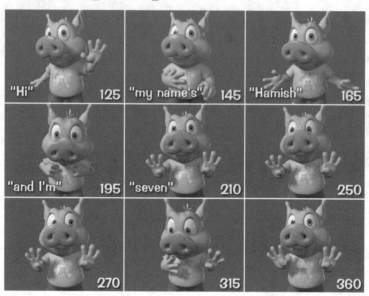

Figure 5.5-4. Some frames from my body animation to the audio track.

Facial Expressions

The basic principle of animation is to start with the broad motions and gradually work in toward detailed and subtle motion. This is why it's good to start with the body animation, and is also why it's useful to create the facial animation in order. You can always go back and tweak or adjust other aspects, but creating the animation in order makes facial animation fast and efficient.

1. Start by adding the directional blinks. These are more related to the existing eye rotation than the emotion of the character, so they're quick and easy to create.

2. Create the eye and mouth expressions. You can animate the eyes before the mouth or the mouth before the eyes, or animate them both at the same time; it really depends on the scene.

3. Finally, create the emotive blinks to enhance the existing facial animation.

Expression Animation

Without further ado, let's jump into animating the facial expressions.

1. Load **Hamish_TestAnim_v002.lws** and save the scene incrementally as **Hamish_TestAnim_v003.lws**.

2. Select the **Hamish01** object. Open **Object Properties**≻**Deform** and open **Morph Mixer**.

> **Note:**   You can also open Morph Mixer for the selected object by selecting Plugs≻Additional≻Morph Mixer. This Morph Mixer launcher is included with Custom Character Picker.

3. In Morph Mixer, select the **Eye** group and add directional blinks to the animation.

4. Add eye and mouth expressions to the animation. Don't do too much during the dialogue; create most of the expression animation before and after the dialogue.

5. Add emotive blinks if necessary, emphasizing the transition between expressions or to break up long holds.

You can find my expression animation scene for Hamish in \Scenes\Chapters\ Hamish_TestAnim_v003.lws or see the rendered version in \Movies\Hamish_ TestAnim_v003.mov.

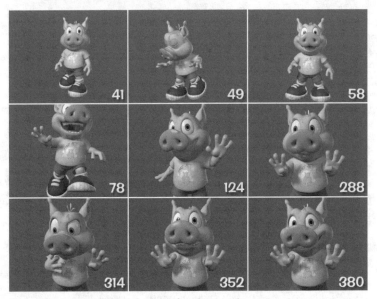

Figure 5.5-5. Some frames from my facial expression pass.

Lip Sync

Lip sync can be done at any point in the animation process. When it's done is
largely up to each individual animator or based on the requirements of the scene.
I sometimes find it useful to animate the lip sync before the other facial expressions so I can create the other expressions more easily based on what the
character is saying. If you leave it until last as we've done here, it's a good idea
to go back afterward and tweak or enhance the facial expressions during the dialogue. Other times lip sync can be done before body animation, especially if the
character is close to the camera for most, or all, of the scene.

> **Tip:** It's useful to parent a new camera to the head bone of a character
> when animating the facial morphs. This way you have a consistent view of the
> face at all times.

During dialogue it's a good idea to use the mouth expressions to emphasize
what's being said rather than leaving the mouth in the same pose or expression
throughout an entire phrase. This helps to make sure that you don't have conflicting morphs between the mouth expressions and the phonemes or other
mouth shapes. Make sure if you do have expressive mouth morphs active during
dialogue that you reduce the expressive morphs when the mouth narrows, puck-
ers, or widens during the lip sync, leaving the eyes to convey the majority of
expression during that time.

> **Tip:** In larger scenes, make sure the object you're performing morph anima-
> tion for is selected. The selected object will update much faster than the other
> objects in the scene, allowing for more responsive feedback as you scrub the
> timeline.

1. Load **Hamish_TestAnim_v003.lws** and save the scene incrementally as
   Hamish_TestAnim_v004.lws.
2. Select the **Hamish01** object and open **Morph Mixer**.
3. Select the **Phoneme** group and add lip sync to the animation following the
   essential rules of lip sync.

You can find my lip sync animation scene for Hamish in \Scenes\Chapters\
Hamish_TestAnim_v004.lws or see the rendered version in \Movies\Hamish_
TestAnim_v004.mov.

Final Pass

The last stage is tweaking the existing animation and adding secondary animation for things like the clothes, ears, and any other floppy bits. It's important to
leave this until last because it's this finer detail that relies most on the other animation. If you do this any earlier, you may well find that you have to redo it if a
change is required after an animation review.

Figure 6.2-5. Using the default settings, the dynamic effect
is far too exaggerated.

5.   Adjust the EffectSize values for each map until the effect is the right size.
     Notice the object is updated automatically as you adjust the values. I've set
     FX_Soft to **15%** and Hair to **20%**.

6.   Adjust the WaveCycle and WaveSize(s) values to determine how fast the
     area springs back and how long it takes to stop wobbling. For FX_Soft I've
     set WaveCycle to **2** and left WaveSize(s) at **0.5**. For Hair I've set WaveCycle
     to **3** and WaveSize(s) to **0.4**.

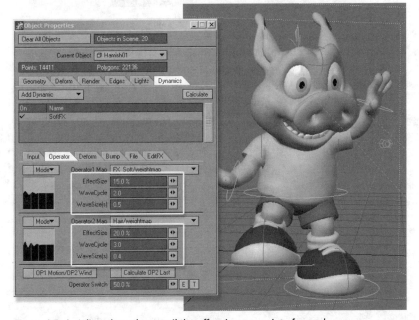

Figure 6.2-6. Adjust the values until the effect is appropriate for each area.

7. Create a preview (**Preview**➤**Make Preview**) to check the dynamics at the right speed in context with the rest of the animation. Continue adjusting the values if necessary.

8. When you're happy with the dynamic motion, select the **File** tab and select **Save**, saving the settings as **Motions\Hamish_SoftFX.txt**.

Note: This file is used when applying the SoftFX settings to the final rig.

9. Select **Save Motion**, saving as **Motions\TestAnim_Hamish_SoftFX.mdd**.

Note: When saving motions it's good practice to save as <Scene>_<Object>_<Dynamic type>.mdd. This way the motion files are easily distinguished for each scene, character, and dynamic type.

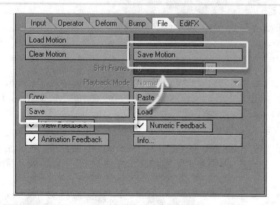

Figure 6.2-7. Save settings, then save the motion.

10. Save the scene, storing the calculated dynamics.

Applying SoftFX dynamics really is quick and easy. We've covered the basics, but there are many other settings in SoftFX to explore. Soft FX also has many uses in addition to what we've covered here. You can use SoftFX for other areas of the body, such as the tummy, simple clothing motion, and much more.

If these are the only dynamics your character requires, then all you need to do is to apply the SoftFX settings to the final rig, and your character is finished. But we'll continue on to apply dynamics to Hamish's shirt using ClothFX.

6.3 Shirt Dynamics

ClothFX is more complicated than SoftFX. This is reflected in the number and type of settings or dynamic characteristics, and in the preparation of the object.

Preparation

Preparing the Scene — Part 1

The first part of the preparation involves creating a new character object for the dynamics. This means the original object and rig can still be used for scenes where clothing dynamics aren't necessary.

1. Load **Hamish_TestAnimDynamic_v001.lws** into Layout.
2. Select the **Hamish01** object and **File▷Save▷Save Current Object** as **Hamish01_Dynamic.lwo**.
3. Open the SoftFX properties for **Hamish01_Dynamic**, select the **File** tab, and **Clear Motion**.

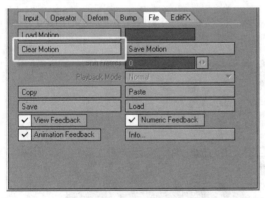

Figure 6.3-1. Clear the SoftFX motion. The object is about to change, so the SoftFX dynamics will need to be recalculated.

4. Select **File▷Save▷Save Scene As**, saving the scene as **Hamish_TestAnimDynamic_v001a.lws**.
5. Select the **Hamish01_Dynamic** object and press **F12** to open the object in Modeler.

Preparing the Object

We'll use proxy objects for the dynamic calculation and the collision. To keep things easier to manage it's best to use additional layers in the character object for the proxies instead of separate objects.

1. Select all the polygons of the shirt and **Cut. Paste** the shirt into layers 2 and 3 so you have two copies of the shirt.
2. In layer 1, select the polygons shown in Figure 6.3-2. **Copy** and **Paste** into layer 4.

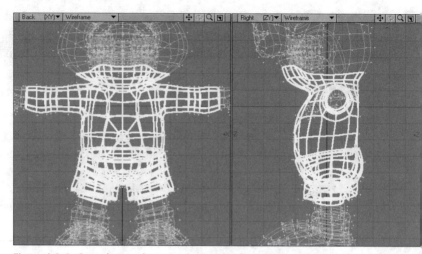

Figure 6.3-2. Copy these polygons to layer 4 for the collision object.

3. In the Layers window, double-click on the layer name (**unnamed**) for layer 1 and rename it **Body**.

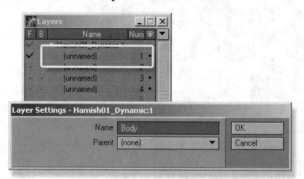

Figure 6.3-3. Name the layers so they're easy to identify.

4. Rename layer 2 to **Shirt_Dynamic** and set Parent to **1: Body**.
5. Rename layer 3 to **Shirt** and set Parent to **2: Shirt_Dynamic**.
6. Rename layer 4 to **Collision** and set Parent to **1: Body**.

We now have the four layers we need, but there are some adjustments that still need to be done.

7. In layer **2: Shirt_Dynamic**, delete the polygons of the Shirt_Inner surface.
8. Select two polygons of the second and third bands from the bottom and **Construct▸Reduce▸More▸Band Glue**. This makes the polygons closer in size; otherwise the extra detail at the bottom would become noticeable in the motion of the cloth.

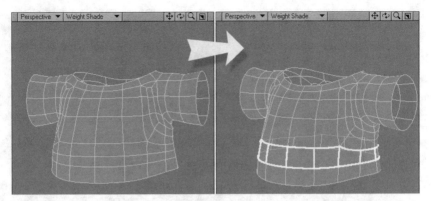

Figure 6.3-4. It's best to keep the polygons close to the same scale to achieve consistent dynamic motion.

9. In layer **4: Collision**, remove the belly button by deleting the polygons and welding the points. Turn off **Symmetry** and merge each pair of triangles.

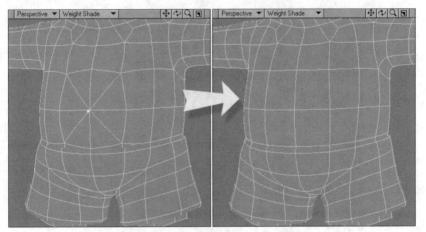

Figure 6.3-5. Remove superfluous detail from the collision object.

10. Turn **Symmetry** on and delete the top two rows of polygons of the pants. Then select the top row of points of the pants and, from the Top view, stretch them until they're just inside the body.

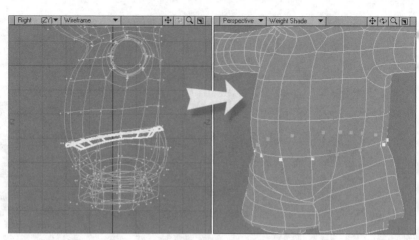

Figure 6.3-6. Leaving the top edge of the pants might cause the shirt to get caught on it.

11. Select the polygons of the body inside the pants, leaving one band overlap, and delete them.

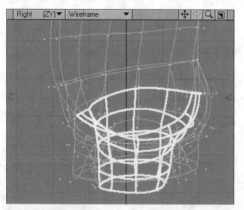

Figure 6.3-7. Remove the legs under the pants as only one layer of geometry is needed for the collision.

12. Select the inside two rows of polygons for the pant legs. Move them down a little and delete them.

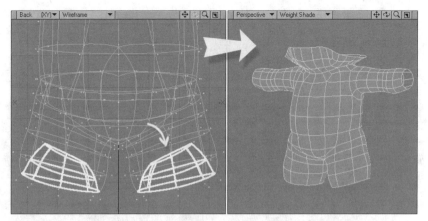

Figure 6.3-8. Because they're short, lengthening the pant legs makes sure the shirt won't go through or past the edges.

Creating Dynamic Weight Maps

With the layers established, the dynamic weight maps can be created. We'll create weight maps to influence the fixed area, the dynamic area, and the hold area.

> **Note:** It's usually good practice to adjust the initial ClothFX settings without weight maps, then create weight maps where they're needed. I already know where the weight maps are needed, so doing it now means we don't have to switch back to Modeler later on.

1. In layer **2: Shirt_Dynamic**, select the top two rows of points around the neck and the single row of points under each armpit. Create a new weight map called **FX_Fix** with an initial value of **100%**.

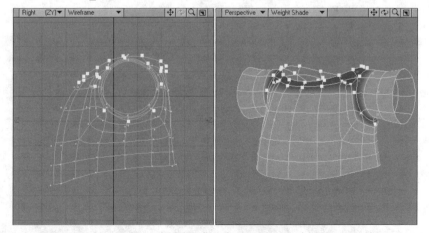

Figure 6.3-9. Fix doesn't respect weight values between 0% and 100%. Any value between those will be 100% fixed.

2. Select the bottom three rows of points on the torso and the last row of points on the arms. **Expand Selection** twice. Create a new weight map called **FX_Dynamic** with an initial value of **25%**.

3. **Contract Selection** and set the value to **50%**. **Contract Selection** again and set the value to **100%**, creating a gradient for the dynamic effect.

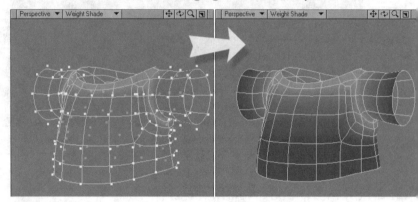

Figure 6.3-10. The dynamic weight map determines where the dynamic effect is strongest.

4. Deselect all the points and create a new weight map called **FX_Hold** with an initial value of **100%**. Select the same points as the previous map and set the value to **75%**. **Contract Selection** and set the value to **50%**. **Contract Selection** again and **Clear Map**.

5. With the weight maps complete, flip (**f**) the polygons of the Shirt_Dynamic layer so they're facing inward.

Note: Collision works on both sides of the polygons, but tends to favor the side the polygon normals are facing.

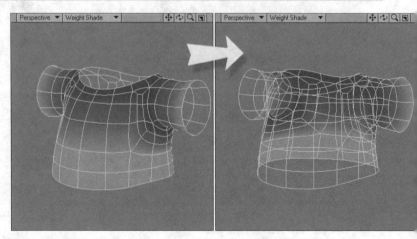

Figure 6.3-11. The hold weight map provides stability under the arms, a common trouble spot, and helps keep the cloth from folding in on itself.

6. Save the object.

Preparing the Scene — Part 2

With the object ready, the additional layers need to be included in the scene and set up ready for the dynamics.

When including layers, the expressions need to be updated. Integrated expressions automatically update when the object is replaced, but don't update when adding layers dynamically. Motion modifier expressions don't update with object replacement, so they need to be updated differently from integrated expressions.

We also need to prepare a neutral pose. If you know you'll be using ClothFX it's useful to retain the setup pose in the initial animation, copying it to frame −10 so you can start the animation at frame 0. Starting with a neutral pose is important as ClothFX treats the first calculated frame as its rest state. You can use this to your advantage if you want the cloth to come to rest in a different pose from what it's been modeled in, but in this case we want the rest state to be the same as the modeled pose.

1. Switch to Layout and check that the new layers have been imported.
   Save≻Save Scene (very important for the next step).

Figure 6.3-12. The new layers included in the scene.

2. Select **Plugs≻Additional≻Renamer JG**. In tab 1, change Find to [**Hamish01_Dynamic** and change Replace to [**Hamish01_Dynamic: Body**. In tab 2, change Find to **Hamish01.** and change Replace to **Hamish01_Dynamic:Body.** (making sure to include the period at the end of both). In the File tab, change New File to **Hamish_TestAnimDynamic_ v001b.lws**. The new scene will load with the name changes.

Figure 6.3-13. The first find and replace updates the integrated expressions. The second find and replace updates the motion modifier expressions.

3. Turn **Parent in Place** off and parent **Hamish01_Dynamic:Shirt** to **Hamish01_Dynamic:Shirt_Dynamic**.

4. Parent **Hamish01_Dynamic:Shirt_Dynamic** and **Hamish01_ Dynamic:Collision** to **Hamish01_Dynamic:Body**.

> **Note:** To make it easier I'll reference the objects by layer name from here on, so the Body layer means Hamish01_Dynamic:Body.

5. Change the Shirt_Dynamic and Collision layers to display Front Face wireframe.

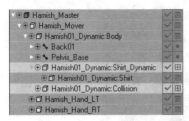

Figure 6.3-14. New layers parented and display options set.

6. Select the **Shirt_Dynamic** and **Collision** layers and open Object Properties. Change Subdivision Order to **Last** and both SubPatch Level settings to **1**. (Leave the properties panel open for the next few steps.)

7. Select the **Render** tab, turn on **Unseen by Rays** and **Unseen by Camera**, and turn off all the shadow options.

> **Note:** You could just deactivate the proxy layers instead of adjusting the object properties, but it's a bit too easy to accidentally activate them when working in the Scene Editor. Setting the object properties prevents them from being rendered under any circumstances.

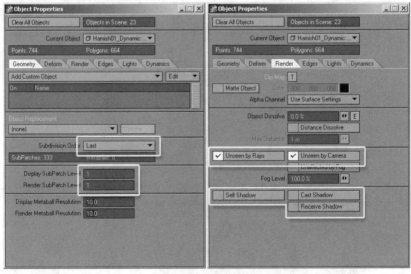

Figure 6.3-15. Object properties for the dynamic objects.

8. Select the **Shirt_Dynamic** layer and press **Shift+b** for Bones mode. In the Bone properties, set Use Bones From Object to the **Body** layer. Do the same for the **Shirt** and **Collision** layers.

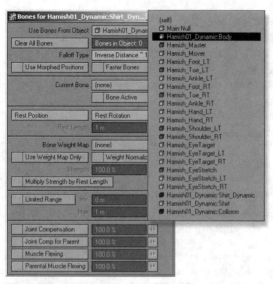

Figure 6.3-16. Set all layers to use the bones from the main object.

9. Select the **Shirt** layer and the **Geometry** tab. Set Subdivision Order to **Last,** Display SubPatch Level to **2,** and Render SubPatch Level to **4.**

10. Select the **Deform** tab and **Add Displacement**➢**FX_MetaLink.**

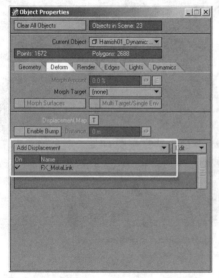

Figure 6.3-17. FX_MetaLink deforms an object to the dynamic motion of its parent.

11. Set the first frame in the frame range to **–10** and move to frame **–10.**

12. Select all bones of Hamish and reset their rotation.

• Dynamics

13. Move the hand and foot IK goals so the body is in a neutral pose, similar to the modeled pose but with the arms slightly lowered.

Figure 6.3-18. The neutral pose for Hamish at frame –10.

14. Save the scene as **Hamish_TestAnimDynamics_v002.lws**.

Applying ClothFX

The scene is set up and ready for dynamics. We need to recalculate the SoftFX since the main object has changed, apply collision to the Collision layer and apply ClothFX to the Shirt_Dynamic layer.

1. Select the **Body** layer and the **Dynamics** tab. Click the **Calculate** button to recalculate the SoftFX dynamics.

2. Open the SoftFX properties, select the **File** tab, and select **Save Motion**, saving as **TestAnim_Hamish_SoftFX2.mdd**. Save the scene, saving the SoftFX calculation into the scene.

3. Select the **Collision** layer and **Add Dynamic▸Collision**. Open the properties and change Type to **object-subdiv**, Radius/Level to **10 mm**, and Bounce/Bind power to **20%**.

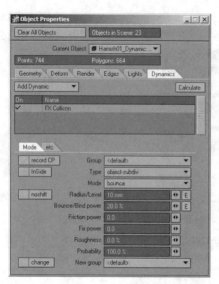

Figure 6.3-19. Collision settings.

4. Select the **Shirt_Dynamic** layer and **Add Dynamic**≻**ClothFX**.
5. Select the **Basic** tab and set Fix to **FX_Fix/weightmap**.

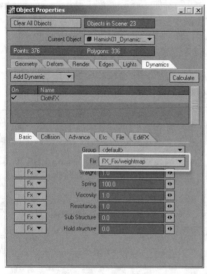

Figure 6.3-20. Setting the fixed area.

6. Select the **Collision** tab, and set Collision Detect to **<all>** and Exclusive
    Collision to the **Collision** layer.

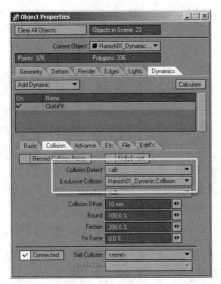

Figure 6.3-21. Initial collision settings.

7. Open the ClothFX properties and select the **Etc** tab. Set Gravity Y to **–9.8 m** and select the **Cotton(thin)** preset.

Note: The Cotton(thin) preset is already listed but is not activated until you select it.

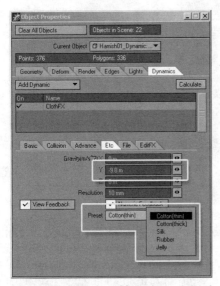

Figure 6.3-22. Real-world gravity is –9.8 m/s. It's best to have a default gravity value that all the dynamics use. It doesn't really matter what the default gravity value is, as long as it's consistent throughout the production, but it's usually easiest to use –9.8 m so you can more easily determine the correct weight for dynamic objects.

8. Calculate the dynamics, then check the preview to see the results at the right speed.

Tweaking the Settings

The default thin cotton settings are a good starting point, but don't work too well for the shirt. It's from here that the tweaking begins.

When you're tweaking the settings, don't worry too much about collision errors on fast motion. The default calculation resolution isn't enough to account for fast motion but creates fast calculation so you're not waiting around too long to see the results of your tweaking. The resolution is increased after the basic motion is correct.

Instead of going step by step through the tweaking process, I'll show you my adjusted settings and how I came to decide on them.

Basic Tab

The basic settings are where most of the work is done. These values determine the type of material and behavior of the dynamic object.

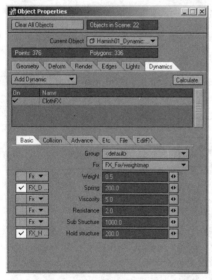

Figure 6.3-23. Basic settings.

Because the gravity is set to a standard value, the weight needs to be adjusted to suit. At a Weight of 1 the shirt seems too heavy, so I've set it to 0.5.

With a high Spring value the shirt seems more like rubber than cloth. I've lowered the Spring to 200 so it's not as bouncy. I applied the FX_Dynamic weight map to the Spring value so the edges have the most motion, and the midsection moves less. This keeps the shirt from folding into itself so it doesn't need self collision.

Giving the shirt more viscosity makes it move and react a little slower, as well as stopping it from deforming too drastically. For cartoon characters a bit more viscosity than you might normally use can help give the motion a more caricatured feel. Setting Viscosity over 5 tends to make the cloth seem too gelatinous, so test values between 1 and 5 to get the motion you require.

A little bit more resistance makes the material react more to air pressure, or the environment around the character, making its motion more believable. Lighter material tends to have more resistance than heavier material, so reducing the weight and increasing the Resistance value to 2 makes the shirt appear lighter.

Sub Structure is good at 1000. The shirt isn't distorting too much.

Hold structure helps the material keep its shape. Setting Hold structure to 200 with the FX_Hold weight map keeps the shirt stable, especially under the armpits (a common trouble area), without affecting the major dynamic areas.

Collision Tab

The collision settings determine how the material reacts to collisions.

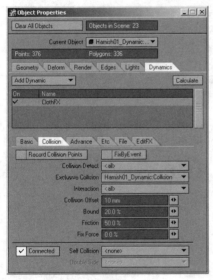

Figure 6.3-24. Collision settings.

A Collision Offset setting of 10 mm is about right. Because the dynamic object is a single layer and the final shirt has thickness, the collision offset needs to be fairly high. Thinner material might need a lower offset so it doesn't float above the collision surface.

Cloth doesn't tend to bounce off the body too much. Lowering the Bound setting to 20% gives better results.

Giving the cloth some friction can help stabilize the cloth, but too much will make the cloth stick to the body too much. 50% is a good amount for the shirt.

Advance Tab

The main settings to adjust in the Advance tab control the stretchiness of the material.

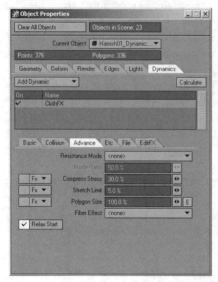

Figure 6.3-25. Advance settings.

Setting Compress Stress to 30% is a good value for the cloth, allowing it to contract a little bit but not too much. Increasing Compress Stress stiffens the cloth.

The shirt is stretching more than cloth should. Setting Stretch Limit to 5% lets it stretch just a little, but not so much that it becomes rubbery, losing the appearance of cloth.

Final Calculation

When you're happy with the basic motion of the shirt, it's time to save the settings and do the final calculation.

The Resolution setting in the Etc tab determines the accuracy of the calculation. Lower values result in more accurate calculation, which is especially useful if there's fast movement in the scene or collision object. Setting Resolution to 1 mm is usually low enough to provide decent results without slowing the calculation too much. For complex cloth simulations or long scenes you may need to leave the final calculation working overnight.

You can also choose to leave the resolution at a higher value for faster calculation, and do more adjustment using EditFX.

1. Select the **Collision** layer and open the Collision properties. In the Etc tab, select **Save**, saving as **Motions\Hamish_Collision.txt**.

2. Select the **Shirt_Dynamic** layer and open the ClothFX properties. In the File tab, select **Save**, saving the settings as **Motions\ Hamish_ClothFX.txt**.

> **Note:** These files are used when applying the dynamic settings to the final rig.

3. In the Etc tab, set the Resolution to **1 mm** and **Calculate**.

Figure 6.3-26. A frame from the final calculation.

Fixing Calculation Errors

Check through the animation for any places where the body shows through the clothing. There shouldn't be many errors in the shirt motion. The only error in my calculation is on the sleeve where the collision object squashed the shirt into the arm.

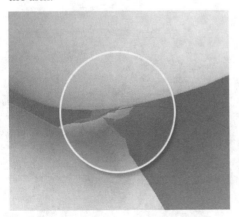

Figure 6.3-27. Collision error on frame 83.

1. Select the **EditFX** tab and set EditStart and EditEnd to either side of the frame with the error. If the error is on a single frame, then set EditStart and EditEnd to one frame on either side of the error. If the error occurs over a number of frames, set EditStart and EditEnd to just before and after the frame range where the error is occurring.

2. Set EditSize depending on the size of the error. Setting a larger EditSize makes EditFX work a bit like the Magnet tool in Modeler. To move a single point, set it to **0.01**.

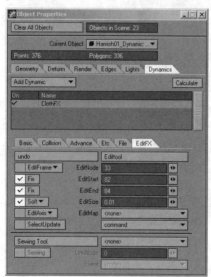

Figure 6.3-28. EditFX settings for editing frame 83.

3. Select and move the appropriate points.

> **Note:**   It can be a bit tricky to find the correct points when the object is sub-divided. If you accidentally move the wrong point you can use the Undo feature on the EditFX tab.

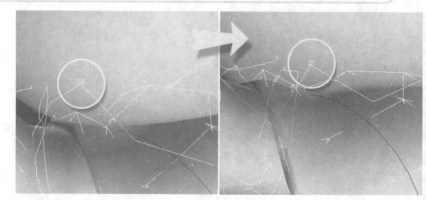

Figure 6.3-29. Moving the offending points.

Repeat steps 1 to 3 for any frames containing errors.

4. Once all the errors are fixed, select the **File** tab and **Save Motion**, saving as **Motions\TestAnim_Hamish_ClothFX.mdd**.

5. Save the scene, storing the final calculated dynamics.

6.4 Updating the Rig

Updating the final rig for dynamics is similar to preparing the test animation for dynamics. The additional layers need to be included and dynamic settings applied to the appropriate objects.

Applying SoftFX

SoftFX can be applied to the existing rig because it doesn't require any object changes.

1. Load your Hamish rig into Layout (you can find a preprepared scene in \Scenes\Chapters\Hamish_Rig01.lws).

2. Select **Hamish01**, open Object Properties, and add **SoftFX**.

3. Open the SoftFX properties and select **Load** from the File tab. Choose **Motions\Hamish_SoftFX.txt**.

4. Save the scene.

Applying ClothFX

It's useful to save the rig with ClothFX under a different name, as not every scene will require the shirt dynamics.

1. Select **Hamish01** and **Items▹Replace▹Replace with Object**, choosing **Hamish01_Dynamic.lwo**.

2. Select **Items▹Load▹Object Layer**, choose **Hamish01_Dynamic.lwo**, and specify layer **2**. Repeat to load layers **3** and **4**.

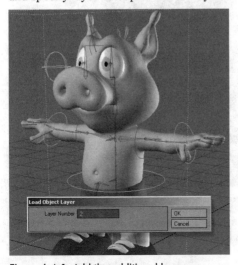

Figure 6.4-1. Add the additional layers.

3. Save the scene as **Hamish_Rig01_ClothFX.lws**.

4. Select **Plugs**≻**Additional**≻**Renamer JG**. In tab 1, change Find to **Hamish01.** and change Replace to **Hamish01_Dynamic:Body.** (making sure to include the period at the end of both). The scene will reload with the name changes.

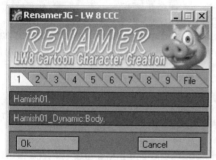

Figure 6.4-2. The integrated expressions are updated correctly when the main object is replaced, so just the Motion Modifier expressions need updating.

5. Make sure **Parent in Place** is off and parent the **Shirt** layer to the **Shirt_Dynamic** layer.

6. Parent the **Shirt_Dynamic** and **Collision** layers to the **Body** layer.

7. Hide the **Shirt_Dynamic** and **Collision** layers, as they don't need to be visible until calculating the dynamics.

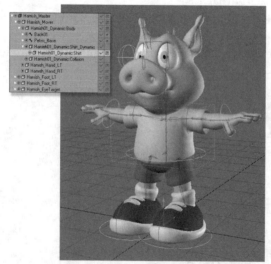

Figure 6.4-3. New layers parented and initial display options set.

8. Select the **Shirt_Dynamic** and **Collision** layers and open Object Properties. Change Subdivision Order to **Last** and both SubPatch Level settings to **1**.

9. Select the **Render** tab, turn on **Unseen by Rays** and **Unseen by Camera**, and turn off all the shadow options.

10. Select the **Shirt_Dynamic** layer and press **Shift+b** for Bones mode. In the Bone properties, set Use Bones From Object to the **Body** layer. Do the same for the **Shirt** and **Collision** layers.

11. Select the **Shirt** layer and the **Geometry** tab. Set the Subdivision Order to **Last**, Display SubPatch Level to **2**, and Render SubPatch Level to **4**.

12. Select the **Deform** tab and **Add Displacement**➤**FX_Metalink**.

13. Apply FX Collision to the **Collision** layer. Load the previously saved Collision settings.

14. Apply ClothFX to the **Shirt_Dynamic** layer. Load the previously saved ClothFX settings.

15. Select **Hamish_Master** and press **Enter**. Create a keyframe for **Current Item and Descendants** at frame **–10**, creating the neutral pose.

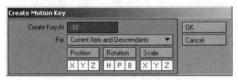

Figure 6.4-4. Set up a neutral pose on frame –10.

16. Save the scene.

You now have two dynamic rigs. The primary rig with simple body dynamics can be used for scenes that don't require the more complex shirt dynamics, and the rig containing ClothFX can be used when required.

There is much more to explore in the realm of dynamics. Take some time to experiment with the various settings so you're well equipped to simulate any type of soft body that you might need. Remember when tweaking to save the settings every now and then. It's easy to lose track of what changes you've made, so it's useful to have a few milestones saved that you can revert to if you go too far down the wrong track.

6.5 Conclusion

You now have the skills to do the complex problem solving necessary for rigging characters and the knowledge of how to bring it all together to breathe life into the character through animation, but keep in mind your learning has only just begun. The next stage of your learning is to develop and enhance those skills through practice — creating and animating your own characters.

One of my favorite aspects of character creation and animation is that it's a constantly evolving art form. I've been creating and animating 3D characters for over ten years and I still learn something new almost every day, whether it's a new technique, a new way to use a tool, or an aspect of the software I hadn't used before. The constant challenge means that even when character creation is your job, it never becomes boring.

I hope this series has been as useful and fun to read as it's been for me to write. Character creation is undoubtedly a challenge, but it's a lot of fun and very rewarding. I wish you the very best of luck in your character creation efforts. I look forward to seeing your characters online or on a screen somewhere so they can inspire us all.

Appendix

There are hundreds of plug-ins available for LightWave 3D. Some are useful on a regular basis, shaving small amounts of time off common tasks. Others are useful for less common, more demanding tasks, but save much more time or do things that are otherwise impossible. The following is by no means a comprehensive list of useful plug-ins, but includes the plug-ins that I find most useful on a regular basis for character creation.

Free Plug-ins

All of the following free plug-ins are included on the companion CD, but make sure you check the developer web sites for updates and other useful plug-ins.

> **Note:** Make sure you read the manuals provided with each plug-in.

Combine Weightmaps

Kevin Phillips — www.kevman3d.com

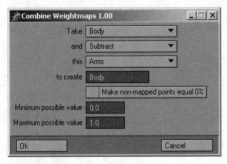

Figure A-1. Combine Weightmaps.

One of the most frustrating parts of weight mapping is working out the correct values for adjoining bone weight maps. Combine Weightmaps makes it easy to create the weight values by letting you subtract one weight map from another. You can also add weight maps together and multiply or divide them into an existing weight map or a new one.

In addition to setting values for adjoining weight maps as shown in the tutorials, Combine Weightmaps can also be used to create more blending between left and right weight maps. You can do this by creating an additional weight map to determine the blending amount and multiplying the symmetrical weight maps with the additional weight map.

MSort

Scott Martindale

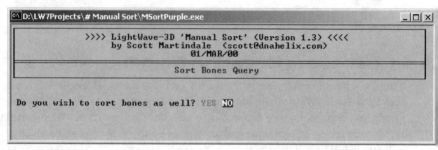

Figure A-2. MSort.

MSort isn't actually a plug-in, but a separate program that works with LightWave scene files. It's most useful for character rigging as it allows you to adjust the order of the bones and control objects so it's easy to change the selected item by pressing the up and down arrows. It's also useful for making the bone and object order the same for every character in a production so moving from character to character in a scene is a seamless transition.

It takes a lot of extra time to create items in the proper order when rigging. If you're not careful to create items in order, then extra time is spent during animation. MSort saves that time by giving you the ability to quickly change the order in which bones or objects appear in the selection lists.

A new version of MSort is currently in development as a plug-in instead of a separate program. The new version includes drag and drop editing and much more functionality. When it's finished, the updated version of MSort will be available from my web site.

MorphMap Mixer

DStorm — www.dstorm.co.jp/dslib/index-e.html

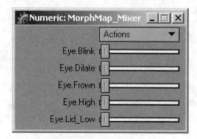

Figure A-3. MorphMap Mixer.

MorphMap Mixer allows the mixing of morphs within Modeler. This is useful for creating new morphs based on the combination of existing morphs. It's also useful for quickly testing how the modular morphs mix together, so you can find trouble spots early on.

Custom Character Picker

Jacobo Barreiro — www.jacobobarreiro.com

Figure A-4. Custom Character Picker.

Custom Character Picker is, as the name suggests, a character picker plug-in. Character pickers are great, providing a panel where you can click to select various items in the scene. You can create your own background, choose where the nodes or buttons appear, and choose which items selected when you click on each node. Using a character picker to select the most commonly used bones can make animating a character much easier.

Expresso JG

Samuel Kvaalen — www.kvaalen.com

Expresso sets up predetermined morph joystick controls, providing an easy interface to choose which morphs are assigned to each control. This custom version of Expresso features controls that I've designed specifically for the basic list of morphs described in this book.

Expresso is only used in the setup phase, so others using the character don't need to have Expresso to animate the character using the joystick controls. The disadvantage to Expresso is that the controls are predetermined. You can edit the controls and their expressions to some degree after they've been set up, but the price for easy setup is being restricted to the controls that are provided.

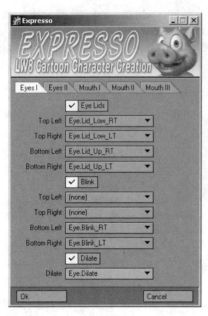

Figure A-5. Expresso JG.

Renamer JG

Samuel Kvaalen — www.kvaalen.com

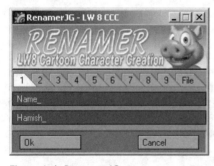

Figure A-6. Renamer JG.

Renaming can be done within Layout, but having to rename a number of items can be very time consuming. One of the benefits of LightWave scene files is that they're saved as plaintext, so you can perform global name changes by doing a find and replace in a text editor, but that requires leaving LightWave. Renamer does the same find and replace as a text editor, but you don't have to leave LightWave.

Renamer is not just useful for renaming items; it's also very useful if you need to update expressions when you replace or add layers to a referenced object.

Masked Morph Copy

Kevin Phillips — www.kevman3d.com

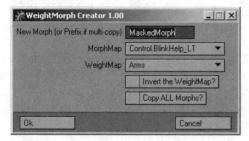

Figure A-7. Masked Morph Copy.

Masked Morph Copy allows you to copy a morph based on a weight map. This has many uses, including creating left- and right-sided versions of symmetrical morphs from within Modeler instead of creating them in Layout as demonstrated in the tutorials.

Commercial Plug-ins

Demo versions or examples from the following commercial plug-ins are included on the companion CD. Check the developer web sites for updates, pricing, and other information.

Quick Picker Pro

Samuel Kvaalen — www.kvaalen.com/QPP

Quick Picker Pro is a character picker, similar to Custom Character Picker featured in the tutorials, but with a few differences. Included is a demo version of QPP so you can test it out for yourself.

Mimic 2

Daz 3D — www.daz3d.com/Mimic

Mimic 2 automates lip sync for 3D characters by reading audio files. The resulting animation can be imported into LightWave and tweaked or enhanced even further.

While I wouldn't normally recommend automated lip sync for primary characters, Mimic 2 does a great job of getting you 90% of the way with very little effort. You may even find that the results are good enough on their own for secondary or background characters. Regardless of how you choose to use it in your production, if you have a lot of lip sync to do in a short amount of time, Mimic 2 can be a great time-saver.

Relativity

Prem Subrahmanyam — www.premdesign.com

Relativity is an alternative to LightWave expressions. Relativity has many advantages over LightWave expressions, including greater functionality with fewer limitations.

LightWave expressions are very useful and will serve you well in many situations. I recommend learning and using LightWave expressions first, as it'll give you a good basis for understanding how to use Relativity. It'll also give you a better understanding of the advantages of Relativity once you run into problems that LightWave expressions aren't equipped to handle.

FPrime

Worley Labs — www.worley.com

FPrime is an invaluable preview tool for character creation. It creates very quick renders with every change you make to the model, providing real-time feedback instead of having to wait for F9 renders to check your results. FPrime is most useful for texturing and lighting, allowing you to make changes and see the results immediately, which saves considerable time and allows you to work as fast as you can think. Because of the time savings you can spend more time experimenting, ending up with superior results, and still finish well under the time it would take traditionally.

A.2 Auto Rigging Plug-ins

What you've learned in this book and *Volume 1: Modeling & Texturing*, together with the improved rigging tools in LightWave 8, give you the ability to create custom character rigs and apply them to multiple characters. Before LightWave 8, it was quite time consuming to transfer rigs from one character to another, so some enterprising plug-in authors wrote some tools to make the job easier.

The main downfall of most auto rigging tools (with the exception of ACS4) is that you're stuck with creating the one rig. While you can add to the rig easily enough once it's been created, this doesn't really help when you have a unique rig of your own that you want to apply to multiple characters. An auto rigging tool gives you a way to quickly rig a character for test poses or to check deformations before sending the character model for final rigging. For character creators comfortable with modeling but less experienced in rigging, this can be very useful. Auto rigging can also be useful for rigging background characters that don't need complex or unique rigs.

Free Plug-ins

All of the following free plug-ins are included on the companion CD, but make sure you check the developer web sites for updates and other useful plug-ins.

> **Note:** Make sure you read the manuals provided with each plug-in.

Simple Rigger

Christopher Lutz — www.animationsnippets.com/plugins

Simple Rigger creates the animation controls and sets IK for a character object with skelegons, allowing you to choose between FK or IK arms. There are few options available to you, but Simple Rigger creates a decent rig and you can adjust it for your preferred control methods once the rig has been created.

Also look for other useful plug-ins available from Christopher's web site, including a useful replacement for LightWave's Match Goal Orientation.

J Auto Rig

Jacobo Barreiro — www.jacobobarreiro.com

J Auto Rig sets IK for a character object with skelegons. The resulting rig is a little different from the rigs I've covered in this book. Instead of using null objects as the animation controls, the null objects are hidden, allowing you to use the bones themselves as animation controls. This rigging method was made popular by Timothy Albee in his book *LightWave 3D 7 Character Animation*.

Also look for other useful plug-ins available from Jacobo's web site, including a Pose Saver plug-in.

Commercial Plug-ins

Demo versions or examples from the following commercial plug-ins are included on the CD. Check the developer web sites for updates, pricing, and other information.

Auto Character Setup 4

Lukasz Pazera and Pawel Olas — acs.polas.net/acs

Auto Character Setup 4 is a very powerful auto rigging tool. There are many different rigs available to choose from, which puts it ahead of most other auto rigging tools, but it's most useful feature is the ability to customize any rig for use with ACS4, allowing you to store IK settings, modifiers, expressions, and more. If you have a lot of characters to rig in a short amount of time, ACS4 will pay for itself very quickly whether you use the provided rigs or put the extra effort into converting a custom rig.

T4D Rigging Tools

Peter Thomas and Samuel Kvaalen — www.thomas4d.com

Thomas 4D Rigging Tools is a suite of tools for rigging and animating characters. Version 2 offers the choice between using bones or null objects as animation controls and IK or FK arms and legs. It also includes a pose saver, a character picker, and joystick controls for facial morphs.

A.3 Internet Resources

The following are some Internet sites useful for character creation, some geared toward LightWave, others geared toward 3D regardless of package. The following resource sites contain tutorials, tips, and plug-ins that will help save your time and sanity when creating characters. The community sites contain inspiring characters and other artwork created by people from all over the world. These communities also offer help; you'll always find someone who can answer a particular question to help solve a problem.

Lightwave Resources

These LightWave resource sites will help you use LightWave 3D to its fullest extent.

Official LightWave 3D Web Site

www.lightwave3d.com

The official LightWave 3D web site includes the latest patches and downloads, tutorials, and interviews with artists using LightWave for production work in many different areas. You can also visit the NewTek forums, which offers a meeting place for everything NewTek.

SpinQuad

www.spinquad.com

SpinQuad is a web site created by William "Proton" Vaughan to be the ultimate LightWave 3D resource.

Flay

www.flay.com

Flay includes the most comprehensive database of LightWave plug-ins available. It also features the latest news, job postings, and tutorials.

LightWave Tutorials on the Web

members.shaw.ca/lightwavetutorials

LightWave Tutorials on the Web contains links to hundreds of LightWave tutorials covering almost every possible use of the package, as well as tutorials for related plug-ins and other packages. If you want to know how to accomplish a task in LightWave 3D, this should be your first stop.

Communities

These community sites are meeting places for 3D artists from around the world. They allow you to find answers to problems and are a great source of inspiration, letting you see the great work that others are doing.

LightWave 3D Mailing List

groups.yahoo.com/group/lw3d

The official LightWave 3D mailing list.

SpinQuad Forums

www.spinquad.com/forums

SpinQuad forums are dedicated to LightWave 3D, where people can meet and discuss pure LightWave issues in a fun and productive way. SpinQuad forums are a great place to visit to find out about recent developments, if you want constructive criticism, or just to show off your latest work.

LightWave Group Forums

www.lwg3d.org

LightWave Group forums include galleries, articles, interviews, and tutorials.

CGTalk

www.cgtalk.com

CGTalk is a huge forum that caters to everything related to computer graphics, both 2D and 3D. There is a forum dedicated to LightWave, but the great benefit is that you can meet people and see work done using a multitude of 3D packages.

Friends of NewTek

www.friendsofNewTek.com

Friends of NewTek is a site dedicated to LightWave user groups all over the world. If you're looking for your local user group for face-to-face meetings, this is where you'll find it.

Index

surface,
    changing, 214
    selecting, 59
symmetry,
    morphs, 74
    weight mapping, 116

T
T4D Rigging Tools, 407
Target Item, 143, 171
tension, 320-321
test animation,
    body, 363-365
    facial expressions, 366-367
    lip sync, 368
Tip Move, 138, 274
tongue morphs, 51, 52, 332
torso weight mapping, 117-118
Track Item Selections, 358

U
Unaffected by IK of Descendants, 205
Undo
    Levels, 4
    shortcut, 15
Unseen by Camera, 387
Unseen by Rays, 387
Unweld Points, creating a button for, 8
UV.Test, 73-74

V
vertex map,
    copying, 56
    creating, 54
Vertex Maps panel, 6
viewport settings
    Layout, 10
    Modeler, 5
visibility options, 123

W
weight mapping, 102-107
    bone weights, 103
    hard bodies, 104-105
    separating left and right, 116
weight maps,
    adding, 189-190
    adjusting, 191-192
    basic list, 106
    creating, 108-120
    for gradients, 75-77
Weight Shade, 108

Y
Y scale (expression), 228-230

Z
Z axis, 136, 316
Z scale (expression), 226-230

Essential LightWave 3D 7.5
1-55622-226-2 • $44.95
6 x 9 • 424 pp.

LightWave 3D 7.5 Lighting
1-55622-354-4 • $69.95
6 x 9 • 496 pp.

LightWave 3D 8 Lighting
1-55622-094-4 • $54.95
6 x 9 • 536 pp.

**LightWave 3D 8 Cartoon
Creation: Volume I Mode
Texturing**
1-55622-253-X • $
6 x 9 • 496 pp.

LightWave 3D 8 Texturing
1-55622-285-8 • $49.95
6 x 9 • 504 pp.

LightWave 3D 8: 1001 Tips and Tricks
1-55622-090-1 • $39.95
6 x 9 • 648 pp.

**CGI Filmmaking: The Creation of Ghost
Warrior**
1-55622-227-0 • $49.95
9 x 7 • 344 pp.

Just Released

**Advanced Lighting and Materials with
Shaders**
1-55622-292-0 • $44.95
9 x 7 • 360 pp.

Coming Soon

**Essential LightWave 3D 8:
The Fastest Way to Master
LightWave 3D**
1-55622-082-0 • $44.95
6 x 9 • 450 pp.

**LightWave 3D 8 Character
Animation**
1-55622-099-5 • $49.95
6 x 9 • 400 pp.

**LightWave 3D 8 Modeli
A Definitive Guide**
1-55622-289-0 • $
6 x 9 • 500 pp.

Visit us online at **www.wordware.com** for more informat

...klist, and upcoming titles.

...ling a Character in 3DS Max
...622-815-5 • $44.95
...9¼ • 544 pp.

Coming Soon

Modeling a Character in 3DS Max
(2nd Edition)
1-55622-088-X • $44.95
6 x 9 • 550 pp.

Game Design: Theory and Practice,
Second Edition
1-55622-912-7 • $49.95
6 x 9 • 728 pp.

...e Development and Production
...622-951-8 • $49.95
... • 432 pp.

Game Design Foundations
1-55622-973-9 • $39.95
6 x 9 • 400 pp.

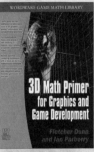

3D Math Primer for Graphics and
Game Development
1-55622-911-9 • $49.95
7½ x 9¼ • 448 pp.

...r Game Math Processors
...622-921-6 • $59.95
... • 528 pp.

Memory Management Algorithms
and Implementation in C/C++
1-55622-347-1 • $59.95
6 x 9 • 392 pp.

Learn FileMaker Pro 7
1-55622-098-7 • $36.95
6 x 9 • 544 pp.

Use the following coupon code for online specials: car2-2548

Introduction to 3D Game Programming with DirectX 9.0
1-55622-913-5 • $49.95
6 x 9 • 424 pp.

Advanced 3D Game Programming with DirectX 9.0
1-55622-968-2 • $59.95
6 x 9 • 552 pp.

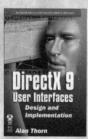

DirectX 9 User Interfaces: Design and Implementation
1-55622-249-1 • $44.95
6 x 9 • 376 pp.

Strategy Game Program with DirectX 9.0
1-55622-922-4 • $.
6 x 9 • 560 pp.

DirectX 9 Audio Exposed: Interactive Audio Development
1-55622-288-2 • $59.95
6 x 9 • 568 pp.

Learn Vertex and Pixel Shader Programming with DirectX 9
1-55622-287-4 • $34.95
6 x 9 • 304 pp.

ShaderX2: Introductions and Tutorials with DirectX 9
1-55622-902-X • $44.95
6 x 9 • 384 pp.

ShaderX2: Shader Progr Tips & Tricks with DirectX
1-55622-988-7 • $.
6 x 9 • 728 pp.

New Releases

Programming Multiplayer Games
1-55622-076-6 • $59.95
6 x 9 • 576 pp.

Wireless Game Development in Java with MIDP 2.0
1-55622-998-4 • $39.95
6 x 9 • 360 pp.

Official Butterfly.net Game Developer's Guide
1-55622-044-8 • $49.95
6 x 9 • 424 pp.

Visit us online at **www.wordware.com** for more information

Use the following coupon code for online specials: **car2-2548**

About the CD

The companion CD is organized into the following directories:

- Book_Illustrations contains all the illustrations from the book.
- LWProjects contains all the files necessary to follow the tutorials, along with plug-in demos and examples.
- LWProjects\LW8_CartoonCreation\Objects\Extra includes extra objects created by William "Proton" Vaughan.
- Movies contains the movies from the book.

Note: For the advanced rigging tutorials to work correctly, it's very important to install the LightWave 8.0.1 update. (See www.newtek.com.)

Warning: By opening the CD package, you accept the terms and conditions of the CD/Source Code Usage License Agreement. Additionally, opening the CD package makes this book nonreturnable.

CD/Source Code Usage License Agreement

Please read the following CD/Source Code usage license agreement before opening the CD and using the contents therein:

1. By opening the accompanying software package, you are indicating that you have read and agree to be bound by all terms and conditions of this CD/Source Code usage license agreement.

2. The compilation of code and utilities contained on the CD and in the book are copyrighted and protected by both U.S. copyright law and international copyright treaties, and is owned by Wordware Publishing, Inc. Individual source code, example programs, help files, freeware, shareware, utilities, and evaluation packages, including their copyrights, are owned by the respective authors.

3. No part of the enclosed CD or this book, including all source code, help files, shareware, freeware, utilities, example programs, or evaluation programs, may be made available on a public forum (such as a World Wide Web page, FTP site, bulletin board, or Internet news group) without the express written permission of Wordware Publishing, Inc. or the author of the respective source code, help files, shareware, freeware, utilities, example programs, or evaluation programs.

4. You may not decompile, reverse engineer, disassemble, create a derivative work, or otherwise use the enclosed programs, help files, freeware, shareware, utilities, or evaluation programs except as stated in this agreement.

5. The software, contained on the CD and/or as source code in this book, is sold without warranty of any kind. Wordware Publishing, Inc. and the authors specifically disclaim all other warranties, express or implied, including but not limited to implied warranties of merchantability and fitness for a particular purpose with respect to defects in the disk, the program, source code, sample files, help files, freeware, shareware, utilities, and evaluation programs contained therein, and/or the techniques described in the book and implemented in the example programs. In no event shall Wordware Publishing, Inc., its dealers, its distributors, or the authors be liable or held responsible for any loss of profit or any other alleged or actual private or commercial damage, including but not limited to special, incidental, consequential, or other damages.

6. One (1) copy of the CD or any source code therein may be created for backup purposes. The CD and all accompanying source code, sample files, help files, freeware, shareware, utilities, and evaluation programs may be copied to your hard drive. With the exception of freeware and shareware programs, at no time can any part of the contents of this CD reside on more than one computer at one time. The contents of the CD can be copied to another computer, as long as the contents of the CD contained on the original computer are deleted.

7. You may not include any part of the CD contents, including all source code, example programs, shareware, freeware, help files, utilities, or evaluation programs in any compilation of source code, utilities, help files, example programs, freeware, shareware, or evaluation programs on any media, including but not limited to CD, disk, or Internet distribution, without the express written permission of Wordware Publishing, Inc. or the owner of the individual source code, utilities, help files, example programs, freeware, shareware, or evaluation programs.

8. You may use the source code, techniques, and example programs in your own commercial or private applications unless otherwise noted by additional usage agreements as found on the CD.

Warning: By opening the CD package, you accept the terms and conditions of the CD/Source Code Usage License Agreement.
Additionally, opening the CD package makes this book nonreturnable.